THE FINEST CREW IN THE FLEET

The Next Generation Cast On Screen and Off

ADAM SHRAGER

Introduction by David Gerrold

WOLF VALLEY BOOKS
New York City

First published by Wolf Valley Books 1997

Copyright © 1997 by Adam Shrager
Introduction copyright © 1997 by David Gerrold
All rights reserved. No part of this book may be used or reproduced in
any manner whatsoever without prior permission from Wolf Valley Books,
99 Bank Street, Suite 5E, New York, NY 10014.

Dedication reprinted by permission. Originally written (in the
masculine voice) as a eulogy for his son-in-law. June 1992.

Published by
Wolf Valley Books
99 Bank Street, Suite 5E
New York, NY 10014

Distributed by
The Talman Company
89 Fifth Ave., Suite 802
New York, NY 10003

Library of Congress Cataloging-in-Publication Data

Shrager, Adam, 1966–
    The finest crew in the fleet: the next generation cast on screen and
off / Adam Shrager.
        p.   cm.
    Includes bibliographic references.
    ISBN 1-888149-03-5
    1. Star Trek, the next generation (Television program).   2. Television
actors and actresses—United States—Biography.   I. Title.
PN1992.77.S732S56   1997
791.45'72—dc21   96-46744
                                                              CIP

10 9 8 7 6 5 4 3 2 1
Design by Catherine Lau Hunt

Star Trek and Star Trek: The Next Generation are trademarks of
Paramount Pictures.

This book has not been licensed or approved by any entity involved
in the production of Star Trek.

Contents

ACKNOWLEDGMENTS   *iv*

INTRODUCTION BY DAVID GERROLD   *viii*

PREFACE   *x*

1. PATRICK STEWART—*Thespian on the Bridge*   *1*

2. JONATHAN FRAKES—*Number One Behind the Camera*   43

3. LeVAR BURTON—*Roots, Reactors, Role Model*   69

4. MICHAEL DORN—*A Great* Trek *Record*   93

5. GATES McFADDEN—*The Dancing Doctor*   120

6. MARINA SIRTIS—*From Hoi Polloi to Counselor Troi*   144

7. BRENT SPINER—*Handy Android, Versatile Actor*   165

8. WIL WHEATON—*Stand by Him*   191

9. REGULAR PLAYERS—*Denise Crosby (Tasha Yar),
Whoopi Goldberg (Guinan), Colm Meaney
(Chief O'Brien), and Diana Muldaur (Dr. Pulaski)*   203

10. FACES YOU KNOW—*Majel Barrett Roddenberry
(Lwaxana Troi), Brian Bonsall (Alexander),
Rosalind Chao (Keiko O'Brien), John de Lancie (Q),
Michelle Forbes (Ro), Dwight Shultz (Barclay),
and Patti Yasutake (Nurse Ogawa)*   241

POSTSCRIPT   265

BIBLIOGRAPHY   266

FOR MY MOTHER,
WHO WOULD HAVE BEEN PROUD

Let us not speak of the unspeakable
Let us not dwell on the inferno that enveloped her
and turned the golden days into leaden nights.
Let us remember the radiance that warmed our lives,
the questing nature ever seeking the perfect way
and measuring the clues with churning hope.
Let us speak of the lover of foods and children,
and music and books
and all that is sensitive and kind.
Let us say that in a world that festers year by year
she was the tender plant that never could survive,
but in the flourishing the leaves gave out
a touch of beauty that will never die.

—Eugene T. Maleska, *"The Tender Plant"*

ACKNOWLEDGMENTS

When I agreed to write this book, I knew that I would be seeking advice, assistance, and information from many disparate sources. Had I realized up front just how much reference material existed, and how wide a net *Star Trek* fandom cast, I may not have taken it on. Nonetheless, what you are holding in your hands could not have come into being without the generous assistance of many people.

The first thing I did upon deciding to write *The Finest Crew in the Fleet* was to log on to the World Wide Web and head toward Luca Sambucci's incredible *Star Trek* site (www.vol.it/luca/startrek/). Luca and I have never met, but we have corresponded via e-mail, and his "mother of all *Star Trek* sites" is a must-visit for fans of *any* aspect of *any* of the *Star Trek* incarnations. From Luca's site, I befriended much of fandom, learned about countless fan clubs, and realized that I had my work cut out for me. The Internet has provided me a steady stream of articles and information, some more reliable than others. For being of particular usefulness, I am indebted to Jim "The Big Dweeb" Griffith (moderator of rec.arts.startrek.info), Ruben Macias (compiler of the weekly *Warp 10* newsletter), and Mike "Vidiot" Brown (www. cdsnet.net/vidiot/).

Fan clubs, "officially sanctioned" and otherwise, have proved absolutely invaluable in my research. The single most remarkable among these clubs has to be the former International Audience Alliance for Patrick Stewart (IAAPS). Although the IAAPS is defunct, members (who now operate the fan club The Patrick Stewart Network) continue to operate the Patrick Stewart Research Library (PSRL) in West Islip, New York. The curators of the PSRL—Janet D'Airo, Joan Rumerman, Regina Hewston, and Cindy Thomas—opened their doors for me, answered my questions, and allowed me to garner an incredible trove of information about Mr. Stewart. The folks at the PSRL guard Mr. Stewart's privacy and possessions (many of which he has donated) very carefully, and have created a genuine reference center for Stewart fans and *Star Trek* fans alike. I cannot thank them enough for their hospitality and generosity, and I sincerely hope that my efforts reflect the respect and deference the PSRL folks hold for this great actor. While *Star Trek: The Next Generation* was on the air, the IAAPS published *The Stargazer*, simply the finest fan club publication ever produced. One glance through the bibliography of *The Finest Crew in the Fleet* will attest to the level upon which I have relied upon this fine magazine. For anyone interested in creating a fan club publication, you can do no better than to emulate *The Stargazer*.

I am indebted to many other fans who have collected and shared their extensive stores of information about their favorite *Next Generation* actors: Judi Megna-George and Louise Jacobson run Imzadi International, a club (still going strong) dedicated to Jonathan Frakes and Marina Sirtis, and sanctioned by Sirtis. They currently publish, out of their own small Pipedream Publishers operation, two magazines, *Red Alert* and *Imzadi International*. They have been more than generous with their time and resources, and have become both friends and colleagues to whom I will remain indebted Raymond Ko maintains an excellent Gates McFadden Web page (www.sis.port.ac. uk/~dis12886/beverly.html), and we have been communicating now for many months. Melody and Jim Rondeau publish *DataEntries*, and have generously sent me copies for my research. I made many of these friends and discovered many of these sources with the assistance of the Star Trek Welcommittee, a group of fans dedicated solely to helping other fans find local or special-interest fan clubs appropriate to their *Trek* interest. Wow.

The filmographies at the end of each chapter, and throughout chapters 9 and 10, have been compiled from extensive research, "television encyclopedias," cross-referencing of articles and reviews, and fan publications. However, the foundation of each (except Patrick Stewart's) was realized by building with permission on similar lists compiled by Ron Carman, who compiles "*Star Trek* Actors' Other Roles" (www.cris.com/~Carman/reg.html). Much of this information is elusive, and Ron has spent years compiling it. He unselfishly has allowed me to build upon his work, and I in turn have allowed him to utilize mine. Visit his Web site for the most updated résumés of the stars of *The Next Generation*, as well as those of the other *Star Trek* series. The basis for the Patrick Stewart filmography was compiled by Joan Rumerman of the PSRL/IAAPS, a hefty and thankless job to which I can only say, thank you.

Three writers, none of whom I know personally, deserve special acknowledgment. Larry Nemecek is the author of *The Star Trek: The Next Generation Companion* (Revised 1995 Edition: Pocket Books $14.00). He provides insight on the goings-on behind each individual *Next Generation* episode, and offers explanations as to the impact the individual episodes had on the actors, the characters they play, and the future of the franchise. His book was an invaluable reference tool, and I encourage all readers who do not yet own a copy of his tome to purchase one today. His volume truly must be on the bookshelf of every *Next Generation* fan. Dan Madsen is the editor and publisher of *Star Trek: The Official Fan Club* magazine (now known as *Star Trek Communicator*). Each issue includes in-depth interviews with the stars of *Star Trek*, many of them conducted by Madsen himself, interviews that not only detail the goings-on in the world of *Star Trek*, but also include intimate details of the actors' lives. I have relied upon dozens of back issues of his quality publication in writing this book. Finally, Ian Spelling, a newspaper columnist, publishes a weekly syndicated "Inside Trek" column and contributes *Trek* articles to mainstream and science fiction publications alike. A peek at my bibliography offers a testament as to how much I relied on Spelling's articles.

Part of the reason we watch *Star Trek* is to discuss it, debate it, argue over it, pick it apart, postulate over it, complain about it, and anxiously await the next one. To enjoy it fully, I have spent the last few years watching and discussing *Trek* with Sam Ramer, Rob Rudnitsky,

Alan Dickar, Ezra Angrist, and Matt Webster, all of whom contributed on some level to this book. Amy Worlton gave up many lunch hours on my behalf to seek out nooks and crannies of the World Wide Web I had not yet found. I am also indebted to a couple of sources at Paramount, who have requested anonymity. You know who you are. I think you'll see I have maintained respect and integrity for the program and for the actors involved, as promised. Like I said, who would want to read anything else?

The first thing that made this book possible was a gem of an idea by Bill Wolfsthal, publisher of Wolf Valley Books. With one phone call, he placed his trust in me, and I in him. I only hope that I have come through with my end of the deal. Bill (an incredible *Star Trek* fan in his own right, and someone with whom I have debated over the Vulcan's appearance in *First Contact*) has hired a group of fantastic people to run his operation—and I need to give a special acknowledgment to my hardworking editor, Amy Stout. Her ideas and persuasive honesty have made this book immeasurably stronger. For someone who is not a professed trekker, she's spent her share of time associated with *Star Trek*–related projects—having edited both Gene Roddenberry's authorized biography and a number of novels by David Gerrold.

Before my Brooklyn prose ever made it under my editor's pen, it suffered under the unrelenting critical eye of my wife, Lisa. She read every page, every word, backtracked, cross-referenced, questioned, fixed my grammar, and improved my writing tremendously. She was honest, critical, and judgmental, while bearing with me as I slaved through chapter after chapter, life story after life story. She did a lot of other things, too, for which I thank her from the bottom of my heart. The rest of my family, particularly my brother, Paul, and my father, Ed, although not the least bit interested in this subject matter, have unquestioningly supported me both in my efforts on this book and through the recent loss that we all suffered.

I took unblushing advantage of all of the above, as well as many others whom I've unintentionally neglected to mention. This book would be much less without all of their input. For all that is good about the following, I have them to thank. For the errors and mistakes that inevitably creep into such a project, I personally take full responsibility.

—Adam Shrager

INTRODUCTION

One of the things I have learned in the past thirty years is that just about everybody in the world wants to be a part of *Star Trek*—not simply because they want to be part of a successful television show, and not simply because they want to be part of a cultural phenomenon—but because they need to be part of the dream.

I remember when Bob Justman began lobbying for Patrick Stewart as Captain Picard. Meeting after meeting, he would talk about Stewart's compelling performance as the Machiavellian Sejanus in the astonishing BBC production of Robert Graves' epic novel of the first four Roman emperors, *I, Claudius*.

At first, Gene Roddenberry was reluctant to consider Stewart—even after he met him in person. But after interviewing several other candidates for the role of Picard, it became obvious that Patrick Stewart was the most qualified. His theatrical training came through as a strong sense of authority. Today it's hard to believe that there was ever any doubt about Patrick Stewart.

Another piece of casting, however, was probably inevitable. When the character of Wesley was first created—first Wesley, then Leslie (a fifteen-year-old girl), then Wesley again—it happened almost the same week that *St. Elsewhere* broadcast an episode starring Wil Wheaton as a child prodigy who had just completed medical school. The following day, I wrote a memo to Bob Justman and Gene Roddenberry suggesting Wil Wheaton as Wesley. But it was months before that part was cast—and by then, Wil Wheaton's name had been submitted by a number of individuals. One way or another, there was no way that Wil Wheaton was not going to be considered for the role, and there was no one else who was as right for the part as he was. Wil's youth and enthusiasm were considerable.

LeVar Burton was also an inevitable choice for the role of Geordi LaForge. What may not be as well known is that his character is based on a real individual. In 1974, a group of Detroit fans held a *Star Trek* convention and invited Gene Roddenberry, several cast members, and several writers (including myself). The emotional high point of the convention occurred when teenage muscular dystrophy patient George LaForge entered the convention masquerade as Captain Christopher Pike. He and his wheelchair had been made up to look like Pike in "The Menagerie."

George LaForge was one of the most enthusiastic of *Star Trek*'s fans and this was one of the greatest moments in his life, meeting so many of *Star Trek*'s people in person. Later, Gene Roddenberry made him an honorary admiral in Starfleet, the first and only time this honor has been granted. George LaForge died a few years later, but he was warmly remembered by everyone who was at that convention.

So, in 1986, when Gene Roddenberry decided to add a disabled person to *Star Trek*'s crew, we considered various disabilities. Gene finally decided on blindness. (When this information was passed on to the studio executives, one of them sent back a memo asking if we thought it was appropriate for LaForge to have this handicap in addition to being black. Say what—?) About this same time, I reminded Gene of George LaForge and suggested that we name this character after that young man. Gene thought it was a good idea, and that's how Geordi LaForge got his name. (Incidentally, that thing he wears across his eyes—? That's a hair beret.)

The one piece of casting that happened almost by accident was Jonathan Frakes as Will Riker. Another actor was originally on the inside track, and it was assumed his casting was a done deal. All that remained was for him to be seen (and approved) by the studio executives. Unfortunately, he choked in that final reading. Everyone involved was disappointed. But they were so sure he was right for the part that they brought him back—and he choked a second time. So they went with Jonathan Frakes instead—a brilliant decision stumbled into almost by accident.

What sets *Star Trek* apart from the rest of television is the way the audience has responded to it. To judge by the fans, *Star Trek* represents another way of being, one that suggests that the way the world is today is not necessarily the way it has to be—and the way we are is not the way we will always be. To see the show this way is to understand that it is not just a dream—it is also a responsibility.

Why? Because space is not the final frontier. The final frontier is the human soul. Space is where we will meet the challenge.

—David Gerrold

PREFACE

"They're betting they can catch lightning in a bottle again."
—LEONARD NIMOY, QUOTED IN A 1987 *TV GUIDE* ARTICLE

Patrick Stewart is not Captain Jean-Luc Picard. He is English, *not* French, prefers tennis to fencing, and Darjeeling over Earl Grey tea. He loves roller coasters, his Nintendo Gameboy, *Beavis and Butt-head*, and valet parking. Picard flies one of the most technologically advanced pieces of machinery in our galaxy, but Stewart makes no pretenses regarding his inability to program a VCR.

You can find Jonathan Frakes (Commander Riker) behind the camera these days or at home with his actress wife of ten years, Genie Francis, and their two young children. Brent Spiner (Data) is an avowed "television junkie" and veteran of the Broadway stage. LeVar Burton (Geordi LaForge) enjoys a legion of fans from his role on *Star Trek: The Next Generation*, from his Emmy-nominated role on *Roots*, and (perhaps most significantly) from his hosting duties on the venerable PBS series *Reading Rainbow*. Marina Sirtis (Counselor Troi) can often be found astride her Harley-Davidson or caring for her Yorkshire terrier and five cats. Gates McFadden (Dr. Crusher) has taught at the university level and worked extensively with Jim Henson's muppets. Michael Dorn (Worf) now holds the record for being the actor to have appeared on the greatest number of episodes of *Star Trek* (including his time aboard *Deep Space Nine*), but off camera, you can find him piloting jets.

When we reminisce about the crew of the *Enterprise-D*, we remember the exploits of her French captain and swashbuckling Alaskan first officer. We revel in the adventures of the Klingon security officer, Betazoid counselor, android from parts unknown (eventually revealed to have been built at the Omicron Theta colony), blind chief engineer, and beautiful doctor. (Where *were* those latter two from? It was never revealed, though we do know that Dr. Crusher's grandmother lived at the Arvada III colony, and that LaForge's parents moved around quite often.) However, what we are really remembering are the exploits of seven talented actors: two Brits (Stewart and Sirtis), two native Texans (Dorn and Spiner), a Pennsylvanian (Frakes), an Ohioan (McFadden), and an American born in West Germany (LeVar Burton). Their lives and careers, triumphs and disappointments, are the subjects of this book.

Other actors in addition to the seven featured players made their marks on *Star Trek: The Next Generation*. Most notably Wil Wheaton (Wesley Crusher)—one of the four teenagers who starred in the hit film *Stand by Me*—saved the *Enterprise* nearly a dozen times, and ultimately left the show to pursue other offers. Denise Crosby (Tasha Yar) is best remembered by some as the granddaughter of Bing, but is also thought of as "the security chief *before* Worf." Colm Meaney (O'Brien) has a successful movie career, as well as being a regular cast member on *Star Trek: Deep Space Nine*. Diana Muldaur (Dr. Pulaski) was the first female president of the Academy of Television Arts and Sciences. After her single season as the *Enterprise*'s chief physician, she achieved great notoriety plummeting down an elevator shaft on *L.A. Law*. Whoopi Goldberg (Guinan), comedian and movie star, joined the crew of *The Next Generation* as a result of both her genuine love for the show and the impact Nichelle Nichols (Uhura) made on her as she was growing up. These twelve actors may be recognized for many divergent roles throughout their careers, but they will always be remembered for their roles in exploring deep space at warp speed.

It has been said by fans and critics alike that the only star of *The Next Generation* is the *Enterprise* herself. They are wrong. Without the actors portraying characters whom millions of viewers learned to love, depend upon, and root for, the program would be little more than a video game. It is a lot more than that, it is a cultural phenomenon that its stars are inexorably linked to.

All fans of *Star Trek*, from the most casual viewer of the show to the most avid, have their favorite actor or character. Fan clubs exist for each individual cast member, a claim that no other television program with as large a cast can boast. From the "Electronic Male Network" (for fans of Brent Spiner), to "Imzadi International" (for those who prefer Frakes and Sirtis), to "WilPower" (Wil Wheaton's admirers), to "The Temporal Mechanic" (Colm Meaney's fans), fan clubs have proved a way for avid devotees of particular actors to learn more about their favorite stars. Patrick Stewart has not only a number of fan clubs devoted to him, but also an American honor usually accorded only retiring presidents: a library detailing his life and illustrious career, located in West Islip, New York (the Patrick Stewart Research Library). Whomever *your* favorite *Star Trek: The Next Generation* actors (or if perhaps you like them all), this book endeavors to bring you closer to them: it delves behind the scenes of their lives growing up, their early careers, the set of *The Next Generation*, and the years since the program ceased production.

"Encounter at Farpoint," the two-hour pilot episode, aired the week of September 28, 1987. The first casting call went out to talent agencies on December 10, 1986. It included calls for series "regulars" Captain *Julien* Picard, "Number One" William *Ryker*, Security Chief Lieutenant *Macha Hernandez*, and fifteen-year-old teenage *girl Leslie* Crusher. These four, along with Troi, Dr. Crusher, and LaForge, comprised the original core crew. Worf, originally conceived as something of a Klingon marine, was added very late, and was not even included in the first-season official cast portrait taken June 1, 1987.

Patrick Stewart was cast after being "discovered" by producer Robert Justman at a dramatic reading at UCLA. Stewart did not initially win over executive producer and series creator Gene Roddenberry as the man for the captain's chair, and was actually cast on October 10, 1986, by Justman for the role of Data. Although Stewart did not fit Roddenberry's image of what a captain should be (he really did want a Frenchman), Justman kept insisting that Stewart was the perfect captain, and finally Roddenberry gave in. Fans familiar with Stewart's résumé probably think of him as "that British Shakespearean actor," but recall that he was previously best known to American television audiences as Sejanus on the BBC-PBS miniseries *I, Claudius*.

Jonathan Frakes suffered through seven auditions in six weeks to win the role of Riker. LeVar Burton's casting received the greatest amount of media attention, his being the most "recognizable" face in the cast. Gates McFadden turned down the role of Dr. Crusher, having committed to appear in a play for $400 a week. Brent Spiner was a Broadway stage veteran, and had replaced Rene Auberjonois—later of *Star Trek: Deep Space Nine*—in the musical *Big River*. Despite an extensive Broadway résumé, Spiner was most recognizable to television audiences from a recurring role on the comedy *Night Court*. Marina

Sirtis was originally auditioning for the role of Security Chief Macha Hernandez, while Denise Crosby was after that of Counselor Troi. However, Gene Roddenberry stepped in and switched them, deciding that Sirtis' European beauty was better suited for Troi's empathic role, and Denise Crosby had the look of a security chief. The only avowed trekkers on the cast, Michael Dorn and Wil Wheaton, rounded out the main first-season cast. Wesley was named after Gene Wesley Roddenberry, and Roddenberry often thought of Wesley as "a seventeen-year-old version of myself." Michael Dorn, in true Klingon fashion, walked into his Paramount audition in character: "No jokes. No laughing with the other actors. I sat by myself waiting for my interview. When my turn came, I walked in, didn't smile, did the reading, thanked them, and walked right out."

What the future holds for *Star Trek* is, of course, impossible to determine. Fans have probably seen the last movie to feature the original cast. Most devotees hope that the *Next Generation* cast will continue to appear on the big screen, and the overwhelming success of *Star Trek: First Contact* makes that appear likely. *Star Trek: Deep Space Nine* and *Star Trek: Voyager* continue to impress, and to build upon the universe that Gene Roddenberry conceived—and of course, they offer opportunities for *The Next Generation* cast to appear and to direct. Rumors of a series or continuing projects featuring Captain Sulu persist. Novels and comic books will surely continue to be published into the next millennium.

Star Trek: The Next Generation is the single most successful hour-long syndicated drama in television history. It has spawned two feature films thus far, as well as two sequel series. It is a cultural phenomenon, enjoyed by college professors and nine-year-olds alike. It is a business, and fans understand that. But it is more than that. It is a weekly morality play, an escape from worldly problems, a dream of what might be to come. Some fans enjoy debating starship design, others warp theory. (Physicist Stephen Hawking likes to joke he's "working on it," or is he joking?) Other fans rant about how much they love the Wesley character; some vehemently disagree. For some, their admiration of Patrick Stewart has led them to Broadway and his one-man rendition of *A Christmas Carol*, or to New York City's Central Park where he performed Shakespeare. When thousands of people at the sold-out Ziegfield theater in the heart of Manhattan scream "DATA! DATA!

DATA!" upon Brent Spiner's appearance as Dr. Okun halfway through the 1996 blockbuster *Independence Day*, it is clear that the show has made an impact. "Engage" and "make it so" are as much a part of the popular lexicon as "beam me up" ever was.

What follows is a tribute, detailing the good—and occasionally the bad—the past, the present, and the foreseeable future, of the only cast that can truly be called "The Finest Crew in the Fleet."

—Adam Shrager
Princeton, New Jersey
February 1997

CHAPTER 1

PATRICK STEWART

Thespian on the Bridge

"There are those who would say sitting in the captain's chair on the
USS Enterprise is far more important than sitting
on the throne of England."
—PATRICK STEWART, RECALLING ONE OF THE LAST ROLES HE PLAYED WITH
THE ROYAL SHAKESPEARE COMPANY, *KING HENRY IV*

P atrick Stewart was born July 13, 1940, in Mirfield, Yorkshire, England, the third son of Alfred Stewart and Gladys Barraclough. His childhood could not be deemed happy, and his family was anything but prosperous. Yet from very humble beginnings grew an actor who would resurrect the role of *Star Trek's* captain and imbue it with his own humanity and style, as well as introduce thousands to the joys of Shakespeare. He would come to be regarded as a sex symbol, leading man, and genuine Hollywood personality. He would accomplish all of this despite impoverished beginnings and the lack of an extensive formal education.

NOT AN EASY CHILDHOOD

Stewart's household was poor and violent. He spent much of his childhood being afraid. His mother, a weaver, raised him and did all she could to shield him from an abusive father, but she was forced to work full time, "operating an enormous, terrifying machine in a huge, drafty weaving shed with two hundred other women." His father, who had spent eight years in the army in India, returned home in 1933 only to reenlist for World War II, where he was accorded the rank of regimental sergeant major.

"You don't get that rank without being a disciplinarian so there were certain rules [in the home]," recalled Patrick's brother Trevor, four years his senior. Eldest brother Geoffrey, sixteen years

1

older than Patrick, stated, "Everything ran to a timetable. He ruled with a rod of iron and had a terrible temper. Patrick was very close to my mother and adored her but she had an extremely hard life because of my father. We always hoped he would die first so she could have a few years' peace."

Patrick himself told an interviewer in 1995, "My family home was run very much as a regimental mess—a lot of discipline, order, and organization. I had the cleanest fingernails in school because my father inspected them every day."

Initially, acting was an escape from a violent home. Every night, Stewart had a legitimate excuse to go out. He reported, "It cauterized the hurt and the pain. Being able to go somewhere else and say 'What if?' or 'Once upon a time' was comforting." Mirfield supported twelve drama clubs, with a population of eleven thousand, so the opportunities for escape were ever present. He was also encouraged by the example of his grandparents. His grandfather made his living as a stage carpenter, and his grandmother cared for the children of stage workers, including a young Stan Laurel.

"One of the reasons I started acting when I was twelve or thirteen," Stewart stated in 1995, "was that I found the stage, and putting on other personalities, much safer, much more comfortable than my own skin. My own problems always started when the curtain came down. Stage life had a beginning, a middle, and an end. I could feel in control there. In fact, I have always had difficulty with letting myself lose control onstage, with letting any strong emotion possess me. I had trouble making emotions seem authentic. Now, in my brand-new fifty-fifth year, I'm trying to achieve more of a balance. I'm getting more control over my life, and I can take more chances in my acting."

Although Stewart's father reportedly never struck his sons, "We were frightened to death of him," brother Geoffrey stated. Yet this difficult family life brought Patrick closer to his brothers, inspired him to get out of the house and participate in local theater; his father's anger and disciplined style provided inspiration for later theatrical roles, including certain aspects of Captain Picard. Although Alfred frequently chastised Geoffrey for sitting up nights reading "that bloody rubbish" (Shakespeare) to his baby brother, Geoffrey still sat up and read the four-year-old Patrick bedtime stories—*MacBeth, Hamlet,* and *King Lear.* "I barely understood a word of it . . . but I liked the sounds. The sounds did something to me viscerally," Patrick recalls. Of course, decades later, when Patrick Stewart was relatively famous in England as an associate with the Royal Shakespeare Company (RSC), father Alfred would find opportunities to quote *Henry V* and *MacBeth.*

Patrick agreed with his brother's assessment of the fear they lived with growing up, but realizes it may have been misplaced. "I'm the one son of his who never did any military service," Stewart said in 1993, "and I know he always held this against me. But now I think I didn't really have anything to be terrified of at all. He would have a good laugh at me being called 'captain' now!" Yet Stewart was always close to his brothers, whether they were reading Shakespeare or engaging in mischief. Referring to the British holiday Guy Fawkes Day (November 5), when children perform pranks similar to those in the United States on Halloween, Stewart admitted to Jay Leno, "It was the only time I crossed paths with the law. My brothers and I were arrested for chopping down trees in someone's wood that was supposed to be protected. I'm ashamed and embarrassed about it now—but I do have a criminal record. . . . I also put a banger [a powerful firecracker] in the lock of my aunt's door and blew it off. We were dumb in those days, we were young."

SEDUCED BY THE STAGE

Because Stewart did not own a television until he was twenty-three, the first time he heard a play in its entirety was on the radio. He listened to *The Tempest* when he was about ten. From his local Mirfield church he had gotten a copy of *The Complete Works of Shakespeare.* There were very few books in the Stewart household, but this volume is one that Patrick still remembers fondly. "I listened to the play on radio, and I followed along in the published text . . . which was very exciting for me—to have in my hands the same lines that the actors were speaking."

Besides participating in theater as a youngster, Patrick was an avid cinemagoer. Every week, he would lose himself in the exploits of Doris Day, Debbie Reynolds, Tab Hunter, and Rock Hudson. However, one of the defining moments of his childhood, culturally, was the day he went to the theater to see a film he knew nothing about, *On the Waterfront*. "I'd been utterly seduced by Technicolor, and I remember when the titles came up feeling irritably disappointed that the film was in black and white." However, once the movie began, he was transfixed. "Everything changed from that moment on, partly because I saw that people made movies about *me*. I lived in an industrial town in northern England. It was a million miles from the Brooklyn waterfront, but nonetheless, all those values and conditions—the things that people were doing to one another—were recognizable, particularly, of course, in Brando's character. I went back four times, I even took my poor mother, who didn't understand what the hell was going on. It was overwhelming. Still is . . ."

Both as a child and as a grown man, and particularly after his twenty-five-year marriage ended, Stewart considered himself quite unhappy. He related personally to the character Scrooge from *A Christmas Carol*. Years later, he would formally rehearse the role for his one-man version of Dickens' tale on Broadway, but he claimed, "In a way, I think I had been rehearsing it metaphorically for a very long time. I don't think it's accidental that of all the things which have obsessed me is a story about a close, narrow, unhappy, mean individual, not living in society at all, who in the last moments of his life is given a second chance to do better.

"I think there was, and probably still is, a substantial amount of Scrooge in my nature, and one of the things I've attempted to do is de-Scrooge myself." It should be noted that now, living with his girlfriend, Wendy Neuss, a producer for *Star Trek: Voyager*, he has openly commented on how much happier and more fulfilled he is. In retrospect, much of Stewart's past misery may have been linked to the crumbling of a long-term marriage and the requisite emotions that accompany such an event, particularly for a celebrity who, much to his dismay, finds his personal troubles splayed out in the weekly tabloids for all to share. Neuss and he are reportedly very happy together, and Stewart often notes that he knew they would be compatible once he learned that she could name all thirty-seven Shakespeare plays.

As a teenage student, Stewart attended Secondary Modern School, instead of enrolling in an academic school, before he dropped out at age fifteen. All eleven-year-old children in England are required to take an exam, the results of which determine which school they will attend for the rest of their childhood education. "On the day of the exam I set off for school in the morning and got to the road that led to the building where the examination was to take place and walked past it. And I went up into the hills that are outside and a bit above my little town and I spent the day walking in the woods and, actually, it was spring, sitting about the bluebell patch. I remember looking at the view, enjoying the spring sunshine, and feeling extraordinarily happy. . . . And I went home and my mother asked me 'how did it go?' and I said it was great. Had a wonderful day." It was at the Secondary Modern School that he encountered an English teacher who taught him the joys of reading Shakespeare aloud. This is the same teacher who asked him, at fifteen, if he had ever considered becoming a professional actor. "I thought the man was crazed," Stewart recalls.

Yet just before leaving school, never to return, Stewart performed with two friends in a revue at the high school. In *The Great Mesmo*, a mind-reading act, Stewart played Mesmo's sidekick who would go into the audience and ask someone to "hand me something—anything." Patrick would then hold it up and say, "Great Mesmo, tell me, what I am holding in my hand?" The blindfolded Mesmo on stage, aided by a third member of the team behind a curtain, would then announce the item to everyone's surprise and delight. Despite engaging in such joyous times as these, and being named head boy at Mirfield High School, Stewart left school at age fifteen to train as a journalist.

Stewart stated in 1994 that "the next closest thing in terms of distinction to winning an Academy Award would be to get an honorary degree." This dream was fulfilled in 1995, when he was awarded a Doctorate of Humane Letters from California's Pomona College.

Stewart's first job after leaving school was as a beat reporter for a local newspaper. He credits one of his English teachers for helping him develop a flair for languages. This "flair" occasionally got him into trouble. Stewart told a columnist in 1990, "I was suspended from writing reviews for six months one time after I'd used a word that was considered inappropriate. I'd called a particularly small theater 'intimate.'"

His newspaper editor wanted him to abandon the theater projects in which he was participating because they interfered with his journalistic commitments. "More than once I just made up the copy," Stewart has stated. "I would try to cover events in advance or afterward by making phone calls." "Abandon these amateur dramatics, or get out!" were the words yelled at him by the editor of the West Riding weekly newspaper. Although reasonable, this infuriated Stewart. "Reasonable or not, though, this was the kind of ultimatum of the kind I hate most. Out of sheer stubbornness, I got out! And so there I was—sixteen years old, qualified for nothing!" Stewart has been quoted as saying that he became an actor afterward out of spite, to get back at that newspaper editor.

A brief stint selling furniture at Hudson's in the nearby town of Dewsbury followed. "I rather enjoyed it and it was good training in a way. Being an actor, reporter, or salesman all involve fooling people on some level." He won a drama scholarship to the Bristol Old Vic Theatre School in 1957, which eventually led him to the Royal Shakespeare Company. During this time, he also participated in a drama camp at Calder, where he worked with the man who would eventually become "The Dynamite Kid," his good friend to this day, and I, Claudius costar, Brian Blessed. At Calder, Stewart also met one of his most influential drama coaches and teachers, Ruth Wynn Owen. Stewart began acting full time in 1959. In the neary forty years since, he has never been out of work for more than a few months at a time—a record he realizes makes him very lucky among actors.

Ruth Wynn Owen was Patrick Stewart's first real drama teacher. A former student at the Old Vic herself, she had never taught before and needed convincing to spend a week at Calder's Whit Week Youth Drama Course. It was here, during her first teaching experience, that she met a young Patrick Stewart and his good friend Brian Blessed. "One could see at once what was there. He was a 'natural,' natural timing and natural movement. . . . Acting is a gift, and he had it," Owen recounted in an interview. As for Stewart's role on Star Trek, she noted: "His natural authority makes him perfect for the character, and his warmth hinges the authority. . . . He is 'officer class.'"

Stewart is indebted to the local Mirfield authority and in particular Gerald Tyler for being instrumental in helping him receive the grant to study at the Old Vic. Without the scholarship, he simply "wouldn't have become an actor." With his limited educational background—academically the absolute minimum the state required in terms of schooling—he was "as unqualified as was possible to be for the kind of scholarship I was given. I was blessed in having people who felt, despite my lack of educational qualifications, there were other things that made the money well spent."

Enrolling at the Old Vic school at the age of seventeen, Stewart spent the next two years studying acting and focusing on losing his Yorkshire accent. He has referred to leading a "double life" during this period; for while he assiduously studied Received Pronunciation during the day and used it professionally, he continued speaking with his native accent and dialect with family and friends. About halfway through his training, which was at the time only a two-year program (it is now four), Stewart received some advice he has referred to as the best he has ever been given. "The principal of my acting school, an extraordinary man named Duncan Ross, said to me, 'Patrick, you will never achieve success by insuring against failure.' It took me many, many years to understand what he meant. It is still hard to live up to that advice. We all have an inclination to play it safe, not to take that big risk that could see us fall and utterly fail. But if you don't take risks, you will never succeed. I think, in one respect, as I've gotten older, I've also gotten braver. I believe that I have something to say and I have a talent to say it with and I wasn't sure of that for many, many years."

Indeed, an Actor

In August 1959, at the age of nineteen, Stewart made his professional debut at the Theatre Royal in Lincoln, in the role of Morgan in a stage adaptation of *Treasure Island*. After only a month, he left this company and joined the Sheffield Playhouse, where he stayed until 1961.

It was during these two years, before he was twenty-one years old, that Stewart lost nearly all of his hair. "It was absolutely traumatic. I did a number of things to try to prevent it and then, when I saw it was unpreventable, to hide it." Although warned that he would have difficulty landing jobs in lead roles due to his bald-ness, Stewart claimed that "being hairless on top and quite young can have its advantages. When a director gathers a company for a season he is looking for a variety of types. With the aid of a toupee he regards me as two for the price of one. I often felt more like an economic asset than an artistic one."

On *The Tonight Show with Jay Leno*, Stewart revealed that for his final audition for Captain Picard, he actually wore a hairpiece he was then using in a London production of *Who's Afraid of Virginia Woolf?* It was nicknamed the "George" and was, in Stewart's words, "just a few strands of hair."

During the 1962–63 theater season, Stewart was a member of the company of the Library Theatre in Manchester under the direction of David Scase, playing Orsino in *Twelfth Night* with other future Royal Shakespeare Company artists. Also at the Library he performed in *The Caretaker*, his first experience—or, as he put it, "confrontation"—with the plays of Harold Pinter. "It's a tremendous experience acting Pinter, like having a terrible secret." Also at Manchester, Stewart played his first major Shakespeare role, that of Henry V in the play of the same name. "Only David Scase would have had the courage or madness to trust me with this. He had a tremendous effect on my acting at this stage." This performance of *Henry V*, well over thirty-five years ago, is the performance that Patrick's brothers, Trevor and Gregory, consider their favorite of all the performances their baby brother has staged. "His speech before Agincourt brought tears to my eyes. I was absolutely dumbfounded by it! He's got better, and done better things since—he's played more important roles in larger and more important companies—but I personally have never been so moved by anything he's done," recalls Trevor.

Stewart spent the following season in Liverpool and eventually was able to return to the Bristol Old Vic as a leading member of the company, performing there from 1964 to 1966. While fulfilling his dream of returning to his former school, he met Sheila Falconer, a choreographer with the company. They were married March 3, 1966, and in 1968, Daniel Freedom Stewart was born. Now an actor and living in California, Daniel is best known among *Star Trek* fans as Picard's "son" in the episode "Inner Light." Patrick and Sheila's daughter, Sophie Alexandra, was born six years later, and now owns and manages a boutique in London.

Stewart's London debut came in February 1969 at the Aldwych with the internationally famous Royal Shakespeare Company. The RSC was created after World War II as the national theater company of England, devoted to the productions of the country's (the Western world's?) greatest playwright, in order to preserve a culture that it was feared might be lost and forgotten. When Patrick Stewart joined the RSC, subsequently being named an associate artist in one year, it was not for him so much the fulfillment of a life's dream as it was just another, albeit a very important, stepping-stone. At the time, his thought was that he would pick up a few classical credits and move on to greater fame, perhaps following in the footsteps of Laurence Olivier or John Gielgud. However, his time at the RSC was fulfillment enough for many years, and the impact Trevor Nunn and his company would have on him (as both a friend and an inspiration) kept Stewart actively associated with the RSC through the early 1980s. He worked for the RSC exclusively from 1966 to 1975, and then through 1984 appeared occasionally while working on television, in films, or on other stages.

While with the RSC, Stewart not only worked with Trevor Nunn's company, but also spent time with Mary Ann "Buzz" Goodbody's *The Other Place*, RSC's small experimental "third" theater. Also with the RSC and Buzz Goodbody's troupe was Ben Kingsley, with whom Stewart remains good friends to this day. Stewart, Kingsley, and Goodbody, among others, lived off and on for three years during the 1970s in a predominantly female, Marxist collective in London, primarily working on "experimental" theater.

For Stewart, at this time in his life the great "revelation," however unfashionable, was Shakespeare. "I don't like to see him performed badly. It's become like a parent-child relationship—you have to open doors, to make possible all kinds of choice and widen the vision. Never say one of his plays isn't about this or that."

Stewart published an academic essay and treatise on Shylock (from *The Merchant of Venice*) in *Players of Shakespeare: Essays in Shakespearean Performance*. His explanation and interpretation of Shylock's meaning and role was as an embittered outsider who happens to be Jewish. When he performed the part with the RSC in the 1970s, he was aware of the "monstrous stereotype" and told himself the part wasn't about the last sixty years of Jewish history. Yet as Stewart worked on the play, he began to realize that "Shakespeare had anticipated the twentieth century. I discovered that Shylock is a revolutionary character, lining up with the IRA and PLO in that he will risk everything and take a life for what he believes in. He will take a life because of inequality and to oppose the status quo. Shakespeare is often accused of being a conservative, a conformist . . . but he continually howls against the disgrace of injustice, of ignorance, and of a lack of concern and responsibility . . . and that is a radical attitude."

All *Star Trek* actors are asked about their favorite episodes, but Stewart is the only one who is just as frequently asked about his favorite Shakespearean play. "*Henry IV, Part 2*. It shows more potently than any of his other plays the great, soaring range of his talent. It contains some of the finest poetic drama he ever wrote, as well as great scenes of conflict, wonderfully, grotesquely comic sequences, and in some places writing of such detailed naturalism that you could lift it straight out of *The Complete Works* and put it in a film script. The one role I most hunger to play is Falstaff."

An interesting feature was reported by the *Coventry Evening Telegraph* in 1971. Stewart had been performing in *The Two Gentlemen of Verona* at the Royal Shakespeare Theatre in Stratford-upon-Avon. In the production is a walk-on part for a dog, which was played by a pooch from a local kennel, a Labrador named Crab. From August until the play closed in January, Crab lived happily at Stewart's home in Barford. Afterward, Crab returned to the kennel and Stewart went on one of his first tours of America, performing in *A Midsummer Night's Dream*. While his family was in America, son Daniel pined for the pup so much that upon returning to Britain, Stewart went and rescued Crab from the National Canine Defence League kennels at Wickhamford, adopting him permanently.

Stewart's love for animals has not subsided. After the Los Angeles earthquake in 1994, he adopted a homeless cat found wandering the *Star Trek* sets on the Paramount lot. Bella, his feline companion, is a close friend, and he dotes on her like a father.

ENGAGING HIS CAREER

On the personal front, Stewart was married to Sheila

Falconer for twenty-five years; their separate lives on two continents during the years he worked on *Star Trek* as well as their growing professional and personal differences ultimately led to their breakup in 1991. Much was written in the tabloid press about the negative impact his weekly hour-long television program had on their marriage, but Stewart set the record straight. "My marriage broke up, which caused me great, great sadness—but I can't hold the show responsible for that. It was a factor, but the responsibility was mine."

However, for many years, Stewart and Falconer's marriage had been viewed as a model, and at one point was featured in a 1982 London daily under the headline "Making Theatre Marriage Work." Although they did not collaborate on a production together for the first sixteen years of marriage—except of course for the "production" of children and a family—they felt that being in theater together, but not working in the same branch, was truly the best of both worlds. There was no competition, Falconer explained, "[but] what is nice is that, because we both understand the theater, we can start talking immediately about salient points. . . . There are whole areas we don't have to fill in." Stewart concurred: "The pair of us have eaten together between rehearsals and talked over the production in bed. But then Sheila has always been a trusted counselor and adviser."

Although Stewart's focus during the 1960s was on the Shakespearean stage, and he was never really a science fiction fan, he was not unaware of the significance of the space race or of happenings in the scientific world in the 1960s. As he stated to *Astronomy* magazine in December 1995, "I can remember more clearly where I was when Neil Armstrong set foot on the moon than I can where I was when John F. Kennedy was shot. I remember that having an enormous impact on me. My son was then four months old, and I remember holding him up in front of the television and saying, 'Look, pay attention to this. This is important.'"

During the 1970s and early 1980s, Stewart kept very busy. Established at the RSC, he also played Dr. Roebuck in *Maybury*, a BBC series about mental hospitals. To research his role as a psychologist, he mixed with staff and patients at a mental hospital. "At first I was so apprehensive I found an excuse not to go. But when I got to know the people on the wards, my visits became very enjoyable. I learned a lot from the patients as well as the doctors and social workers. They were all very glad the series was being made."

Additionally, these middle years saw Stewart get showered with accolades for his stage work. In 1978, the Society of West End Theatres presented Patrick Stewart with its best supporting actor award for his portrayal of Enobarbus in *Antony and Cleopatra*. In 1979, he also won the Olivier Award for best supporting actor for *Antony and Cleopatra* and was nominated for best actor for *The Merchant of Venice*. In 1987 he won the London Fringe best actor award for his performance in *Who's Afraid of Virginia Woolf?* and had another Olivier nomination for *Hippolytus*.

Of course, during these years, American audiences would be hard pressed to recognize Stewart from his theater roles, but would likely recognize him as Sejanus, the sinister lover of history's most famous nymphomaniac, Messalina, in the miniseries *I, Claudius*, originally airing on PBS in 1976. "I found Sejanus to be one of the most delightful and charming characters that I have ever played, utterly irresistible, witty, sophisticated, gentle, caring, and loving," Stewart exclaimed sarcastically in 1990. "Of course at the time when you are doing something like that, you are just doing a job. You never know that it's going to become what *I, Claudius* finally became, this landmark series. . . . My favorite scene was actually the scene where Augustus died. You remember that scene when he died and the camera stayed a single uncut shot on his face. Brian persuaded the director that he would die with his eyes open. And that you would see him die and his eyes would never close. And if you watch very carefully there is an extraordinary moment when the light, the light seems to go out of those eyes and the face never moves. It's quite magical!" The "Brian" Stewart refers to here is his lifelong friend Brian Blessed, whom he has recently said he would like to stand with arm in arm on the summit of Mount Everest.

Stewart draws analogies between Shylock (the Jewish moneylender from *Merchant of Venice*) and Sejanus, and to the way he found himself typecast before landing the role of Captain Picard. "I was sinister playing Sejanus. The point that I make in a lecture I do about Shylock: it is commonplace among actors that you must find some area of the character that you play that you can love, and the more you can love a character, the more chance you have of explaining him to an audience. Now I would be fascinated by trying to do that, particularly wicked people. I cannot remember liking anything about Sejanus except that he was so monstrously unpleasant that he was kind of 'finger-licking good.'"

Although Stewart's theater credits were vast, and his television work marked by a number of serious, well-known roles, his film career was sparse. However, even in relatively minor roles in films that were not box-office success stories, Stewart took something significant from each experience. His first film role was in 1975's *Hennessey*, playing the thug Tilney. Although he is killed after only five minutes on screen, Stewart was tickled to have acted so extensively in a scene with Rod Steiger, who starred with Marlon Brando in the film that so affected Stewart as a child, *On the Waterfront*.

In 1980 he played Leondegrance—a role he was "thrilled to accept"—in *Excalibur*. "I was a big fan of John Boorman, the director, and wanted very much to do it. The cast was stuffed with friends of mine! And so it was like a wonderful but hot and very uncomfortable holiday. . . . I can tell you that along with *Dune* [three years later], it was the most uncomfortable experience of my life." Uncomfortable because of the unwieldy costumes he had to wear in *Excalibur*, and the occasionally wretched conditions he had to endure while filming, including some very loosely choreographed jousts that were "very free for all—even by film standards they were loose!" Stewart was also forced to sit absolutely motionless for over forty minutes on the back of his horse in full chain-mail armor while the rain poured steadily down around him. Director John Boorman would not let him move because he was searching for a particular quality of light. Finally, to create smoke during the round table scene, which was filmed over the course of an entire evening, Boorman burned tires. "I don't think they can do this on movies anymore. But tires make wonderful smoke. And you shouldn't inhale the smoke but we were inhaling it all night long," Stewart recollected. However, despite what must sound like a torturous ordeal to even the least-knowledgeable person regarding Hollywood moviemaking, Stewart has only praise for Boorman. "What a brilliant filmmaker, what an outstanding moviemaker! I found it a great, great thrill to be working with him."

Of the other significantly uncomfortable film experience in Stewart's career, *Dune* (1983), Stewart remembers, "A great movie. Well, no, I'm sorry, correction—a great flawed movie!" Stewart took the job blind, script sight unseen, because he knew David Lynch was directing, and Lynch had directed what was a very "effective" movie for Stewart, *The Elephant Man*. However, the scripts changed from the one he had read on the plane flying to Mexico to join the cast (as a last-minute replacement for another actor). The revised script was one Stewart felt was much less interesting. The disappointing script, not to mention the rubber suit he had to don in the blazing Mexican heat, made Stewart declare the movie one in which "we [Max von Sydow, Jürgen Prochnow, Kenneth McMillan, and Kyle MacLachlan] all went through such hell!" One scene for *Dune* had Stewart playing the baliset, an instrument that took him weeks of lessons from Sting to learn the art of fingering. It did not make the final cut. In another cut scene, Stewart's character, Gurney Halleck, improvised some poetry. "Halleck is a musician, poet, *and* warrior. . . . All you really saw of him was the warrior side."

Following on the heels of *Dune* was *Lifeforce* (1984), Stewart's only other notable film prior to his *Star Trek* days. Stewart felt fortunate again to be working with such an "interesting director." This time he was Tobe Hooper, whose previous directing credits included *Broadcast*. In *Lifeforce*, Stewart played the director of an institute for the criminally insane whose body had been possessed by a beautiful alien from outer space. *Lifeforce* was notorious for two reasons: its original title was *Vampires from Outer Space* ("I would have loved to have been in a movie called *Vampires from Outer Space!*") and it featured Stewart's first cinematic kiss, a kiss with actor Steve Railsback. "I like Steve. And he's a fantastic actor. But given a choice—it's nothing personal, I'm making no political or sexual statement of any kind—it's the way I feel. Next time I would rather it be someone other than Steve. Another sex than Steve!" Naturally, Stewart got his wish, in both episodes of *Star Trek* and subsequent movies. But Stewart meant his remarks about not making a "political or sexual statement," for as a professed liberal and active Labour Party member in England, his humanistic non-judgmental attitude toward his fellow man is one he takes to heart and carries with him in the roles he selects. For his first major post–*Star Trek* role, he starred in the gay romantic comedy *Jeffrey* and had a very frank interview regarding the film and sexuality (Stewart is heterosexual) published in *The Advocate*, a magazine primarily aimed at the gay community.

Never shy about speaking his mind regarding controversial issues, Stewart has been active in politics since a young age. In a February 1990 interview for his fan club, he stated, "It was impossible not to [be involved in politics], given where I grew up and how I grew up. My politics were essentially left wing—Socialist politics—in support of the Labour Party. It has always seemed to me that most of the people I worked with in theater and TV and so on had similar lively concerned interests in what was happening in their own backyard as well as much farther afield. And it's been one of the curiosities of doing this job that there isn't the same measure of active vocal concern with all of that. Particularly since we have lived through the most extraordinary six months in my life. It has not only produced what, I think, is the man of the century in Gorbachev, but it has brought about a prospect of freedom and independence and civil rights to millions of people that hadn't possessed them before. And it died pretty well bloodlessly too, which is something we could never have expected. And link everything in South Africa and these past six months have been simply astounding."

Brazenly and proudly opinionated, Stewart has called Margaret Thatcher the living person he most despises. And on a visit by President Ronald Reagan to the set of *Star Trek* in 1990: "Meeting Reagan was as grotesque and bizarre as you could imagine, and then more so. It was like being in the presence of a clockwork dummy. People would whisper into his ear and he would repeat what they said." Softening a bit, Stewart concluded, "He was very charming, but just not of this world. I have a happy photograph of us together, taken rather appropriately in the Klingon Great Hall."

Although Americans may not find it a natural inclination, to a member of a working-class British family passionate feelings toward the events of the day are actually quite routine. Using his celebrity status to share his views is less common, but not something Stewart shies away from. Discussing the invasion of Panama, he expressed his view that an "illegal invasion of another country makes me very, very uneasy. I was saying this to a group of fans at a convention two weeks ago when they all fell silent and still. They would cheer my remarks about East Germany and Romania and Hungary, Bulgaria and South Africa, but when I mentioned Panama, they all fell strangely silent as though they couldn't see what the connection might be there. I'm quite sure the good captain would describe the invasion of Panama as a breech of the Prime Directive. Without question."

At a 1991 Chicago benefit for Amnesty International, an organization he has supported for many years, Stewart spoke frankly about his involvement with the group and his lifelong interest in politics. Amnesty International is an independent worldwide movement working impartially for the release of all prisoners of conscience; for fair and prompt trials for political prisoners; and for an end to torture and executions. *Star Trek* fans who remember the torture scene from the *Star Trek: The Next Generation* episode "Chain of Command, Part II" will not find it surprising that Stewart prepared for the scene by viewing tapes of torture victims sent to him by Amnesty International. In what Larry Nemecek has called "a tour de force . . . [Stewart's] most intense and focused acting on the series," method actor Stewart actually insisted on performing nude during the interrogation scene.

"I'm a member of and do a certain amount of work for Amnesty International. It has always seemed to me that to live is to be political. And that it is not possible to draw breath in this world without engaging oneself at some point in activity, in action, even if only in thought, which is essentially political. It seems to me that we are in the process in every continent of the world to be making a mess of our globe, both in terms of human rights as well as the way we are treating our planet. And particularly so far as those less fortunate are concerned, which is my background. I came from a very poor northern England family. That all of us have a need, have a responsibility to take care of those who are less fortunate than ourselves—that is political!

"So far as Amnesty International is concerned, I became involved with them only about eight years ago in England, but simply as a member and did nothing that was in any public context because I had no reason to do it. The public didn't know who I was!

Now, wherever I can I like to publicize their activities and their work. It's one of the charms, one of the attractions that a certain amount of notoriety, fame, infamy, call it what you will, has that it means that one can draw attention to worthwhile causes as a result of one's own particular notoriety."

In addition to drawing attention to the work of Amnesty International, one of Stewart's goals was to inform his audiences during his run of A *Christmas Carol* on Broadway to the plight of street children around the world. "One particular case is the matter of street children in Central America who, because of the economic situation and because of homelessness, because of lack of jobs and because of the savage deprivations that have occurred in that country during and, in fact, throughout Central America during the last ten years, as many as possibly five thousand and some people think it may even be ten thousand children between the ages of six and eighteen are on the city streets. And they're not being left alone. There is sufficient evidence to prove that many of these children have been attacked, brutalized, and tortured officially by the police. And they need a kind of protection that isn't available to them there. One of the things that Amnesty can do is bring the attention of the world to incidents of injustice and inhumanity to individuals whether men, women, or children of any race, color, or creed."

Politics pervades Stewart's speech, his thoughts, and the roles he accepts. Being interviewed by Dick Cavett, Stewart was asked how he felt regarding the state of funding for AIDS research, in light of his recently completed film *Jeffrey*. Stewart could barely spit out an answer, referring to "the unspeakable [Jesse] Helms." Being interviewed on BBC Radio 1 in 1993, Stewart proclaimed to the interviewer, "I tell you: I've already been guaranteed in the United States that I could run for Congress. Then after, the gentleman who proposed it to me says that he could raise enough money for me to get to Congress in two years, having heard me do some public speaking. However, unfortunately, I am not a citizen, and it is required, and I have no intention of giving up my British citizenship. Labour Party, are you listening?"

Besides a passionate interest in politics, Stewart is also an avid sports fan and participant. In a 1968 *Stratford Programme* interview, he exclaimed that if he were not in the theater, "I'd give all my time to Huddersfield Town FC [Football Club] and Yorkshire County Cricket: in fact sport of any kind—except Rugby Union." Still an avid supporter of Huddersfield Town, Stewart wrote in "Me and My Tennis," a 1990 article in *Perspective* magazine, that every Sunday morning when the *Los Angeles Times* crashes onto the mat, he looks first at the tiny print in the sports pages for the British football results. "Sport has always played an important part in my life. When I was a schoolboy I seriously thought of becoming a professional athlete. I was a sprinter and a hurdler for Yorkshire. Then the county finals clashed with the school play and I chose acting rather than athletics."

Brother Trevor adds this insight: "You realize that Patrick hasn't, and won't ever, achieve what is his real-life ambition, and that would be to open the batting for Yorkshire [in cricket]."

When Stewart was with the Royal Shakespeare Company, he captained the cricket team for a season and played right fullback on the soccer team. In London, he played squash three times a week, but since squash is considered in Hollywood to be an "East Coast game," he now plays tennis. "It is treated as far more than a sport. It is almost a social necessity to play well." In 1990, when he was playing tennis at least twice a week, he admitted he was "not quite up to the other Hollywood stars round me who think nothing of six sets before breakfast. . . . After fifteen hours a day pacing the bridge of the *Star Trek* set I find tennis marvelously invigorating. During my early days with the Royal Shakespeare Company I was often cast in roles emphasizing the body beautiful, such as Hector in *Troilus and Cressida*, so I took up weight lifting." While working on *Star Trek*, Stewart bought an exercise bicycle for his home as well as a table tennis kit. He even encouraged the *Star Trek* writers to incorporate into scripts two other sports he enjoys, fencing and horseback riding.

Stewart is also obsessive about walking, but finds that the dull sameness of the Southern California hills does not compare favorably to the "fells" of his native Yorkshire, where he used to walk while learning his lines for the Royal Shakespeare Company. The fells have been described as barren, bleak, and treeless, but when Stewart looks at pictures of them, he claims to actually feel quite homesick. "I sense that this is the most beautiful countryside that I have ever seen, and yet realizing that to a stranger it is probably utterly boring. A lot of it has to do with the light you see. Problem about California is the light doesn't change except in the evenings. But in the north of England where I was brought up, one of the fascinating things about those bare hillsides is that you sit and you look at them. They change perpetually because the quality of the light always changes and shifts." Stewart expressed in 1996 his feelings toward his native Yorkshire: "God practiced on everywhere else in the world, but this bit he got right."

Of course, Stewart cannot walk everywhere. He drives a British racing green Jaguar XJS V12 convertible, which he says he loves "beyond reason," and was his one concession to luxury when he made his first *Next Generation* million. According to *Star Trek* costar Marina Sirtis, the first car Stewart bought when he got to the United States was a simple Honda Prelude. After he got it, Wil Wheaton showed up at the studio with a brand-new Honda Prelude Deluxe. Not to be outdone, Stewart ran out and bought the Jaguar.

As Captain Picard, Stewart is a hero to many, adults and children alike. As a child, his heroes were actors and sportsmen. As he recounted in an interview with *Star Trek: The Official Fan Club* magazine, "One of my earliest heroes in the cinema was the comedian Danny Kaye, whose work I admired enormously and I enjoyed everything he did. I was a great cricket fan when I was younger and my fellow Yorkshireman Len Hutton, and the great Australian batsman Don Bradman, were great heroes of mine. Later on, Sir Edmund Hillary, who was the first man to climb Everest, was a hero. I remember I was a great fan of a very famous English soccer goalkeeper named Frank Swift. Another hero of mine was an English teacher named Cecil Dorman—he was the first person to get me involved in acting. Later on, as I took up acting professionally, among English actors, Alec Guinness and Ralph Richardson were heroes of mine. The young Peter O'Toole, whom I had seen as an astonishingly brilliant young man working in provincial repertory, was a hero. In fact, he still remains, for me, the most charismatic actor I've ever seen on stage. He would actually burn with an extraordinary light when he was performing. I took a lot of inspiration from him." And again, on the experience of seeing *On the*

Waterfront as a child: "To suddenly be exposed to the work, in one movie, of Marlon Brando, Rod Steiger, Lee J. Cobb, Eva Marie Saint, Karl Malden—I didn't know people acted like that! That was a seminal experience for me. Marlon Brando was, and still is, a role model as a performer." When Stewart was a student at the Old Vic, Peter O'Toole was the lead actor in the professional company. At the time, he was so in awe of O'Toole that if Stewart saw him coming down the street he would cross to the other side because O'Toole's presence was so overwhelming to him.

Although politics and sports are at the top of Stewart's list of passions, it would not be complete without the inclusion of music. He has always been passionate about it: from his ability to learn an unfamiliar alien instrument for both *Dune* and *Star Trek: The Next Generation* (in the episode "The Inner Light") to his love of Reba McEntire. ("Literally, my heart skipped a beat when I [first] saw this woman," he told *Movieline* magazine. "Anyone who can sing, 'I walked into the kitchen, silverware's gone, furniture's missing, guess he got it all . . .'—that's my kind of woman." Once, when Stewart appeared on *The Tonight Show with Jay Leno*, Reba McEntire was coincidentally appearing the same evening, prompting the captain of the *USS Enterprise* to state quite plainly, "My knees turned to jelly.")

Though his résumé does not make it clear to the casual reader, Stewart is an accomplished musician who does not shy away from roles that may utilize his talent. Stewart, along with LeVar Burton, Michael Dorn, and Jonathan Frakes, formed The Sunspots, a backup group on Brent Spiner's album *Ol' Yellow Eyes Is Back*.

John McNally of KCRW Santa Monica interviewed Patrick Stewart in October 1988 for his program *Castaway's Choice*, in which this question is posed to famous guests: "If you were to be cast away, perhaps forever, which ten recordings would you take and why?" Stewart's selections (in no particular order) were:

1. *Handel's "Zadok, the Priest"*—a piece that inspires the warmest memories of his days as a young choirboy in Yorkshire.
2. *The incidental music from* On the Waterfront, *by Leonard Bernstein*—for the list had to include some

film music, and no other film has made such an impact on him.

3. *"The Revenger's Tragedy" from Coronation Procession, music by Guy Woolfenden*—a play rehearsed during his first year with the Royal Shakespeare Company, by then–assistant director and close friend Trevor Nunn.

4. *Ella Fitzgerald's rendition of "Every Time We Say Good-Bye"*—for he would have to have some Cole Porter on this island, because of his admiration of Ella Fitzgerald, and to remind him of all the time he has had to spend away from his family. (This album was first given to him by his wife in the early 1970s and Stewart was still married at the time of the interview.)

5. *Every Good Boy Deserves Favour, music by André Previn, from the play by Tom Stoppard.* Stewart referred to this as "the musical highlight of my career." Little did he know that, a few short years after this radio interview, he would be reprising his role as the doctor *and* directing his fellow *Enterprise* crewmates in a revival.

6. *"Hold Tight," by Fats Waller*—because it always makes his daughter smile.

7. *Mozart's "Clarinet Quintet"*—which he takes wherever he is, for he considers it something of a talisman.

8. *Randy Newman's "Rollin."* He's a great fan of all Newman's work, and appreciates "the layers and layers of complexity that lie below what is a superficial surface to many of his songs."

9. *Benjamin Britten's "Serenade for Tenor Horn and Strings"*—which is, for Stewart, "the most powerful evocation of England."

10. *Steven Sondheim's "Sweeny Todd"*—because there would have to be some opera, and because of the brilliance of Sondheim. "I have a feeling that when the second half of this century is added up, the role of Sweeney Todd will prove to be one of the great dramatic roles of all time."

Eclectic interests are as much a part of Stewart's life as his acting. He is a roller-coaster aficionado; has always had a fondness for steam engine railroads; collects masks and World War I posters; and loves his Nintendo Gameboy given to him by his children. He is admittedly addicted to the popular game Tetris. "I have to limit myself to two games a day, otherwise my life and career would disintegrate." He wakes up every morning at 5 A.M. and reads, and once a week visits his chiropractor. He absolutely loves valet parking, an amenity that does not exist in England. He does enjoy some very British cuisine, such as apple sandwiches (soft white bread, butter, and slices of Granny Smith apples) and potato crisp sandwiches (bread, butter, and potato chips). And he never travels without tea bags. "I know it sounds corny for an Englishman, but . . . I actually do."

As for his favorite light entertainment, he thinks *Cheers* was the best program on television, but now that it is off the air, he has turned to *Beavis and Butt-head*. "I can't help thinking that somewhere in that program is a secret metaphor for society," he once told David Letterman. After Letterman played a clip of Beavis and Butt-head parodying *Star Trek: The Next Generation*, and Stewart in particular, the captain of the *Enterprise* exclaimed, without missing a beat, "Being recognized in that way is possibly the highest compliment that can be paid to an actor." His devotion is so strong that while filming the 1996 feature film *Star Trek: First Contact*, Stewart even wore a black *Beavis and Butt-head* T-shirt under his Starfleet regulation captain's uniform.

In a *TV Guide* interview, Stewart also expressed an affinity for *American Gladiators*. "It's like a show in England called *It's a Knockout*. It always seemed to me that you could add a certain element of tension to these shows just by adding trapdoors that would collapse beneath contestants while shark-infested pools or pits of snakes waited below. I think that could do wonders for the ratings."

READY FOR THE ADVENTURE

Since 1980, Stewart has been an associate director of the Alliance for Creative Theater, Education, and Research (ACTER) at the University of California at Santa Barbara. Through ACTER, he has lectured and performed, as well as arranged educational tours by small groups of actors at universities and colleges throughout the United States and Europe. ACTER grew out of a similar program at UCLA, the Artists in Residence program, with which Stewart was involved throughout the 1970s. It was during one of Stewart's lectures/performances with ACTER at UCLA in 1987 that *Star Trek: The Next Generation* producer Robert Justman saw him perform and turned to his wife, exclaiming, "I think we've found our captain!"

Two days before being cast in *Star Trek*, Stewart was having dinner with Kyle MacLachlan, Everett McGill, and an actor he had just met. Both he and the new acquaintance were up for parts, but were too superstitious to discuss them. Within forty-eight hours Stewart had been cast as Jean-Luc Picard and his dinner companion, Ron Perlman, was cast as Vincent in *Beauty and the Beast*.

Stewart auditioned, and was nearly cast as Data. Justman was certain that Stewart was the one they had been looking for to sit in the captain's chair. But Gene Roddenberry had chosen another actor, Steven Mocked. It took weeks of discussion between the two producers before Roddenberry was convinced. Mocked later appeared as Bajoran General Krim in two episodes of *Star Trek: Deep Space Nine*, "The Siege" and "The Circle."

Stewart was back in London when he received the call that he had landed the part of Captain Jean-Luc Picard on *Star Trek: The Next Generation*. The offer caught him during a rare lull in his stage career. He had been performing a critically acclaimed production of *Who's Afraid of Virginia Woolf?* at the Young Vic Theatre, and was attempting to get it transferred to the West End, analogous to having a play moved from off-Broadway to a larger, more prestigious Broadway stage. "I remember I had spent the morning talking to backers and producers that night the closing notice went up. I was brought very low by that. It seemed I wasn't a big enough name for the transfer. It was a painful thing to happen and I did feel a certain amount of resentment. The next day I got the offer of *Star Trek*. I was ready for the adventure."

So *Star Trek: The Next Generation* had this very peculiar actor (by American standards) at the helm, poised to become an icon: raised in difficult circumstances by a strict father, Stewart was a professional Shakespearean, a politically savvy liberal, an athlete, a music lover, a journalist, a furniture salesman, a follicly challenged and virtually *unknown* Brit, a published author of Shakespearean opinion but with the American equivalent of less than a high school degree. He was all this and more. He was expected to take the helm from Captain James T. Kirk, the embodiment of the American television hero: space explorer, adventurer, and romantic.

Paramount was banking heavily on *Star Trek: The Next Generation,* to the tune of a $30 million budget for the inaugural 1987–88 season. *The Next Generation* was the most expensive series on television in the fall of 1987, and the most ambitious syndicated show in the history of television.

But before the new show aired, fans were justifiably skeptical. The media enjoyed the opportunity to run headlines that began with the likes of "Baldly Going . . ." The British press dubbed Stewart "The unlikeliest trekkie of all." As a man who admittedly "did not know *Star Trek* or its cultural significance in America," only occasionally having viewed parts of episodes of the original 1966–68 series with his children, Stewart was "utterly naive about the power of *Star Trek.* Upon reflection, I think that was the best way to approach the project. That way, I wasn't intimidated by the enormity of what I was undertaking," he told a 1990 interviewer.

"When I first went over I was treated with suspicion and a certain amount of hostility, rather than respect," Stewart recounted to London's *Daily Mail.* He recalled a sense of, "What the hell is this limey doing here playing a part that should have gone to an American star?"

"And I have to say that I agreed with them," Stewart continued. "I couldn't understand why they'd gone for a boring old Brit when they had access to so many American stars. I really believed they would replace me after three months. I thought that by then they would have woken up to the grotesque reality that casting a middle-aged, bald, Shakespearean actor as Captain Jean-Luc Picard just wasn't going to work."

Star Trek: The Next Generation fans do not need to be reminded that the first season of the new show was inconsistent. Picard was angry, aloof, and didn't like children. The cast was just getting to know each other, and that led to some clashes. "That first day on the *Next Generation* set—I wasn't just very nervous, I was *more* than nervous. I was *scared*.

"The first thing I had to do was a simple reaction thing. I didn't have any dialogue. I just had to walk through the holodeck doors, and react to Commander Riker and Wesley Crusher, who were coming the other way. Something horrendous happened—I can't remember what. Anyway, I reacted—and the director called 'cut.' In the nervous pause that followed, Jonathan Frakes said: 'I say! That must be what they call British face-acting. Not bad for a Brit!' And we all just burst out laughing. It instantly broke the ice."

Despite these light moments, all was not relaxed on the set. During the first season, Stewart forbid anyone else to sit in Captain Jean-Luc Picard's chair, and was constantly annoyed when the cast would make jokes or flub lines or behave without the proper decorum. "I believe I was something of a pompous ass. All those attitudes belong to my pre-Americanization phase. I was fortunate enough to work with a group who liked me enough not to want me to go on being a pompous ass."

One day, Stewart even called a meeting of the cast. "I felt the set was much too undisciplined. I thought we should all exhibit much more self-control. Can you imagine? I remember Denise Crosby was still on the show. She said, 'C'mon, Patrick, it's just fun.' I said, 'We are not here to have fun!'"

Although "Skin of Evil" was not a happy episode, Stewart finally lightened up while filming this first-season episode that saw Denise Crosby's Natasha Yar get killed. Her hologram farewell scene was filmed on grassy hills and a meadow. While the camera was not rolling, Stewart could be seen skipping around, singing, "The hills are alive . . ."

Stewart was sad to see Denise Crosby leave the series. He had always advocated stronger roles for women on the show, and had reportedly sent back certain scripts, particularly during the early seasons, requesting rewrites because he felt the scripts were sexist or demeaning. "It was a great shame Denise chose to leave. There was so much potential in having a woman as head of the *Enterprise's* security and the wonderful background the writers dreamed up for her added extra dimensions. Here was this homeless child, who'd been living on the streets dodging rape gangs and other unimaginable brutalities—and now she was having to bring controlled violence to her profession," Stewart recalls.

That first season had its summits and its valleys. In "The Big Goodbye," Stewart, Gates McFadden, and Brent Spiner were given the opportunity to show off their comedic talents, a refreshing change from some otherwise stagnant and poorly reviewed writing early on. During "The Arsenal of Freedom," Stewart and McFadden had to endure flea-infested sand while filming in the cave pit set on Paramount's lot. Personal discomfort aside, it was in this and other first-season episodes that important development of individual characters occurred, and the actors themselves had a chance to shine.

The greatest change Stewart hoped for from the first to subsequent seasons was for the female characters to wield more decision-making power. "While they have respectable positions, we all agree that someone should be promoted to make some life-death decisions," he stated. He also emphasized that he wanted to assuage critics' fears of "stiffness" of the characters. "We've just established who the characters are," he said. "Next season, the camaraderie will be more apparent. Like most relationships, this takes time to develop."

The second season succeeded on many levels. The cast worked together more, and the comfort level was apparent in the finished product. However, all was not rosy. Gates McFadden was gone for the season, and her replacement, Diana Muldaur, was not envisioned to fill the gap in Picard's life that McFadden's Dr. Crusher had left. Moreover, other concerns became apparent to Stewart. For one, the other crew members were growing as characters and fleshing out their roles, but Captain Picard was stagnating a bit. His concern heightened after he appeared in a few episodes as little more than an order-giving figurehead.

In October 1988 Stewart sat down to lunch with executive producer Gene Roddenberry and spelled out these concerns. Roddenberry listened and promised that changes in Picard were forthcoming. Stewart followed up their lunch with a letter recapitulating their discussion, which was widely circulated among the writing staff and other insiders at Paramount.

Stewart summed up, in a dense two-page missive, a review of the "state of play with regard to Capt. P." He felt that early second-season episodes, from his character's standpoint, were repetitive and even boring. He noted that to this point in the season, scripts had only featured stories in which the *Enterprise* and her crew were in trouble and Picard in some fashion "deals" with the problem.

Stewart's complaint stemmed from that fact that all Picard was doing was reacting to problems. Nothing new was learned about him. None of the traits that Picard supposedly possessed were being explored. (Stewart wrote, "Picard is leader, negotiator, peacemaker, ombudsman. He thinks, he talks, he assesses, he bluffs.") He cited the second season's first five episodes and their respective plot elements to prove his point: "The Child" (an unstable virus), "Where Silence Has Lease" (the Nagilum entity), "Elementary, Dear Data" (Moriarty), "The Outrageous Okona" (Debin and Kushell), and "The Schizoid Man" (Dr. Graves and Data).

Essentially, Stewart was concerned that the character not only was becoming dry and uninteresting to the fans, but also was not stimulating him as an actor. Stewart emphasized that the role was becoming increasingly less interesting to play, and proposed constructive suggestions for the future of Picard. Specifically, Stewart wanted Picard to exhibit traits one might expect a starship captain to be endowed with.

Stewart pressed for changes in the way Picard was being written. He encouraged Roddenberry to develop a captain who was idiosyncratic, who had attitude, and who occasionally even got involved in some action sequences. He reminded Roddenberry that captains enjoy certain privileges and can even be eccentric. *The Next Generation*, to this point, had provided few opportunities to explore any of these facets of his character.

The two aspects of Picard's character Stewart emphasized most in his letter were humor and action. He felt that without more humor, Picard was too solemn, even boring. As for action sequences, though he acknowledged that the captain must not take unnecessary risks, neither should he be "treated like a Sevre tea service." Stewart assured Roddenberry that he was in excellent shape for a man his age, and there was no reason his athleticism could not become part of Picard's profile. He even reminded Roddenberry that earlier that month, October 1988, he had been held up at knifepoint. Rather than acquiesce to the mugger's demand, Stewart struck him and escaped without injury (and without losing his wallet).

Stewart emphasized that Picard had been established as a competition-level fencer and suggested that Picard might compete in a "rather aristocratic version of modern pentathlon." He also inquired as to whether Starfleet officers ever practice with their phasers and wondered if there was a shooting range on the ship.

A final concern Stewart shared was that of Picard's relationships with his fellow crew members. Nothing much had been done to develop and further the synergy between Riker and Picard. Picard's intrigue with Data needed to be explored more. Picard and Worf could be brought together for something beyond giving and receiving orders. Guinan's few scenes thus far had failed to explore her special relationship with the captain. Stewart also most enjoyed the scenes he played with Wil Wheaton. Although many fans at this point in the series found Wesley Crusher annoying, Stewart held tremendous respect for the actor's talents. He asked Roddenberry, "Have I ever told you what a fan I am of that young man?"

Stewart also mentioned the lack of any private or romantic relationship for his character. Since Dr. Crusher was written off the program, Stewart felt lost in terms of a romantic interest. "I know there is a school of thought that a Picard/Crusher relationship never existed," Stewart wrote, "but I am a little puzzled by this as I spent hours in front of the camera last season assuming—and acting—that it did." He told Roddenberry that Crusher's departure had left a chasm in Picard's life that obviously needed filling with something. The viewers agreed: early second-season fan mail concerning his perceived relationship with Dr. Crusher was exceeded only by fan mail comparing and contrasting Picard with Captain Kirk.

Finally, Stewart assured him that the letter was meant purely constructively; that it should be taken as a cordial recap of their discussion.

Clearly, Stewart's decades of experience as an actor conceiving powerful characters brought him to some profound realizations regarding Picard. His suggestions were for the most part heeded. Future weeks, months, and seasons featured a Picard who continuously evolved into a fleshed-out leader, explorer, lover, and negotiator, among other roles the captain came to embody.

Star Trek: The Next Generation's third season began to see some of the changes in Picard truly come to fruition. In "The

Defector," Stewart himself selected the *Henry V* teaser (opening) scene, and played one of the soldiers, the role of Michael Williams, under heavy makeup. Two episodes later, in "The High Ground," Picard is involved in more action and romance and is even given the opportunity to slug a terrorist on the bridge. "Captain's Holiday," just a few episodes later, also featured Picard in more sexual and shooting escapades, at the request of Stewart. "The Offspring," the third-season episode that marked the first opportunity for one of the cast, Jonathan Frakes, to direct, is also Stewart's all-time favorite among all seven seasons' worth of episodes. "It represents all of the things we have always tried to do on *Star Trek: The Next Generation*. Also, it has another brilliant performance from Brent Spiner matched by an equally fine performance by Hallie Todd . . . and Jonathan Frakes did outstandingly."

The third season ended with the gripping cliff-hanger "Best of Both Worlds, Part I," which, according to Larry Nemecek's *Star Trek: The Next Generation Companion*, "signaled to even the hardest of the hard-core original-trek fans that *The Next Generation* had finally arrived." By the end of the third season, Picard had come into his own as well, fulfilling a destiny Stewart had set for him a year earlier.

Toward the end of the fourth season, following Jonathan Frakes' lead with "The Offspring," Stewart got to direct his first episode, "In Theory." "One's first directing experience is like one's first love affair—you never get over it or forget it," Stewart recalled. The fourth season also featured an episode with a scene that Stewart points to as one of the most emotional for him: the farewell scene with Wesley in "Final Mission." Stewart's fondness for Wil Wheaton as both a friend and a colleague is not something Stewart has ever been shy about expressing, and the good-bye scene was, at the time, very difficult.

Also during the fourth season, Stewart formed an acting troupe that studied in a series of Stewart-led Saturday Shakespeare workshops on the Paramount lot. Each workshop ran ten to twelve weeks, and Stewart hoped eventually these actors, about twenty in each workshop, might form a core group that would coalesce into a company sometime in the future. When Stewart found himself with other commitments on Saturday, he left the group in the hands of his decades-long friend and Royal Shakespeare Company colleague Ben Kingsley.

During the fifth season, one of the most intensely personal episodes, "The Inner Light," premiered to rave reviews. An incredible performance by Stewart was aided by his own son, Daniel, in the role of his Kataanian son, Batai. Over Christmas break Stewart was off to New York City with his one-man *A Christmas Carol*, a solo rendition in which he plays all forty-six of Dickens' characters on a sparsely furnished stage. Although premiering it on Broadway December 17, 1991, Stewart had been performing a solo version of *A Christmas Carol* as early as December 1984, in the Mirfield Parish Church. Stewart had sung in the church choir in Mirfield; in 1984, brother Trevor (who still sings in the same choir) was trying to raise money to refurbish the old church organ. Patrick came up with the idea of performing a reading of *A Christmas Carol*, and put on a show with no props other than an oak table with a glass of water and an oil lamp on it. People came and sat on the hard church pews. It is reported not one of them budged during the entire performance, which lasted over two hours. Stewart went on to perform *A Christmas Carol* at UCLA and other colleges on the West Coast through the late 1980s, ultimately bringing the performance to Broadway. At last, unlike his experience trying to bring *Who's Afraid of Virginia Woolf?* to the West End of London, he was a big enough name to command an audience.

After the fifth season had wrapped up, Stewart directed and acted in a play he had originally performed in 1977—Tom Stoppard and André Previn's *Every Good Boy Deserves Favour*. The play is rarely performed because it requires a seventy-piece orchestra. Significantly, when casting the play, Stewart looked toward his *Star Trek* crewmates. Stewart played the role of a doctor in a Soviet mental hospital, while Jonathan Frakes played Alexander Ivanov, a sane political dissident sent to the hospital because of his political views. Brent Spiner was cast in the role of a lunatic who imagines that he is the triangle player in a symphony orchestra, and is also named Alexander Ivanov. Because they have the same name, Ivanov, Frakes and Spiner are confined to the same cell. Other members of the play's small cast included Gates McFadden as a teacher and Colm Meaney as a colonel.

Star Trek: The Next Generation's sixth season was highlighted by the aforementioned two-parter "Chain of Command," featuring the infamous torture scene. Producer Michael Piller took out a full-page advertisement in *Variety* to back, unsuccessfully, an Emmy nomination for Stewart. "It's not possible that there are five better male actors in this town than Patrick Stewart!" the advertisement read. Coproducer Jeri Taylor agreed. "It's probably his finest performance—he literally threw himself, physically and mentally, into that." The sixth season was also highlighted by the action movie–esque "Starship Mine," a very violent episode in which Stewart performed many of his own stunts.

After the sixth season, Stewart reflected to *Entertainment Weekly* that he had always viewed *The Next Generation* as a show that was still growing. "I've always felt that we aren't doing a series of single episodes but that we're in the process of doing a play—of which, so far, we're done 128 acts. Everything won't be in place until we say 'cut' in the final scene of the last day of the series."

Also after the sixth season, Stewart took an uncredited comic role at union pay scale as King Richard in Mel Brooks' *Robin Hood: Men in Tights*. Although much of Stewart's short part wound up on the cutting room floor—the scenes fell victim to good taste (such as that in which Stewart as King Richard I is introduced, nailed to a cross)—he still appreciated the opportunity to do pure comedy and to work with Brooks. Mel Brooks sincerely appreciated his efforts as well, signing Stewart's script as a memento:

To Patrick
  What a Tyro!
  Such a Talent!
  And a Good Price Too!
  Love, Mel Brooks

The seventh season of *Star Trek: The Next Generation* was, in many ways, a season for resolving story arcs. In "Thine Own Self," Stewart had his smallest role in any single *Star Trek* episode— one line uttered in sickbay—arranged so that Stewart could perform his one-man Olivier Award–winning *A Christmas Carol* on the London stage. Stewart also missed four days of shooting a few months later during the Klingon-heavy episode "Firstborn" in order to rehearse and host the February 5, 1994, *Saturday Night Live*.

During the seventh season, the producers actually asked the actors about any hanging character threads that still "needed" to be turned into stories. Stewart pitched a story about DaiMon Bok and his unsatisfied vengeance from the first season's "The Battle." Stewart's suggestion became the seventh season's "Bloodlines."

ALL GOOD THINGS . . . MUST COME TO AN END

Stewart was exhausted while making *The Next Generation* two-hour grand finale, "All Good Things . . ." The episode featured him in virtually every scene, and the seventeen-day chore of filming the finale was immediately followed by the lensing of the first big-screen movie and the infamous meeting of the two captains Picard and Kirk, *Star Trek: Generations*. "I was at times anxious as to whether I would get through that last period of work, and I'm not being melodramatic." Not only was the pressure of shooting the movie on Stewart's mind, but there was increased stress from the script of the finale episode, "All Good Things . . ." Significant revisions had been made to the first draft of a script the cast had fallen in love with. After major rewrites, the actors were reportedly unhappy and it was up to Stewart to call a meeting to have many of the missing character moments restored.

Despite well-publicized troubles on the set of the last episode, ongoing contract negotiations for the movie, and anxieties among the cast and crew regarding job hunting, the family atmosphere that had been cultivated over seven long seasons did not dwindle. It is a long-standing Hollywood tradition to ask actors and directors with whom one appears to autograph the final script. The scribbled markings on the cover of Stewart's final script speak much louder about the relationships among the crew of *Star Trek: The Next Generation* than any Hollywood gossip column possibly could:

Dear Patrick,
To my favorite leading man! Thanks for your friendship,
your talent, and the laughs. Enjoy
Jonathan

Patrick,
I love you as a friend and a brother!
LeVar Burton

Patrick
Having you as a friend is something I will treasure for the
rest of my life. It's been a joy working with you.
I love you.
Marina
P.S. Nextime XXXX

Patrick—
There's something I've been meaning to tell you—
I'll love you in the past, present, and the future—
Love,
Gates

Patrick—
Thank you for a wonderful voyage.
Love,
Colm Meaney

Pat, my dear
We'll meet again, don't know where, don't know when.
But I'll look forward to it!
Brent

Dearest Patrick—
It has been a real genuine pleasure . . .
All the Best!
Lots of Love
Denise Crosby

The genuine emotion behind these signatures is obvious. Knowledgeable *Star Trek* fans will recognize Gates McFadden's comment as wrapping up a line she began but never finished a handful of times over the course of six seasons during emotional moments between Dr. Crusher and the good captain.

Although many of the cast members were publicly dismayed at *Star Trek*'s demise, Stewart, though sad, did not think the decision to end the show was premature. "I feel their timing was perfect," he told *The Washington Times*. "I like the idea that we left the series while we were really on top. I had started to fear that I, as an actor, might be beginning simply to repeat myself. Days were not as interesting and exciting as they had been, and I was looking for fresh fields and pastures new."

What has followed the television conclusion of *Star Trek: The Next Generation* is a plethora of movie, television, and stage offers. However, despite dire predictions otherwise, Stewart refuses to be typecast, taking roles as a gay interior decorator in *Jeffrey*; a homeless ballroom-dance instructor in *Let It Be Me* (a film in which Stewart dons a wig of white hair and speaks in an American accent); a pesky spirit in *The Canterville Ghost*; and a reclusive ex-spy dealing with a government threat and with Alzheimer's disease in *Safe House*. Stewart has also been the voice of the character Adventure in *Pagemaster* and appeared as himself on *Sesame Street*. Since *Star Trek: The Next Generation* ceased weekly production, Stewart has also won a Grammy Award for the best spoken word album for children for his work on *Peter and the Wolf*. And of course, he has never given up his beloved Shakespeare, playing Prospero in *The Tempest* in New York City's Central Park and on Broadway. He hasn't turned his back on *Star Trek* either, appearing first in *Star Trek: Generations* with William Shatner and more recently in *Star Trek: First Contact*.

Many sources cite Stewart as the catalyst for the inclusion of members of the original crew, and especially William Shatner, in the first *Next Generation* movie. Although many of his castmates did not agree, Stewart insisted, "I felt that this should be seen as a transitional movie, given that Bill Shatner and his colleagues had already made six movies. Just to cut them off with the last one and start off with us was going to be missing a really golden opportunity to do something quite intense and dramatic."

Naturally, rumors abounded regarding how these two men would hit it off, but negative comments Shatner had made years earlier regarding the future of the franchise with an all-new cast had been long forgotten (and disproved). Shatner helped Stewart with the horse he had to ride, and the two captains spent some time together in a private jet. "During the flight, Bill and I talked and laughed, and we ended up friends. I look forward to visiting his horse ranch in Kentucky," Stewart recalled. Of course, the two captains are markedly different: Kirk is a representative of his times, the action type; Picard is more sophisticated and cerebral. Brent Spiner has summed it up this way: "It's like Lucy Ricardo meeting Rob Petrie."

During one scene in Generations, Stewart saves Shatner, but the bridge they were on gives a lurch, and Stewart goes over the side. "We filmed this with Bill hauling me up. None of that is seen. I'm hanging onto Bill's hand, and he said, 'I suppose it's too late to get back on the horses.' And I said, 'I'm afraid so!' We're extremely dismayed this didn't get into the movie."

The other great pleasure for Stewart in doing Star Trek: Generations, although one that received far less media coverage, was the opportunity to work once again with Malcolm McDowell, who performed with Stewart in the Royal Shakespeare Company three decades earlier, in 1966. McDowell told an interviewer, "He's [Stewart's] a lot more relaxed now that he's rich," acknowledging Stewart's previous reputation for being taciturn and uptight. "In other ways he is the same as he was then. He was always as bald as a coot. He could play any age. And he was a good solid actor."

"I was not funny then," Stewart responded when told of McDowell's comments.

Following Star Trek: Generations, "I wanted work that would dynamite the Picard image," Stewart stated. Perhaps no role attracted as much attention or succeeded in "dynamiting" his captainly image more so than his part in Jeffrey. During breaks in the filming of Star Trek: Generations, sitting on a rock in the Nevada desert between shooting violent action scenes with Malcolm McDowell, Stewart found himself crying while reading a draft of the Jeffrey script. "It was 119 in the shade and I was sitting there reading the script. Well, I completed it and found that I needed both wardrobe and makeup to help me because my face was streaming with tears and the tears dripped off onto my spacesuit."

In a startling and revealing interview in The Advocate, Stewart discussed Jeffrey and aspects of Star Trek usually not covered by the mainstream media. Playing a homosexual role was not an issue for Stewart; his only concern was playing up inappropriate stereotypes of gays and the gay community. He told *The Advocate* he was aware that for years many fans were convinced that he was gay. "Well, so far as I'm aware, I'm conventionally a heterosexual male. And yet I find something quite flattering in these suggestions of others that I'm something else," he candidly proclaimed. And, on the *Charlie Rose* program, shown on PBS stations, Stewart simply claimed of his character in *Jeffrey* that "apart from everything else, it is one of the very best roles I've ever had."

Stewart's enthusiasm for this role in *Jeffrey* is an indication of his humanistic attitude. Stressing that "the writers and producers [of *Star Trek*] could not escape from their own essential rigidity in their attitudes to women," he emphasized that women were often featured as sex objects as well as second-class individuals on *Star Trek: The Next Generation*. Because of what *Star Trek* purported to represent, he often felt that in this regard, the show failed. Finally, and perhaps most shocking to some *Star Trek* fans, Stewart admitted that he thought Q might in fact have been gay, a notion due perhaps to the boldness of the character played by John de Lancie (who is not gay), Q's provocative way of looking at Picard, or the brief scene with the two of them in bed.

GETTING REACQUAINTED

"In our wildest dreams, we never anticipated an opening this big," Stewart exclaimed after the record-setting $37 million domestic box-office take for *Star Trek: First Contact's* premiere weekend. Stewart is enthusiastic regarding the future of the franchise. "I want this [*Star Trek*] to go into the next millenium—but I also want to see us getting better and better with every movie we make. I want *The Next Generation* cast to become the dominant force in *Star Trek*." He commented that *First Contact* is everything he always wanted, "a good story that happens to be *Trek*," and that he enjoyed getting "reacquainted" with Picard. "I get to be much more physical in this one. There's a lot of running, jumping, climbing, leaping—and also some ballroom dancing, I might add."

However, not all was smooth in the early stages of creating *First Contact*. Stewart had a clause in his contract that allowed him to demand a rewrite if he was unhappy with the script. Although the executives at Paramount were happy with the submitted script, Stewart was concerned. "I was very conscious of the fact that we created a story line for Picard in *Star Trek: Generations* in which he is hit by these emotional blows early on in the movie. It was, in fact, a little too downbeat and we didn't want to let that happen here. Although this film begins with a very dramatic sequence involving the Borg, we didn't want it to appear as though Picard is somehow mentally or emotionally unstable because of this experience. On the contrary, his experience gives him the ability to tune into the Borg in a way no one else can. He reacts in a very human way to having been violated but he rises above it. It's very *Star Trek*."

"It seemed like a pain in the ass at first," admitted screenwriter Brannon Braga, about making the changes Stewart insisted upon, "but Patrick was right. It was good for the script ultimately."

Stewart's one voiced complaint with the finished product was simply the timing. "I did feel two years between these films is not enough. I've always said—and will keep saying it—that at least three years between would be best. But I find myself in a very fortunate situation: I'm at the center of a high-quality, extremely popular entertainment franchise and I have a whole life and career apart from it that is exciting, fulfilling, and utterly different. And I don't see why the two should not go hand in hand."

Which is why, despite persistent rumors that Stewart is ready to walk away from Picard altogether, his fans can rest easier. "The general suspicion is that at any moment Patrick Stewart is going to hand in his communicator," he told *Entertainment Weekly* in November 1996. "That is simply not true. If I can help keep this populist commercial franchise going while continuing to have a varied and rich career elsewhere in other movies, theater, and so forth, I'll be very happy."

Stewart does not believe in slowing down. Recently certified in scuba diving, he commented, "Acting is a lot like learning to adjust to different depths as you dive. With each new depth, more technique and certain skills are required, and it may seem harder and even a little alarming as you go deeper, but it is good." Stewart has also made a well-publicized appearance on *Sesame Street* (in a scene with the muppet The Count, he admonished a misbehaving stick-puppet of the numeral "1," "Make it so, Number One!"); recorded a wake-up call for the space shuttle astronauts; and hosted a bicoastal bell-ringing in June 1996 for the opening of the American Stock Exchange's first Los Angeles office. Despite all of these peripheral activities, he remains first and foremost an actor. "Acting is telling beautiful lies," he told *The Washington Times.*

And Stewart's calendar is quite full. He has filmed *Smart Alec*, in which he plays Bentley, a role Stewart relished. "Bentley is not only the villian protagonist in the story, but he's also utterly obnoxious as well." Stewart has also been cast opposite Mel Gibson and Julia Roberts in the big-budget feature *The Conspiracy Theory*, in which again he will play the villain. Stewart has agreed to star as Captain Ahab in *Moby Dick*, a four-hour 1997 television miniseries (which proves to those filmgoers who remember the scene from *First Contact* that he really has read the book). The animated feature *Prince of Egypt*, not due for release until 1998, will feature a veritable A-list of Hollywood voices: Sandra Bullock, Steve Martin, Michelle Pfeiffer, Martin Short, Val Kilmer, Ralph Fiennes, Jeff Goldblum, and of course Patrick Stewart.

On December 16, 1996, Patrick Stewart was honored with a star on Hollywood's Walk of Fame for a lifetime of performance on the stage and screen, becoming the second cast member of *Star Trek: The Next Generation* to be so honored. (The first? LeVar Burton, honored for his prior credits on *Roots* and *Reading Rainbow*.) Each year, over three hundred different Hollywood stars and executives are nominated for stars, but only twelve are awarded. His star is located on the same block as fellow Brit Stan Laurel, whom his grandmother had cared for decades earlier. To the cheers of the assembled crowd watching Stewart unveil his star, he humbly exclaimed, "Being on the same block as Stan Laurel is unbearably exciting and almost too much of an honor."

In the initial press package of biographies for the cast of *Star Trek: The Next Generation*, Stewart stated that "[being on the series] is a little like rock climbing, which I've done. Your concentration stays on the area of rock immediately in front of your face and above your fingers. *Star Trek* is like that for me. If I look down or look up, maybe I'll be in trouble. But the demands of doing this are so great and so intense."

At the conclusion of the series, he commented, "Looking back . . . I feel very content at having *Star Trek* as the dominant association in my career." He realized that his time spent aboard the Federation's flagship was an experience not terribly removed from his decades spent on the English stage. "I was looking at the bridge of the *Enterprise*, and was thinking about how very theatrical it is — it actually has some of the classic elements of the Tudor and Jacobean stage: it has a raised area at the rear, it has a main acting area here, there the throne sits — the captain's chair, right in the center — it has downstage left and right entrances, upstage left and right entrances. What you've got there is an Elizabethan theater." He also noted that when visitors came to the set of *The Next Generation*, they could look in on the action taking place on the bridge through a hollow rectangle that, when filming was completed, became the *Enterprise's* view-screen — "so there you even have your theater audience too."

Will *Star Trek* ever end for Stewart? "Oh, I'd like Picard to die eventually. As Claudius says in *Hamlet*, 'Everything that lives must die.'"

Acknowledging *Star Trek* as the "dominant association" in his career, Stewart spoke movingly at the November 1991 memorial service for Gene Roddenberry, a tribute that not only saluted Roddenberry, but also served to sum up Stewart's feelings toward the impact of *Star Trek* on his own career. "Gene's gift to me was this job, and that endowment will last a lifetime — sometimes as a curse, but much more as an unexpected, life-transforming, life-bestowing blessing. Five years ago [early 1987], first in his home, then twice in his office, he looked at and listened to a middle-aged, bald, opinionated, working-class British Shakespearean actor and he said, 'He will be Captain.' Inexplicable!"

PATRICK STEWART

*Captain Jean-Luc Picard**
Also appeared on Star Trek: Deep Space Nine

STAGE:

As You Like It ('58, '61, '67, '68)
Cyrano de Bergerac ('58)
Eighty in the Shade ('59)
Treasure Island ('59)
An Inspector Calls ('60)
Hans, the Witch & the Goblin ('60)
Not in the Book ('60)
Pygmalion ('60)
Romersholm ('60)
Sailor Beware! ('60)
The Edwardian ('60)
The Great Sebastians ('60)
The Ring of Truth ('60)
The Seagull ('60)
Twelfth Night ('60, '61, '62)
Don't Listen Ladies ('61)
Duel of Angels ('61–'62)
Lady of Camelias ('61–'62)
Naked Island ('61)
The Bastard Country ('61)
The Man in the Moon ('61)
Strip the Willow ('62)
The Buried Man ('62)
The Princess & The Swineherd ('62–'63)
Your Obedient Servant ('62)
Antigone ('63)
Billy Liar ('63)
Dandy Dick ('63)
Hay Fever ('63)
Summer and Smoke ('63)
Summertime ('63)
The Caretaker ('63)
The Entertainer ('63)
The Hamlet of Stepney Green ('63)
The Hostage ('63)

The One Day of the Year ('63)
The Rough & Ready Lot ('63)
A Little Winter Love ('64)
A Midsummer Night's Dream ('64, '71, '77)
A View from the Bridge ('64)
Cockade ('64)
Dr. Angelus ('64)
Heartbreak House ('64)
Hindle Wakes ('64)
Pinocchio ('64)
Poor Bitos ('64)
The Beaux Stratagem ('64)
The Closing Door ('64)
The Little Hut ('64)
The Skin of Our Teeth ('64)
A Little Further ('65)
A Scent of Flowers ('65)
Conditions of Agreement ('65)
Galileo ('65)
Lock Up Your Daughters ('65)
Mary, Mary ('65)
Saint Joan ('65)
The Birthday Party ('65)
The Cherry Orchard ('65)
The Merchant of Venice ('65, '78, '79)
The Quare Fellow ('65)
Battle of Agincourt ('66)
Hamlet ('66)
Henry IV Part I ('66, '82)
Henry IV Part II ('66, '82)
Henry V ('63, '66)
The Happiest Days of Your Life ('66)
The Investigation ('66)
The Revengers Tragedy ('66, '67, '69)

The Taming of the Shrew ('67)
King Lear ('68)
Much Ado about Nothing ('68, '69)
The Relapse ('68)
Troilus and Cressida ('68, '69)
Bartholemew Fair ('69)
The Silver Tassie ('69)
King John ('70)
Richard III ('70)
The Tempest ('70, '95, '96)
The Two Gentlemen of Verona ('70, '81)
Enemies ('71)
Occupations ('71)
The Balcony ('71)
Antony and Cleopatra ('72, '73, '78, '79)
Coriolanus ('72)
Julius Caesar ('72, '73)
The Hollow Crown ('72, '77)
Titus Andronicus ('73, '81)
Uncle Vanya ('74)
Hedda Gabler ('75)
Miss Julie ('75)
Bingo ('76, '77)
The Iceman Cometh ('76)
Every Good Boy Deserves Favour ('77, '92, '93)
That Good between Us ('77)
The Bundle ('77)
A Miserable and Lonely Death ('78)
Hippolytus ('78, '79)
The Biko Inquest ('79)
The White Guard ('79)
A Winter's Tale ('81, '82)
Body & Soul ('83)
Camelot (excerpts) ('83)
A Christmas Carol ('84, '88–'95, annually)
Yonodab ('85, '86)
Who's Afraid of Virginia Woolf? ('87)

Garden Grove: Festival of Britain ('90)
Morte D'Arthur ('90, '91)
Phantom & Phriends ('90)
Shylock: Shakespeare's Alien ('90, '93)
So Many People Have Heads ('90, '91)
Uneasy Lies the Head ('90, '92, '93)
Tom Stoppard's Works ('91)
Celebrity Reading for Literacy ('92)
'Twas the Night Before Christmas ('94)

TELEVISION:
Civilization (Protest & Communication) ('70)
Death Train ('73)
Fall of Eagles ('73)
The Artist's Story ('73)
The Love Girl and the Innocent ('73)
A Walk with Destiny ('74)
Alfred the Great ('74)
Conrad ('74)
Joby ('74)
Antony aand Cleopatra ('75)
Eleventh Hour ('75)
Jackonary ('75)
North and South ('75)
Inquest for Mozart ('76)
Oedipus Rex ('76)
The Madness ('76)
I, Claudius ('77)
Miss Julie ('77)
When the Actors Come ('78)
Tinker, Tailor, Soldier, Spy ('79)
Tolstoy, A Question of Faith ('79)
Hamlet, Prince of Denmark ('80)
Little Lord Fauntleroy ('80)

Maybury ('80, '82)
The Anatomist ('80)
Smiley's People ('82)
Playing Shakespeare ('83)
Twelfth Night ('83)
Pope John Paul II ('84)
The Holy Experiment ('84)
The Mozart Inquest ('85)
Great Plains Massacre ('86)
Henry VII ('86)
Reflections on a River ('86)
The Devil's Disciple ('86)
The Making of Modern
    London: London at War ('86)
Star Trek: The Next Generation
    ('87–'94)
The Cage—A Star Trek Saga
    ('87)
Reading Rainbow ('88)
Star Trek: From One
    Generation to the Next ('88)
Nova: Neptune's Cold Fury ('90)
Nova: The Voyager Encounters
    ('90)
Nova: To Boldly Go ('90)
Shape of the World ('91)
MGM When the Lion Roars ('92)
Space Age ('92)
Nova: The Mind of a Serial
    Killer ('93)
Star Trek: Deep Space Nine
    ('93)
The Planets ('93)
In Search of Dr. Seuss ('94)
Saturday Night Live ('94)
Science Fiction: A Journey into
    the Unknown ('94)
Skiing with Style and Elegance
    ('94)
Star Trek: A Captain's Log ('94)
Stargazers ('94)
500 Nations ('95)
From Here to Infinity: The
    Ultimate Voyage ('95)

Screen Actors Guild Awards
    ('95)
Sesame Street ('95)
The Canterville Ghost ('95)
The Simpsons ('95)
Dad Savage ('97)
Moby Dick ('97)

FILM:
Churchill: The Gathering
    Storm ('74)
Hedda ('75)
Hennessey ('75)
Excalibur ('81)
Gorky Park ('83)
Dune ('84)
The Plague Dogs ('84)
Code Name: Emerald ('85)
Lifeforce ('85)
The Doctor and the Devils ('85)
Wild Geese II ('85)
Lady Jane ('86)
L.A. Story ('91)
Robin Hood: Men in Tights
    ('93)
The Nightmare Before
    Christmas ('93)
Gunmen ('94)
Liberation ('94)
Star Trek: Generations ('94)
The Pagemaster ('94)
Jeffrey ('95)
Star Trek: First Contact ('96)
Conspiracy Theory ('97)
Let It Be Me (direct to video)
    ('97)
Safe House ('97)
Smart Alec ('97)
Prince of Egypt ('98)

*also Michael Williams in the
episode "The Defector"*

---------- CHAPTER 2 ----------

JONATHAN FRAKES

Number One Behind the Camera

*"I've been told that I bear a resemblance to Bill Shatner. . . . Maybe
subconsciously that's why they gave me the job."*
—JONATHAN FRAKES, IN A 1995 STARLOG INTERVIEW

An accomplished field commander who demurs whenever any-
one suggests that he is needed in the captain's chair, Jonathan
Frakes' Will Riker has been called "the Colin Powell of *Star
Trek: The Next Generation*." Yet as an accomplished television
actor, "musical-theater guy," and a hot film and television director,
Frakes has taken decisive command of his career and his destiny.

"Who wouldn't want a crack at directing it?" Jonathan
Frakes responded when asked about the impending big-screen film,
Star Trek: First Contact. "I'm pursuing it, but will it happen? I wish,
but I don't imagine it will happen on this film." Rather, he was
resigned to set his sights on the third *Next Generation* film. "I'll just
keep trying and asking until it's my time." Five days after this quote
was published (on January 24, 1996), it was noted in the late edi-
tions of newspapers nationwide that Frakes had been named director of the Thanksgiving release.

It would be the most financially successful of all eight *Trek*
films to date: breaking box-office records in its opening weekend,
proving immensely popular with fans and reviewers alike, and
impacting profoundly upon Frakes' career. But spending eleven
months of 1996 creating *Star Trek: First Contact* was not a gift;
Frakes had earned the opportunity to direct the film. Every decision
he had made in his twenty-year career led up to it.

DRUG DEALER, FATHER-KILLER, NE'ER-DO-WELL

He was born August 19, 1952, and grew up in Bellefonte in
Pennsylvania's Lehigh Valley. To this day, Jonathan Frakes still considers himself an East Coaster. His family warmly welcomes him

43

home to Bethlehem, Pennsylvania, every Thanksgiving. Frakes' father, James (a native of Little Washington, Pennsylvania), is a tenured professor with an endowed chair at Lehigh University: the Edmund W. Fairchild Professor of American Studies. His childhood was filled with visits to his grandmother's home in Altoona, Pennsylvania, accompanied by his brother, Dan, and mother, Doris. Frakes' upbringing and family values, along with his work ethic and even his diction, are evident in his professional life. Speaking in Pittsburghese slang, "I move the camera when it needs moved," he commented on his role as director of *First Contact*.

The young Frakes was frequently taken to the movies by his father, a film buff and occasional movie critic. He fondly reminisced in 1987 about attending the movies with his father, and winding up in hysterics. "One of my favorite memories is the time my father and I almost got thrown out of the Boyd Theater in Bethlehem for laughing too loudly at the movie *M*A*S*H*. We stayed to see it twice. We were kicking the back of the seats, having a great time. Imagine, almost getting thrown out of a theater—with your father!" When Frakes ultimately decided to pursue an acting career, his father supported his every effort.

Although Frakes acted in school plays in junior high and high school, he never considered it anything more than a hobby. He attended Penn State University and was a declared psychology major. To earn spending money over the summer, Frakes worked as an usher at the Festival of America Theater at Penn State, where the producer and director of the play *Indians* spotted him standing in the aisle before rehearsals had begun. "Gee, you're a tall guy," Frakes remembers the director saying to him. (Frakes stands six feet, four inches.) "Would you like to be in the chorus of this play?" "Why not?" he responded. "And I saw that people were making a living doing something that they clearly loved, performing at night, rehearsing another play during the day in a creative, open, inspirational atmosphere. I thought, 'This looks like a good job!' So I transferred over from the psychology department to the theater department with the hopes of becoming a professional actor."

However, Frakes' change of majors was motivated by other factors as well. He confessed that the real reason he began auditioning for roles in Penn State's musical productions was to meet women. Nonetheless, Frakes took his studies seriously. After graduating from Penn State in 1973 with a BA in theater arts, he attended Harvard. While there he spent several seasons with the Loeb Drama Center. Upon graduating with his master's degree, he moved to New York City and gave himself five years to find success as an actor. "If I hadn't begun to make a living five years out of college I think I would've gone back to grad school and gotten a degree in something more practical," he recalls.

As he sought out auditions, Frakes worked as a waiter, the self-professed "worst waiter in the history of New York." Yet perhaps most notable was his stint as Captain America making public appearances around the country for Marvel Comics. In this heroic role he attended supermarket ribbon cuttings, made visits to hospitalized children, signed comic books in publicized appearances, and even visited the White House, where first daughter Amy Carter posed for a "photo-op" on Jonathan "Captain America" Frakes' lap. Frakes' agent was not pleased with his choosing to personify a costumed superhero. "He preferred I had another job. He said he would rather have seen me moving furniture, which I did and severely screwed up my back in the process, than be labeled 'Captain America' for the rest of my life."

Although a young actor takes the odd jobs he needs to survive, Frakes' professional career did not take long to engage. In 1976, Frakes landed the first Broadway chorus part he auditioned for, after surviving the "cattle call" process, in the Broadway musical *Shenandoah*. Following his professional debut, he landed a one-year contract on the daytime soap opera *The Doctors*. Although roles on daytime soaps are often derided, Frakes' role on *The Doctors* portended a greater career. *The Doctors*, which aired from 1963 to 1982, launched the careers of actors such as Armande Assante, Dyan Cannon, Julia Duffy, and Gil Gerard. Frakes was also something of a closet soap opera fan himself, admitting devotion to *Ryan's Hope*, and in particular to the actress who played Mary Ryan, Kate Mulgrew. In 1978, after his character on *The Doctors* was killed off, Frakes felt it was time to leave New York. He relocated to Los Angeles to pursue his acting career.

Frakes found work relatively quickly, the television industry welcoming the big man with impressive acting credentials. He appeared on dozens of television programs, almost always as a guest villain, and played a recurring role as the cad hillbilly Jamie Lee Hogg on *The Dukes of Hazzard*. Reminiscing, he can only say of his stint on *Dukes of Hazzard*, "Isn't that scary?" Regarding his overall career track at the time, he remembers, "I did a lot of TV. Some good. Some not so good. That's all I used to do, guest spots on TV shows. I was a big guest villain on all the hour-long dramas—*The Waltons, Barnaby Jones, Quincy*. I used to play drug dealers, father-killers, ne'er-do-wells."

During the early 1980s, Frakes split his time between episodic television and regional theater. He joined the company of the Sharon (Connecticut) Playhouse in 1982, and received critical mention in two stage plays, Philip Barry's 1928 comedy *Holiday* and the country-western musical *Prairie Passion*. *The New York Times* reviewer enjoyed *Holiday*, and hailed the "right cast and the right director—the flair and the feeling." The same reviewer panned *Prairie Passion*, calling it a "mixed-up mess." Nonetheless, he singled out a few of the cast members, including Frakes' role as Curly, saying he "hurled [him]self into the hapless proceedings with a real prairie—and professional—passion . . . [he's] first rate."

Frakes' Progress

In 1983, back in Hollywood, Frakes was cast as the nervous, conniving, "slimeball" Marcus Marshall in the short-lived NBC prime-time soap opera, *Bare Essence*. It was on this set that he first met the headlining star, Genie Francis, Laura of *General Hospital* fame. They would meet again within the next two years, and after much flirtation, dating, and a Hollywood romance, would become engaged and marry. On *Bare Essence* Frakes also worked with actor Bruce Boxleitner (perhaps best known to science fiction television fans for his popular role on *Babylon 5*), who has remained a close friend. One year later, Frakes was cast in another regular series role, that of Morgan Fairchild's bisexual male secretary on the very short-lived *Paper Dolls*, which also starred future *Star Trek: Deep Space Nine* regular Terry Farrell. He also landed a recurring role on *Falcon Crest*. However, his first significant television success would arrive with the critically derided but highly rated miniseries adaptation of the best-selling novel by John Jakes, *North and South*.

In November 1985, ABC programmed twelve hours of *North and South* over a six-night period. The miniseries was filmed over five months, and was budgeted at $25 million (equivalent to, as a 1985 reviewer noted, "about nine episodes of *Miami Vice*"). The miniseries was the second most ambitious and expensive ever produced at the time, trailing just behind *Roots*, the 1977 miniseries starring *Next Generation* cohort LeVar Burton. Frakes' most significant scenes in *North and South* came during the second evening. As Stanley Hazard, the wimpy, conniving brother of George Hazard (James Read), Frakes is but a secondary character in this miniseries, although in later sequels his role would be increased. In *North and South Book II*, another twelve-hour miniseries broadcast one year later, viewers saw much more of Frakes. Critics panned the writing and the inferior and unrealistic characterizations, yet the miniseries was still a hit with fans. Reviewer Tom Shales wrote, "Virtually every character in the miniseries is either a pillar of goodness or a font of evil; the writers don't mess with Mr. In-Between. Mary Crosby and Jonathan Frakes as an evil Northern couple proudly declare their nastiness." *Star Trek* trivia buffs will note that, although Mary and Denise Crosby are roughly the same age, Mary is the aunt of *Star Trek: The Next Generation*'s Denise Crosby.

North and South also marked the beginning of Jonathan Frakes and Genie Francis' offscreen romance. Frakes commented that on screen they barely even shared a scene. "We sat opposite each other at a dining table. We never seem to speak to each other on this series." While working together on *Bare Essence*, the two had a flirtatious relationship. Frakes recalled that "she was young and had a smile that lit up a room." However, in his eyes she was simply too young to consider pursuing romantically (he is ten years her senior). Yet, less than two years later, during the filming of *North and South*, Frakes revealed, "She had that same smile but was no longer a kid. We flirted and flirted constantly. I asked her out and we ended up eating McDonald's in a rented car in a church parking lot!" In his backyard shortly thereafter, Frakes got down on one knee and proposed. The September 26, 1987, wedding was attended by the casts of both the venerable *General Hospital* and the just-premiered *Star Trek: The Next Generation*. On their honeymoon in Italy, Frakes recalled to Arsenio Hall, "Genie was recognized, I was not."

Following his success in *North and South Book II* but just prior to being cast on *Star Trek: The Next Generation*, Jonathan Frakes was, quite literally, a goat. The Victor Steinbach stage play *My Life in Art*, which ran at Los Angeles' Tiffany Theater during March 1987, featured a bizarre plot in which a goat escapes from a farm, heads for New York City, and ultimately stars in the Broadway production of *The King and I*. Although the *Los Angeles Times* critic, Robert Koehler, was confused by the production and felt that it was, for all its absurdity, not an imaginative staging, he hailed both Frakes and costar Ron Perlman (who was cast in *Beauty and the Beast* later the same year). He praised Frakes as "an actor with an instinct for danger," which in context was a compliment, and concluded his review by stating, "After you see Frakes, you'll never look at goats the same way again." In the *Los Angeles Times* of January 1, 1988, Koehler reviewed the previous year's "best theater," and made mention of Frakes' performance in *My Life in Art*, requesting a curtain call.

SEVEN AUDITIONS, ONE SHIRT

Enterprise first officer William "Bill" Ryker (the spelling in the original December 1986 casting call) and Counselor Deanna Troi were originally modeled upon Decker and Ilia from the stalled *Star Trek II* television series that became *Star Trek: The Motion Picture*. Riker was called William by Picard and Bill by "female friends," although in seven seasons he was ultimately only referred to as "Bill" twice (in the episodes "The Naked Now" and "Haven"). Commander Riker, Captain Picard, and young Wesley Crusher were each, according to Gene Roddenberry, modeled after all the elements Captain Horatio Hornblower would have embodied at different stages of his life. (Hornblower was the eighteenth-century English seaman who rose from midshipman to admiral in the adventure stories and books by C. S. Forester.) Frakes survived seven grueling auditions over a six-week period to finally win the role of Number One, wearing the same shirt to each one for good luck. "I started with the cattle call, then the casting director, the producers, then other directors, to Gene Roddenberry, and then through the Paramount execs, including the vice-president himself and the heads of television." The process actually got easier after Frakes had met with Roddenberry, who claims he saw a "Machiavellian glint" in Frakes' eyes that he recognized in himself. Before each subsequent audition, Roddenberry took Frakes under his tutelage, helping to guide him and explaining how he wanted the character portrayed. "Gene [was] so very non-Hollywood and really quite paternal," Frakes recounted.

Star Trek: The Next Generation's first season offered Frakes the opportunity to develop his character in unique ways. Four first-season stories stand out as significant for Riker, and Frakes made the most of his opportunities. In "The Last Outpost," viewers were treated to the first Federation contact with the Ferengi. Although Riker's away team is taken advantage of by the fur-clad, whip-bearing Ferengi, it is ultimately Riker's intelligence and the ethics of the Federation that impress the evil-yet-misunderstood alien entity of the week. The entity had been holding the away teams and both ships hostage, and Riker's actions induce it to free the *Enterprise* and the Ferengi ship. This was Frakes' first significant episode, yet "The Last Outpost" is considered by fans and Paramount insiders alike to be an episode that essentially failed. The Ferengi, hoped to be a significant "new alien threat," instead came across as quite silly and not terribly threatening at all.

"Hide and Q," four episodes later, featured the first return of John de Lancie's Q since the two-hour premiere. Riker, being granted the powers of Q, learns a lesson in humanity and humiliates Q in the process. In "Angel One," four more episodes later, Riker leads the away team to a matriarchal planet, but must abdicate his leadership role to Troi and Yar. Nonetheless, Riker walks away from this episode the hero as he gains the matriarch Beata's trust through more personal means.

Finally, the episode "11001001" gave fans some insight into Riker's character. In a holodeck fantasy with the sultry Minuet, Riker romances her in a holo–New Orleans jazz bar where he performs on his trombone. Frakes, who has played the trombone since the fourth grade, actually performed the rendition of "Nearness of You" heard in this episode. Marina Sirtis has mockingly stated that the cast never liked the episodes where there was a scene displaying Frakes' musical talent, because he would bring his instrument to the set and would not "stop all day long with that bloody trombone!" Of all the episodes throughout the seven seasons, Frakes cites the first season's "11001001" as his personal favorite from an acting standpoint.

However, the first-season episode that perhaps gave the greatest insight into Frakes' offscreen character was the episode "Conspiracy." It featured a famous, if unpleasant, maggot-eating scene with alien-controlled Starfleet officers, along with Captain Picard and Riker. Patrick Stewart queasily remembered filming the scene, and upon being asked whether or not the maggots were real, responded, "The ones Jonathan Frakes had certainly were! He's the type of person who will always accept a dare. Even looking at them, [they] were too much for me—I made sure I had fakes. When Jonathan had his they were real, and they cut at the last moment. It earned him considerable kudos!"

The impact of appearing week after week on a hit series full of positive messages was not lost on Frakes, especially given his history of portraying less-than-honorable characters. In a lengthy 1987 interview, as *The Next Generation* was just getting under way, Frakes emphasized, "I like the fact that each week we have a morality play to do and that they're very clear and clean and have a beginning, a middle, and an end, and that a problem is solved and a moral, ethical statement is made. I think Roddenberry's vision is very positive and to work with that as your goal, your prime directive so to speak, is really a great way to go to work. What we're doing is not portraying depressing realism. I worked on shows where you can really get depressed because you're playing somebody terribly cynical. When you're playing a lot of negative emotions for twelve to fourteen hours a day, it's very different from going to work on an 'Enterprise' in the twenty-fourth century where the vision is so positive. It's really something you can believe in and appreciate."

He continued, emphasizing both the quality and the new-found job security that came with appearing on a successful weekly television drama. "I would like to maintain the level that we're achieving now. It's provided me with a security that I've never known before. I'm really content and satisfied when I go home at the end of the day. I feel like I've done a good honest day's work for an honest day's pay and I genuinely like the people I work with. I respect all of them."

The role of the hero, the good guy, was one that was relatively new in Frakes' acting career, but not one he found difficult. Comparing Riker to the slew of nefarious characters he had previously portrayed, Frakes said, "Well, my hair is a lot neater, and my posture is a lot better as Riker. My character, of all the regulars in the crew, is more straight ahead than most. And Riker's principles and qualities are very positive. I have those ethics and drives, too, so it's not too huge a stretch despite the fact that I've played a lot of horrible, despicable characters in the past. The hero is fun to play if you don't take him too seriously."

A new experience, and one that took some getting used to, was his sudden introduction to fame. Attending his first *Star Trek* convention early during the first season, Frakes casually walked through the hotel lobby, convinced that he would go unrecognized. What he found was a line of autograph-seeking fans that snaked out of the convention ballroom, through the hotel corridors, and into the lobby. Frakes was swamped. He credits his wife with teaching him how to handle fame, fans, and public appearances. As Laura, Genie Francis made her debut on *General Hospital* at the tender age of fourteen, and was featured on the highest-rated soap opera event to date, the infamous wedding of Luke (Tony Geary) and Laura. Frakes was able to pick up a few pointers from his wife, and "got to see the way she handled her fans and see what happened when we went out in public. I give her a lot of credit for teaching me the ins and outs, and the courtesy and responsibility you have to your fans."

Around the *Star Trek* set, Frakes was known for being exceedingly casual and would often wear a ratty pink bathrobe when not in costume. His costars teased him incessantly about his odd attire, but Frakes ignored their jibes. Oddly, the bathrobe disappeared during the first season, coinciding with Denise Crosby's departure from the program. Whether she is guilty of taking it, either as a souvenir or to put her friends out of their fashion misery, is something to which she has never owned up. Although he lost his bathrobe, a few months later during the hiatus between the first and second seasons of *Star Trek: The Next Generation*, Frakes gained a beard. Far from being a fashion faux pas, the beard, in Gene Roddenberry's eyes, made Frakes look more senior, more authoritative, and more "nautical," and he insisted the actor keep it.

The second season's "A Matter of Honor" featured Frakes' most significant *Star Trek* role thus far, involving a plot in which Riker participates in an officer exchange program with the Klingon ship *Pagh*. Larry Nemecek's *Star Trek: The Next Generation Companion* recounts the director of this episode, Rob Bowman, exclaiming, "Every day it was Jonathan and I doing high-fives and trying to put forth on film all the energy and the spirit and adventure that was in that script." He also recalls one particularly impressive scene in which Frakes' Riker trains on the firing range to become ambidextrous in the use of his phaser. However, Frakes cites as one of his least-favorite memories of *Star Trek* his encounter with Klingon cuisine in "A Matter of Honor." He had to eat a "Klingon dish with an unpronounceable name," which was really kimchee (Korean pickled cabbage) and raw octopus, sprayed down with plastic. "Lovely," Frakes reported sarcastically.

Also during the second season, "The Icarus Factor" featured Riker being offered, for the second time, command of his own ship, the *USS Aries* (the first was the *USS Drake*, and was mentioned as happening before Riker took up his post aboard the *Enterprise*). This episode revealed much about Riker's troubled relationship with his father, civilian strategist Kyle Riker. Finally, the second season included "Peak Performance," in which Riker takes command of the revived derelict *USS Hathaway* to participate in a battle simulation. He ends up saving the *Enterprise* and crew against a Ferengi ambush.

During the hiatus between the second and third seasons, Frakes filmed the NBC television movie *The Cover Girl and the Cop*, starring Julia Duffy. The film, which left critics unimpressed, featured Frakes as Duffy's boyfriend, a member of the inner circle of Washington, D.C., elite who leads her astray with his questionable advice. Despite the movie's poor reception, Frakes kept his résumé active with roles outside of the *Star Trek* universe.

LOOKING OUT FOR NUMBER ONE

Throughout the first two seasons of *Star Trek: The Next Generation*, Frakes had been looking for another way to expand his horizons beyond his Commander Riker role. He asked, nudged, pleaded, and cajoled producer Rick Berman into offering him a chance to direct. Finally acquiescing, Berman insisted that Frakes go to school. "So I did," Frakes recalls. "I spent three hundred hours in editing, watching them cut the show, then I was in dubbing, and then watched all the other directors as they were casting, and I just focused all my energy on the whole project. I went to seminars, read books, lots of books. . . . I think the producers were hoping I'd lose interest, but I didn't."

Frakes finally received the opportunity to direct during the third season, and his successful efforts and dedication paved the way for *Next Generation* cohorts LeVar Burton, Gates McFadden, and Patrick Stewart to direct episodes as well. His breaking the barrier between actor and director—and creating a precedent that allowed actors, after lengthy study, to have the opportunity to direct—has also impacted sister programs *Star Trek: Deep Space Nine* and *Star Trek: Voyager.* Among half a dozen actors who have stepped behind the camera on those programs, *The Next Generation*'s Michael Dorn has directed *Deep Space Nine* since joining its cast. All of these actors have heaped gratitude upon Jonathan Frakes for taking the lead and providing them with the opportunity to take the reins. In all, Frakes directed eight episodes of *The Next Generation,* ranking him among the show's most prolific directors.

"The Offspring," Frakes' third-season directorial debut, featured a story in which Data innocently builds a daughter, "Lal." Frakes admitted to having "a real soft spot for 'The Offspring' . . . I loved that episode. That was also the luck of the draw that I would get that one. But it happened to be a great story, a Data episode, which meant you would get that high end of acting out of Brent." Naturally, such a close and friendly cast did not make life easy for Frakes in his directorial debut. "They refused to come out of their dressing rooms," Frakes told Arsenio Hall. "They declared, 'We won't work for Frakes!' "

Two episodes in particular of the third season of *Star Trek: The Next Generation* also provided Jonathan Frakes opportunities to stretch his acting muscles. In "A Matter of Perspective," Riker is accused of murder and extradited, ultimately to be cleared of his guilt through the investigative efforts of the rest of the crew.

More significantly, in the season finale, "The Best of Both Worlds, Part I," Riker finds himself again with a career advancement decision, being offered command of the USS *Melbourne* (the third such captaincy offered to Riker in his career). Although it initially appeared that this was a recurring plot device the writers of *The Next Generation* utilized, it should be noted that this episode marked the last time Riker was to face such a dilemma over the course of the program. While Frakes acted convincingly in his professional quandary and dealt well with the friction provided by guest Elizabeth "Commander Shelby" Dennehy, the significance of the season-ending "The Best of Both Worlds, Part I" goes much deeper. "I've said this many times but I think the best television we did was the two-part Borg episode 'The Best of Both Worlds.'" The conclusion of the two-parter, "The Best of Both Worlds, Part II," the opening episode of the fourth season, provided Riker's only opportunity over the course of seven seasons to be officially placed in permanent command of the USS *Enterprise-D*. (Of course, the two-part episode, considered the most popular pair of episodes among fans, was also the basis for the immensely popular Frakes-directed feature film starring *The Next Generation* crew, *Star Trek: First Contact*.)

The third season provided some smaller moments that were much less significant, but nonetheless memorable for Frakes. For instance, in "The Enemy," the flashlights needed to give off more light than batteries could provide, for filming purposes. The actors therefore had to wear power cords running through their sleeves and down their pant legs to a power source. At one point during filming, Frakes stretched a bit too far and received quite a shock in a relatively sensitive body part. In the following episode, "The Price," Frakes was reunited with Matt McCoy, his costar from the short-lived *Dream West*. McCoy guest starred on *Star Trek* as Deanna Troi's love interest, the charismatic Devinoni Ral.

The Next Generation's fourth season provided two more opportunities for Frakes to step behind the camera. "Reunion," a Klingon saga of family and power, introduced Worf's son, Alexander, and former lover K'Ehleyr. It also featured popular Klingons Gowron and Duras and included battles and grunting galore. Frakes' other directorial turn that season, "The Drumhead," was a tale of inquisition by a special council investigating an apparent sabotage of the *Enterprise*'s dilithium chamber. Chief Investigator Norah Satie was played by Oscar nominee and "unabashed trekker" Jean Simmons, with whom Frakes had acted on *North and South*. When informed that "The Offspring" and "The Drumhead" were among fans' picks for the series' finest episodes, Frakes responded, "That's very kind, and I don't take it for granted. A lot of it is just the luck of the draw, to be honest." Frakes has stated that when directing, he tries to create an atmosphere in which the actors feel comfortable enough to experiment with a scene, a philosophy that generates the apparent chemistry between the actors so notable in these episodes.

"The Drumhead," as well as fourth-season episodes "The Wounded" and "The Mind's Eye," were written during the days leading up to, and the weeks following, the Gulf War. Frakes commented, "I feel it *[Star Trek]* has always been a more conscious show than a lot of the other stuff that's out there. I admire, and am proud of being a part of that. What fascinated me the most during that time was the fact that here we were playing war games where there was no real violence, and we were on the brink of a real war! Others were complaining, 'Why are we doing this when we are so close to the real thing happening?' Certain members of the company were tied into the whole thing. It became kind of hawkish, frightening to me. The political crossover became so much more evident then, and I found that fascinating. People I never would have considered otherwise, became closet 'John Birchers' and showed their true colors. It became a bit unnerving at times."

Frakes' fair share of featured scripts also came his way during the fourth season. "Future Imperfect" featured Riker, awakening as a twenty-fourth-century Rip Van Winkle, to find that sixteen years have passed and his life has changed: he is captain of the *Enterprise*, a widower, and a father. Only later does he learn that the entire episode was an elaborate scheme concocted by a powerful alien who was merely lonely. It has been noted that in this episode, Frakes proved that he could bring his character to the level of Stewart's Picard and play with similar intensity such moments as the ones Stewart played in episodes like "Family."

In "First Contact" (no relation to the movie), Riker escapes a hospital on the planet Malcor III, populated by a culture that is in the earliest stages of space flight but has not yet learned of other life in the universe. Riker receives invaluable aid from a Malcorian nurse, played by *Trek* fan Bebe Neuwirth, in exchange for his fulfillment of her greatest fantasy: making love to an alien. In the episode "QPid," Frakes received a severe cut under his eye when his stunt sword broke after being hit. Rushed to the hospital for stitches, Frakes was amused that he attracted no undue attention, considering he was surrounded by half of the cast of *Star Trek: The Next Generation* still in costume— dressed as characters out of Robin Hood.

The Next Generation's fifth season continued to offer Frakes the opportunity to shine both in front of and behind the camera. In "Unification, Part I" and "Unification, Part II," Riker commands the *Enterprise* and uncovers a complicated plot involving both Ferengi and Romulans, while Picard sets off on a mission to find Spock. In "Ethics," Worf asks Riker to assist him in performing ritual suicide, setting the scene for a face-off between the two testosterone-charged characters. "The Outcast" was the first *Star Trek* script to dally with homosexuality, as Riker admits his feelings for a member of the androgynous race the J'naii. This episode allowed Riker to lose control over an emotional attachment, a freedom only previously allowed Worf, with whom it was always explained away as his "Klingon nature." Although the producers did in fact set out to create an episode about sexual intolerance, all of the J'naii were portrayed by women. "Having Riker engaged in passionate kisses with a male actor might have been a little unpalatable to viewers," producer Rick Berman commented.

The fifth season's "Cause and Effect" sent the *Enterprise* and her crew spiraling through a time loop, exploding in a collision with another ship at the conclusion of each loop. A fan favorite (it featured Kelsey Grammer as Captain Morgan Bateson), it was a subtle episode to create, as it was a genuine challenge to slowly reveal the subtle differences in each time loop. Frakes' direction of this episode was the one he has labeled his trickiest. "I was concerned about shooting the poker scene, because it's one act being done five times. Thank goodness it was a great act. I dealt with this episode like a directorial test, an exercise. It had to be shot differently each time." Of course, not only did Frakes direct this episode, but it is also Riker's suggestion that ultimately saves the ship and breaks the time loop.

In February 1992, Frakes appeared on stage in Los Angeles with Gates McFadden, Colm Meaney, Brent Spiner, and Patrick

Stewart in the Stewart-directed *Every Good Boy Deserves Favour*. Frakes, as Russian political dissident Alexander Ivanov, who is mistaken for same-named mental patient Alexander Ivanov (played by Spiner), was cited by *Variety* as "communicating Ivanov's anguish and the heroic nature of his resistance." The following year, the four took the show on a brief three-city road tour, during which Frakes' performance was hailed as "superb" by the *Chicago Tribune*.

The sixth season of *Star Trek: The Next Generation* again saw Frakes behind the camera, this time for "The Quality of Life." The episode featured the problem-solving smart machines called the exocomps and starred Ellen Bry as Dr. Farallon, the exocomp's creator. Frakes felt the episode succeeded "because of Ellen Bry. When she did her reading she just took to the technobabble like a fish to water, wrapping her mouth around the words. She humanized the language like no other auditioner did. She made that show." Frakes also directed the sixth-season "The Chase," in which the *Enterprise* joins the hunt for the pieces of a genetic puzzle scattered across the galaxy after Richard Galen (Picard's former archaeology professor) appears. Infighting and trickery among the Romulans, Klingons, and Cardassians made this a very popular episode, and the moral it contained was true to the very nature of *Star Trek*. "This was a real homage to Gene and his philosophy," Frakes commented. "Classic *Trek* with a brilliant guest cast."

After twenty sixth-season episodes (out of a full slate of twenty-six) that failed to feature Riker in any notable fashion, "Frame of Mind" remedied the slight. Riker, haunted by a strange alien lieutenant, finds himself shifting among realities. Unsure of who or where he really is, he is being held captive and drugged in actuality. Writer Brannon Braga is quoted in Nemecek's book as stating that this episode was Frakes' single best performance to date. "Riker's a friendly character, he's the one human you can do humor with, you can do action—and here you can jerk him around and drive him crazy."

Three episodes later, LeVar Burton's directorial debut, "Second Chances," featured what almost became the single biggest plot twist in the history of *Star Trek*: the death of Riker. In this episode it was revealed that a one-in-a-million transporter accident had created a double of Riker years ago, and that this double, christened Thomas Riker, had been surviving alone on the planet for the previous eight years. The implications in this episode were staggering. First, Lieutenant Thomas Riker was prepared to rekindle the romance with Deanna Troi. For six years, fans had clamored for Riker and Troi to "get back together," and the actors themselves thought it was foolish for the writers not to allow the relationship to advance. However, many fans felt that the evolution of Riker and Troi's love affair into a beautiful friendship was accomplished in a manner that was gradual, hesitant, and touchingly credible. Nonetheless, this episode fanned the flames of desire.

Under consideration by the writers and producers behind "Second Chances" was the possibility of killing off Commander Riker and placing Data in the role of first officer. Hungry, ambitious Lieutenant Thomas Riker would take over at helm controls on the bridge, and also succeed in greatly complicating Troi's life. The idea was squashed, with an eye to the future of the franchise on the big screen. "While it would have been really cool to have the new Riker struggling as the hothead, cockier Riker of his youth," commented staff writer Naren Shankar, "the risk you run is you dissociate the character from his past, which is the only past the audience knows. I think it was the right decision [to keep Commander Riker alive], but it was very enticing. Suddenly, you energize that character in a whole new way. It's got some real selling points, but [executive producers] Michael Piller and Rick Berman said, 'No way, what kind of drugs are you taking?'" However, Piller made the suggestion of keeping both alive. "I mean, what other show could do it?" he asked. Although Frakes as Thomas Riker never cropped up again on The Next Generation, he was featured in a third-season Deep Space Nine episode, "The Defiant," and the actor has indicated a willingness and desire to portray the character again.

"Second Chances" did emphasize one element of his character that Frakes is sorry the program never took full advantage of: the romantic ties with Marina Sirtis' Counselor Troi. "I think they really missed the boat on that one. They established it, and it became quite clear that it was a favorite with the fans. In fact, my wife thinks the scenes I did with Marina on the series were some of the best work I've ever done. The idea of not marrying us and not letting us have a family was a big mistake. It was just sitting in their lap. And the [seventh-season] Troi/Worf idea is just absurd! It makes for great material at the conventions but for real character development I think it's ridiculous."

In 1993, at the start of the seventh and final season of *Star Trek: The Next Generation*, Frakes took off one episode to shoot *North and South Book III: Heaven and Hell*. In that third and final installment, set during Reconstruction, his character, Stanley Hazard, is found working for black rights via the Freedman's Bureau (proving that he ultimately turned out decently). Genie Francis also reprised her role as Brett Main Hazard, marking the first time the two had worked together professionally in six years of marriage.

Before the premiere of the seventh season of *Star Trek*, Frakes reflected on the ways he and Riker had changed in the six full seasons that *The Next Generation* had been broadcast. "When I started, I weighed 200 pounds and now I weigh about 210," he joked. "In terms of Riker as a person, we've injected a bit more irony into him. Our writers have written more scenes showing the relationship between Riker and Troi, which I think are essential. I think we, as a cast, have settled into our parts over the years. Our clothes fit us better than they did at the beginning."

The seventh and final season again offered Frakes the opportunity to shine as both director and actor. Throughout it, however, as the show's cancellation had been announced and was imminent, Frakes was particularly outspoken about the tremendous mistake he believed Paramount was making. It was a bittersweet season, although one that paved the way for a prosperous future for an actor and director who had made a significant name for himself in just seven short years.

The Frakes-directed "Attached" explored the much-hinted-at romance between Captain Picard and Dr. Crusher. Frakes felt it was an important set of events and credited the lead actors. "Gates and Patrick were terrific. We had a great year together. I thought Gates was at her best here. The best scene for me was the fireplace scene, where they are talking about their feelings. Throughout the show we learn so much about the two of them, questions are answered. It was a very interesting and emotional show."

Later in the season, "Sub Rosa" was a vehicle for Gates McFadden to stretch her acting talents. Directed by Frakes, it gave her the opportunity to run with the off-format *Star Trek* episode in which Crusher discovers that her grandmother had a young ghostly lover. Frakes remarked, "It was a very exciting and different-looking show. It reminded me more of *Tales from the Crypt* than *Trek*. I've never seen Gates look better than she did in this episode. We saw a different Crusher—Gates and I thought that was interesting."

Frakes' acting highlight of the season came in the LeVar Burton–directed "Pegasus." When Riker's former captain, Erik Pressman, comes on board the *Enterprise* to lead a mission to retrieve their old ship, Riker is caught between Pressman and Picard. He must contend with a Warbird full of threatening Romulans as well. This episode was also notable because it finally answered the nagging, decades-old question, "Why doesn't the Federation have a cloaking device?"

During the filming of "All Good Things . . . ," the show's two-hour grand finale, the cast, despite their anger, frustration, exhaustion, and tension leading into the filming of the feature film *Star Trek: Generations*, simply could not get serious during filming. Marina Sirtis read her lines in a goofy Cockney accent. Gates McFadden delivered hers in a monotone. Veteran director Winrich Kolbe was losing his cool with the undisciplined cast when Frakes flubbed a line. Then flubbed it again. Again. And a fourth time. Finally, an exasperated Frakes threw his hands hopelessly into the air and yelled, "Hey, what are they going to do—FIRE ME!!??"

"If there's any truth to the rumor that our show makes Paramount $80 million a year, why in God's name do they take off the cash cow?" Frakes later posed in a *TV Guide* interview given during the filming of the final episode. "But they don't ask us, do they? One wonders if they aren't going to the well one too many times. I hope not. But it's certainly got to be a fear the creators have."

It was also announced during this time that Genie Francis was pregnant with the couple's first child. Frakes and Francis publicly announced she was pregnant via *USA Today* and *Entertainment Tonight*. "It was to be a revenge on *TV Guide*, which had printed an inaccurate report on us trying to have this kid when it was a complete surprise to us," Frakes explained. The *TV Guide* report was picked up by the media at large and snowballed into all kinds of false, unwanted, and embarrassing coverage. "With the baby coming, I really would have liked to do another year on the show. I could afford to send him or her to Lehigh [University, where his father teaches] then. Do you know what it costs to send a kid to college now? It's astonishing, their decision to pull the plug on this series, which seems to be doing very well. Still they canceled it and with another year on our contracts. But then, corporate decisions sometimes elude me."

Jameson Patrick Ivor Frakes was born August 20, 1994, named after Jonathan's father, James; Genie's father, Ivor; and Patrick Stewart.

FRAKES' FIRST FEATURE FILM

Filming on the feature *Star Trek: Generations* began just days after the wrapping of "All Good Things . . . ," which according to Frakes caused mixed feelings. "There was something that took the onus off the shooting of the last day of the series since we knew we would all get together on the sailing ship in a couple of weeks for the film. There is a certain finality when you finish a movie-of-the-week or a TV series or a play or whatever. It is really bittersweet. We didn't have a full taste of that because we all knew that we were coming together again in a couple of weeks. I'm not sure if that was a blessing or not. It might've been cleaner had it ended differently. It would have been a real sense of completion."

Although every other member of the cast had been in movies previously, and Frakes owned an impressively long list of television and stage credits, *Generations* was his first feature. His overall impression? He thought it was successful and enjoyed the experience. "I liked the movie very much. I liked the tone of it. I liked the look of it and I thought William Shatner was fabulous. He had his tongue so deeply embedded in his cheek—his character was so perfectly tuned that he was just on the edge. He had that twinkle in his eye. I thought he and Patrick worked brilliantly together. I think Malcolm McDowell was great and I was very impressed with the way we all made our transition to the big screen. I think the movie came off better than people anticipated. I think it's the best *Star Trek* movie ever made."

However, like most of his fellow cast members save Patrick Stewart, Frakes fretted that his role was not very large. "I actually didn't have much to do in the movie. I think, though, it's a complaint that actors always make. But I was pleased with what I did. Better that than to have too much to do and stink the place up! I'm sure I'll have more to do in the next movie," he concluded. He had no idea how much more responsibility he would assume.

Following *Star Trek: Generations*, Frakes found employment opportunities both plentiful and diverse. He is featured as the voice of the evil Xantos on the Disney animated series *Gargoyles*, opposite Marina Sirtis' equally villainous Demona. He is also the spokesperson for software maker Boole & Babbage. He made guest appearances on the situation comedies *Cybill* and *Wings*, and appeared with Morgan Fairchild and Joe Piscopo in a CD-ROM interactive poker game, "Multimedia Celebrity Poker." He and wife Francis had cameo roles as themselves in the teen-oriented summer camp feature *Camp Nowhere*. The couple also appeared on the popular comedy-drama *Lois & Clark: The New Adventures of Superman* as campy guest villains.

Frakes has continued directing as well as maintaining his relationship with *Star Trek*. He directed several episodes of *Star Trek: Deep Space Nine* and the nascent *Star Trek: Voyager*. He is impressed with the casts of both series and has also welcomed the opportunity to appear on either (including a well-received cameo reuniting him with John de Lancie's Q on *Star Trek: Voyager*). Frakes has also been involved in the world of high technology, directing the CD-ROM "Star Trek Klingon," which he describes as "a Klingon training film." He has also directed Aaron Spelling's syndicated *University Hospital* as well as Dick Van Dyke's *Diagnosis: Murder*. "It's been a good year for directing," he said late in 1994. "But the project I'm most interested in is raising my beautiful son, Jameson. I've been turning down work, which is something I'm not used to."

Despite insisting his heart will always be on the East Coast, in late 1994 Frakes purchased for a reported $1.6 million a Beverly Hills–area home built by Jane Seymour and her then-husband David Flynn. The home is a ten-thousand-square-foot Georgian Colonial on slightly more than an acre. The brick estate has five bedrooms plus two maid's quarters, a gym, a screening room, a two-story entry, a pool, and a cabana with changing rooms.

Frakes spent 1995 filming many roles that did not hit the air until 1996. Viewers saw him in the television movie *Brothers of the Frontier*, starring Frakes as the father of Joey, Matthew, and Andrew Lawrence. Frakes could also be seen hosting *The Paranormal Borderline, Alien Autopsy: Fact or Fiction*, and *Sights and Sounds*. While viewers suffered through these poorly received programs, Frakes was primed for the most significant opportunity of his career.

Making Contact

Jonathan Frakes was not Paramount's first choice for director of *Star Trek: First Contact*—the eighth feature film in the franchise and the first to star *The Next Generation* crew exclusively. "I didn't start out obvious [the obvious choice]. They had to get past the point where they realized they weren't going to get Ridley Scott *[Alien]* or John McTiernan *[Die Hard]* or one of the other frontline action-adventure directors. Even after they decided to go with someone who knew *Trek*, a lot of us who'd directed episodes threw our hats into the ring. I didn't dare dream I was going to get it. I've only directed maybe twenty hours of television." The film, reportedly budgeted at less than $50 million, has already earned nearly $100 million in theaters domestically, and has been a significant moneymaker abroad and in the home video market.

"Occasionally, I felt that the future of the franchise was resting on my shoulders," Frakes admitted. "We tried to bring the fun back. I mean, one of the great charms of the original *Star Trek* was that relationship that Kirk and Spock and Bones had, where they would kind of kid each other, really, and be ironic and sarcastic, and kind of jab each other in the ribs. And while we don't have that type of relationship, I think a laugh every few minutes in a film that is supposed to be a tense action-adventure is only gonna help. Audiences wanna laugh. And if you take yourself too seriously, it's just the kiss of death, isn't it?"

Frakes genuinely loved the script he was handed for *Star Trek: First Contact*. "It's the best script ever for a *Star Trek* movie, and if I don't screw it up, it will be the best movie in the series. My main goal is to make sure it doesn't look like a TV movie and has a story that captures the flavor of the series, but is big enough for the big screen." Frakes made additions to the script that were obviously designed to inject some crowd-pleasing fun into the story line, while acknowledging his unique *Trek*-loving audience. Frakes was responsible for the cameo appearances by popular and familiar *Trek* stars Dwight Shultz (Barclay), Robert Picardo (*Voyager's* holographic doctor), and Ethan Phillips (*Voyager's* Neelix, in an unbilled role as the holographic maître d'). Frakes also had a hand in the casting of Alfre Woodard (Lily Sloane), who has been a friend for many years, and Alice Krige (the Borg Queen), with whom he starred in the series *Dream West*.

With only twenty television hours, a less-than-impressive number of hours spent directing, Frakes studied the works of his favorite action directors before shooting *First Contact*. He reviewed Ridley Scott's *Blade Runner* and *Alien*, John McTiernan's *Die Hard*, Steven Spielberg's *Jaws* and *Close Encounters of the Third Kind*, as well as Stanley Kubrick's *2001: A Space Odyssey*. Frakes admits that the descent of the Vulcan ship into the Montana clearing was an homage to *Close Encounters*. "My acting teacher always told me to steal from the best," Frakes admitted. "Our goal was to create a genuine action-adventure thriller that could compete on a visual level with blockbusters like *Twister* or *Independence Day* that remains true to *Star Trek* protocol, while possessing an element of heart and peppered with laughs."

He also acknowledged that what he lacked in experience, he would make up for in hard work. "Leonard Nimoy once said, 'When you're an actor they pamper you, and when you're a director you work your ass off.'"

Frakes' most difficult sequence to film? The battle around the deflector dish. ("I steal from Stanley Kubrick for that sequence.") His favorite scenes? "It was kind of a privilege to be in that two-hander with Alfre [Woodard] and Patrick—the Ahab scene—which was two big heavyweights going at it, and my job was to capture it, and shape it, and encourage it. That was a very exciting couple of days— as an actor, as a director, as a friend of these two people."

However, topping that scene was the holographic sequence Picard creates, the 1940s-era supper club with a big-band chanteuse singing while a gangland boss looks on. The scene was actually filmed at the Fred Harvey Restaurant at Union Station in downtown Los Angeles. Frakes views that scene as one he can point to proving his worth as a director. "That's the kind of thing—I can take that scene out of the movie—and say, 'See, I can do a period piece for you. I can do a musical for you.' That was a great couple of days. When you read books about directing, and about people's experiences behind the camera. It was one of those deals where you had five cameras one day, two hundred extras in period costumes, make-up and hairdos, an eighteen-piece orchestra that was actually playing, the band singer, the Borgs, the stuntmen, blowing up the bar. It was a blast, no pun intended."

In scenes where he had extensive acting chores, Frakes generously commented on how helpful it was that his cohorts with *Star Trek* directing experience—particularly LeVar Burton and Patrick Stewart—were on the sidelines to give him advice and tips. Frakes' crewmates complimented the job he accomplished behind the camera. "Right now I can't think of why I should ever want to work with a different director," praised Patrick Stewart. "It's so reassuring to have a man behind the camera who not only understands how actors work, but has a language that he can use to talk to them. It's rare. His focus and concentration on the acting within scenes is terrific. Every day he's observing and responding to things that he sees, making the scenes better and better. On top of that, he's also fully on top of whatever technical aspects there are in the show, which are huge. I couldn't be happier."

Michael Dorn explained, "We all have a great deal of trust in Jonathan." Marina Sirtis complimented him for his "great ideas. The crew love him, so there's this really great feeling that everyone is trying their hardest to make this the best film we can."

The reviewers liked the film, too—and praised Frakes' directing abilities. The *Chicago Sun-Times*' Roger Ebert wrote, "Jonathan Frakes . . . here achieves great energy and clarity." *The Boston Globe*'s Jay Carr noted, "Hiring series veteran Jonathan Frakes to direct it was a smart idea. He preserves its ensemble quality and keeps the narrative from being swamped with detail." *Time*'s Richard Corliss concluded, "Under the suave direction of Jonathan Frakes . . . the movie glides along with purpose and style."

"I went to the [Los Angeles] premiere of *Star Trek: First Contact*," recalled Frakes. "I'd never been to a movie premiere before and it was like I was watching someone else's life unfold. I felt like a kid. It was thrilling. But I did feel like I was having an out-of-body experience." Would he direct the inevitable next *Star Trek* film, the ninth in the series? Acknowledging the quirky galactic curiosity that most fans adhere to, that the best *Star Trek* films are the even-numbered films, Frakes responded, "Call it *Star Trek 10* and you've got a deal."

What does the future hold for Jonathan Frakes? "I'm reading lots and lots of feature scripts." He would also like to have the opportunity to act in a comedy series, and was being touted as a possible addition to the cast of *The John Larroquette Show* before it was placed on hiatus. He continues to direct occasional episodes of *Star Trek: Deep Space Nine* and *Star Trek: Voyager*, and to lend his voice to *Gargoyles*. His name also appears as the byline of a science fiction novel, *The Abductors: Conspiracy*. Frakes did not write it, and was displeased with an early version submitted for his approval. The book was then handed over to a second writer, noted science fiction author Dean Wesley Smith, who submitted a manuscript that Frakes enjoyed quite a bit and is proud to have his name on.

As much as he wants *First Contact* to make a successful contribution to the future of *Star Trek*, Frakes also hopes his first directorial experience leads him to helm more feature films. He commented before the release of the film, "I'm hoping this movie has a big part in returning the audience to *Star Trek*, to raising the level of excitement about *Star Trek* again. On a personal level, I hope *First Contact* will lead to other things for me, to other opportunities as a director. I would love to do a romantic-comedy film. I would love to do a movie that actually takes place in the twentieth century, with people who wear suits, eat normal food, and hold conversations in their kitchen. If I don't screw up *First Contact*, maybe that will happen."

Whatever his professional career may hold, Frakes' priority remains his family. Spending time with his wife and children (his second child was born in 1997), especially after the grueling year creating *Star Trek: First Contact*, remains a priority. Frakes has also put his professional commitments on hold, choosing to spend considerable time with his brother, Daniel, who has been diagnosed with pancreatic cancer.

Frakes acknowledges the impact *Star Trek: The Next Generation* has had on his life and career. Sitting in his trailer as the final season of *The Next Generation* drew to a close, he reflected on the seven seasons he spent starring in and occasionally directing the most popular syndicated television drama in history. "I have seen changes go on around me and I'm sure I've changed, but I kicked around for so long—knowing what it's like being the guest meat on somebody else's show and running out of money—that I've learned to appreciate what a good lick I've been given. Getting the chance to practice your craft on camera for seven years, hour after hour, is something you can't put a price tag on. I only wish we'd found a way to have the irony and tongue-in-cheek banter of the triumvirate of the original. Picard, Data, and Riker should have that. We had our own relationship, but there are moments between Kirk, Spock, and McCoy that I've always envied. That's a small complaint in a show that I was very proud to be a part of."

JONATHAN FRAKES

Commander William Thomas Riker*

Also appeared on and directed Star Trek: Deep Space Nine *and* Star Trek: Voyager

STAGE:

The Common Glory
Henry VIII
Li'l Abner
Shenandoah ('76)
Holiday ('82)
Prairie Passion ('82)
My Life in Art ('87)
Every Good Boy Deserves
    Favour ('92, '93)

TELEVISION:

The Doctors ('77, '78)
Barnaby Jones ('78)
Beach Patrol ('79)
The Waltons ('79)
Beulah Land ('80)
Charlie's Angels ('80)
Here's Boomer ('80)
Paris ('80)
The Night the City Screamed
    ('80)
Five Mile Creek ('81)
Hart to Hart ('82)
Hill Street Blues ('82)
It's a Living ('82)
Quincy, M.E. ('82)
The Blue and the Gray ('82)
Voyagers! ('82)
Bare Essence ('83)
Fantasy Island ('83)
Remington Steele ('83)
The Dukes of Hazzard ('83)
Highway to Heaven ('84)
Paper Dolls ('84)
The Fall Guy ('84)
Falcon Crest ('85)
North and South ('85)
Dream West ('86)

North and South Book II ('86)
Matlock ('87)
Nutcracker: Money, Madness &
    Murder ('87)
Star Trek: The Next Generation
    ('87–'94)
Reading Rainbow ('88)
The Twilight Zone ('88)
The Cover Girl and the Cop
    ('89)
North and South Book III ('94)
Science Fiction: A Journey into
    the Unknown ('94)
Star Trek: Deep Space Nine
    (director) ('94, '95)
Wings ('94)
Alien Autopsy: Fact or Fiction
    ('95)
Cybill ('95)
Gargoyles ('95, '96)
Lois & Clark: The New
    Adventures of Superman ('95)
Star Trek: Voyager ('96)
    (director) ('95, '96)
University Hospital (director)
    ('95)
Brothers of the Frontier ('96)
Diagnosis: Murder (director)
    ('96)
Psychic Detectives ('96)
Sights & Sounds ('96)
The Paranormal Borderline ('96)

FILM:

Camp Nowhere ('94)
Star Trek: Generations ('94)
Star Trek: First Contact
    (director) ('96)

*also Lt. Thomas Riker

CHAPTER 3

LEVAR BURTON

Roots, Reactors, Role Model

*"There is a direct thread between Kunta and Geordi,
and I am in the middle."*
—LEVAR BURTON, IN A 1988 ASSOCIATED PRESS INTERVIEW

evardis Robert Martyn Burton Jr. was born February 16, 1957, in Landstuhl, West Germany. He was the second of three children to Levardis Sr., an army photographer with the United States Army Signal Corps, Third Armored Division, and Erma Christian, an English teacher and social worker. At the age of three, Levar Jr.'s parents separated. He moved with his mother and two sisters, Letitia and Valencia, back to the United States, settling in the small Northern California town of Bakersfield.

Erma Christian, a religious Catholic, sent her children to parochial school and encouraged them to read actively. "My mom was an English teacher, and reading, for my family, was like breathing." Driven to succeed, Burton harbored dreams of performing on stage early in his life. "When I was young, I used to fantasize about being famous. I even practiced my signature . . . for autographs. I wanted to be rich and famous. I asked for it. I created it. So now that it's here, I really can't say it's horrible," he said in 1993. Sitting in front of the television as a child, young Burton watched the original *Star Trek*. Though he admits he never actually fantasized about being on the show, he did look to Nichelle Nichols' Uhura as a role model, feeling reassured that "there was a place for me in the future" as a black man.

TWO INTERRUPTED EDUCATIONS

However, the road to Hollywood success was not straight and narrow. As a preteen adolescent, Burton felt the call to become a priest. "What attracted me to the priesthood was the opportunity to move people, to provide something essential. I was drawn by the elements of history and magic. As a priest, you live beyond the boundaries of the normal existence. It's like joining an elite club. You see, it's not that different from acting, even the Mass is a play, combining these elements of mystery and spectacle."

At the age of thirteen, Burton entered a Catholic seminary, intent upon joining the priesthood. At fifteen, he began reading the existentialist philosophical writings of Lao-tzu, Kierkegaard, and Nietzsche, which led him to question the traditional teachings of the Catholic Church. "I began to wonder how I fit into the grand scheme of things. The more I thought about it, the less sense it made that the dogma of Catholicism was the end-all, be-all of the universe." As Burton's ideology evolved, he realized that he was not destined for the priesthood. He left the seminary at the age of seventeen and entered the prestigious drama school at the University of Southern California (USC) on a full scholarship. Although he moved into a room in a wild USC fraternity house, Burton insists he "wasn't actually in the fraternity, but it was a cheap place to live, close to campus." Burton's freshman year was difficult, and the adjustment from seminary to college life on the campus he calls "Blond Central" was fraught with distractions. "I've never had so much freedom and it was difficult to concentrate that first year."

Although one might wonder at the seemingly opposed career choices, from the ecclesiastical to the glitz and glamour of the stage and screen, Burton feels they complemented each other, that he could fulfill similar roles as an actor and a member of the cloth. "My desire was to be an effective spiritual leader of a small community and I was looking forward to that lifestyle. I had a love of performing and oratory. But I realized that I could apply that side of me to acting and express myself spiritually without a collar. Little did I know at that time how much that decision would dramatically change my life. But my desire to provide value to people has been fulfilled in more grand ways as an actor, producer, and director. In essence, I did not give up anything by not becoming a priest."

At nineteen, during LeVar Burton's sophomore year, he was called to audition at ABC for a role in an upcoming television miniseries, only the second ever produced. At the time, young black television stars were rare, so author Alex Haley and producers at

ABC scoured drama schools searching for a young black man to play the lead in a television adaptation of Haley's book *Roots*. "I think the producers had exhausted all the normal means of finding professional talent and were beating the bushes at the drama school," Burton speculated.

For eight nights in January 1977, nearly one-half of all Americans were riveted to their television sets, engrossed by *Roots*. The television phenomenon of 1977—and, as it turned out, the decade—*Roots* broke all viewing records and is credited with starting a national discussion of slavery and race. The story of Haley's *Roots* follows the life of an African prince named Kunta Kinte, played by Burton, and his family, from his birth in Africa to his capture by white slavers and his family's subsequent fight for dignity on the eighteenth-century plantations of the Deep South. In one of the series' most dramatic moments, an overseer whips Kinte mercilessly in an attempt to have him respond to his slave name, Toby. Kinte refuses to answer to any but his African name. "Finally, as he l[ay] there bleeding and defeated," reviewer Nancy Mills of the *New York Daily News* wrote, "he whisper[ed] the detested [slave name] 'Toby.' Viewers across the nation collectively breathed a sigh—of anguish." Speaking of the impact of *Roots*, Burton in 1993 solemnly reflected, "Those twelve hours of television changed the way a nation dealt with a horrible scar, a wound that had not healed."

Starring in a 1977 miniseries that left a nation spellbound, the twenty-year-old Burton faced a dilemma that many successful actors face: that of being forever typecast, of being overidentified with one famous character. However, he found himself in tremendous demand after *Roots* and his subsequent Emmy nomination. Although he intended to return to college, his acting career kept getting in the way. "From now on," he bragged at the time, "I don't think I'll have any problems in this business." Years later, in 1988, after his career and his life had hit some significant snags, he would reflect on that quote. "That was optimistic," he admitted, "but that's me. I'll own that quote."

Burton found himself a hit on the talk show circuit in 1977. And, although cast in a memorable supporting role in the feature *Looking for Mr. Goodbar* (with Diane Keaton), most of his post-*Roots* roles continued to be in television movies. He played the title character in the 1979 Emmy-nominated *Dummy*, about an illiterate deaf-mute accused of murdering a prostitute. He also starred in *One in a Million: The Ron LeFlore Story*; *Battered*; and *Billy: Portrait of a Street Kid*—all televised in the late 1970s. However, despite three years of steady work and high-profile appearances, nothing came close to matching the success Burton achieved with *Roots*. Hollywood's lack of leading roles for blacks, especially at this time, had finally caught up with Burton, and his career cooled.

The next three years were difficult for Burton. In 1980, his first child, son Eian, was born out of a fleeting relationship. That year Burton appeared in *The Guyana Tragedy: The Story of Jim Jones*, alongside Powers Boothe, Ned Beatty, and Randy Quaid. He also portrayed a young car thief pursued and subsequently befriended by Steve McQueen in the feature film *The Hunter*.

However, the offers were quickly drying up. The inability to match the fame and success he had achieved at such an early age and the realization that perhaps he would have some difficulties in this business left Burton inactive. He sank into a painful depression. His identification as Kunta Kinte had become an albatross around his neck. Realizing a career in which he would be recognized for something other than his role in *Roots* seemed distant indeed.

"The first three years after *Roots* were a whirlwind," Burton recalled, but when the pace of attractive offers slowed, "I took it personally." At the time, Burton blamed his stalled success—and the lack of leading roles coming his way—on "the color of my skin." But this rationalization did little to quell his anger and frustration. "I hadn't come to terms with the bottom line—myself. I wasn't in touch with my feelings. I was floating. I can't point to a particular date in my life, but I finally decided to find some balance within myself, regardless of what was happening in the outside world."

A RAINBOW OF OPPORTUNITIES

The process of rebuilding his career and of shaping a definable identity apart from Kunta Kinte began for Burton in 1983 when he debuted as host of *Reading Rainbow*—a PBS series intended to keep children aged five through eight reading throughout the summer. The series was slated to last only for the duration of the summer of 1983, but its overwhelming success and popularity have kept it on the air for over fourteen years with Burton at the helm. Children nationwide recognize him from his hosting duties on *Reading Rainbow*. Many youngsters have taken to calling him "Mr. Rainbow," although he is clearly identified and introduced on air as LeVar Burton.

Reading Rainbow has followed the same simple format throughout its tenure: Burton begins by reading a story, holding the book in front of his young viewers, and then he explores the day's subject in on-location segments. In one episode that featured *Hill of Fire*—a book that chronicles a volcano that erupted in a Mexican field in the early 1950s—Burton explains, "So we traveled to Mount Kilauea in Hawaii to learn how a seemingly destructive activity actually forms new land. We looked into the power and beauty and cyclical nature of that activity and learned that there are two different kinds of lava in the Hawaiian Islands. Then we visited an artist who lives at the summit who throws pots and glazes and fires them, and talked about the inspiration he gets from the goddess of volcanoes, Pele."

Burton experiences the discovery of a topic along with his audience, yielding a unique hosting style. "We make sure that the show does not condescend to the audience. I talk to the kids as peers." *Daily Variety* claims that consequently the program is also interesting to adults watching it with their children. Burton responded to this phenomenon, drawing from his relationship with his son. "When you have a child, you tend to think about the whole world in terms of that kid and what you want to create and leave to your children." In a program that attempted to dispel social attitudes about the "typical" family, Burton thought back to some difficult days in Northern California. "Returning to my childhood, if you weren't white, middle class, with a mother, father, and station wagon in the driveway, then you weren't considered a family. We talk [on *Reading Rainbow*] about what a family looks and feels like, about love and support. At one point in the show, I talk to the kids by addressing them in the camera dead on, and say, 'If anybody tries to tell you that you are not a family, don't let them.'"

Reviewers have hailed Burton's projection of "warmth, intelligence, and kindness" as *Reading Rainbow*'s host, and have dubbed him "an excellent role model." In 1994, the NAACP honored Burton with an Image Award specifically for his work on *Reading Rainbow*. He told the *Christian Science Monitor* that he is proud of the way *Reading Rainbow* uses television to help create "passionate, literate human beings," and that he is continually amazed to hear from children, "'My favorite author is . . . ,' to be that sophisticated so as to recognize the voice of a writer and to align yourself with that voice as a child is outrageous!"

Burton is serious and supportive regarding *Reading Rainbow's* accomplishments. "There's a huge debate about television being an eroding influence on the developing mind of a child, but I believe TV is potentially the most powerful tool we have at addressing our own growth and change. That's why the idea of *Reading Rainbow* was so exciting to me. It's using the medium to challenge the mind and cause us to want to bring out the best in ourselves."

It is estimated that *Reading Rainbow*, which airs five days a week on nearly 330 PBS stations, reaches eight million children in the target ages of five to eight years old, and is used by more than 132,000 schools. A nationwide survey of children's librarians revealed that 98 percent of them felt that *Reading Rainbow* had stimulated noticeable interest in books among young readers.

In 1985, in addition to shaping an identity with a legion of young fans—albeit with a program that took up only six weeks of his time each year—Burton began rebuilding himself spiritually as well, aggressively focusing on beating his depression. He began to practice yoga, and to work with a mystic masseur who performed rolfing, a rough-handed massage technique. He committed himself to living life to the fullest, studying with Stephen Johnson, a proponent of a form of yogic breathing called rebirthing, which is intended to re-create a womblike sense of security. Burton explained, "Overall we wanted the same things—to get real with ourselves. [He was and is] on the same path I am on," desiring to "push the envelope of human experience."

Pushing the envelope farther than most, around this time Burton participated in an auto race and traveled to Africa on a white-water rafting expedition. He also tried fire walking. "It's a metaphor for turning your fear into power. You put yourself in a state whereby mentally and physically you are congruent, absolutely in alignment, and can walk across hot coals without burning your feet."

In addition to his hosting duties on *Reading Rainbow*, Burton finally was busy professionally again, after an undesired six-year forced hiatus. Burton appeared with childhood role model Nichelle Nichols in the 1986 feature film *The Supernaturals*. He also appeared on television again, being cast in small parts in the television movies *The Jesse Owens Story*, *The Midnight Hour*, and *Liberty*, and making guest appearances on *The Love Boat* and *Fantasy Island*.

A BLIND MAN FLYING THE SHIP

In 1987 before being cast on *Star Trek: The Next Generation*, Burton was living alone, with his German shepherd, Mozart, for constant companionship (although he spent as much time as possible with his son). His home was his "sanctuary," a secluded trilevel house in the San Fernando Valley redolent of incense. Burton chose not to be involved romantically, as he was still engrossed in his deep exploration of self. At this point in his life, he commented, "I love the way life works when you just put out there who it is you are and what it is you want." Perhaps it was this very attitude, and the attainment of true peace in his life, that set the stage for the next turning point in his career—an event as pivotal as the one that landed him the role of Kunta Kinte a decade earlier.

The initial description of Lieutenant Geordi LaForge (named for a quadriplegic fan of the original *Star Trek* series, George LaForge, who had befriended Gene Roddenberry then later passed away in 1975) in the 1986 casting call that went out to talent agencies was as a: "20–25-year-old-black man . . . young . . . but quite mature and is best friends with Data. Please do not submit any 'street' types, as Geordi has perfect diction and might even have a Jamaican accent. Should be able to do comedy well." An hour-long weekly drama set in space was just the vehicle LeVar Burton needed in order to finally throw his *Roots* character aside and get on with his career. The prospect of regular employment—while continuing as host of *Reading Rainbow*—was exactly what Burton desired. In the first *Entertainment Tonight* segment introducing the new *Star*

Trek cast, Burton (easily the highest-profile member of the cast, given his prior successes on American television) commented, "I could get used to this, a five- or six-year mission, yeah, feels good."

Burton auditioned for the role of LaForge at the urging of producer Robert Justman, who had worked with Burton in the television movie pilot *Emergency Room* three years earlier. Unlike castmates Patrick Stewart and Jonathan Frakes, Burton's audition went remarkably smoothly. After his first audition for the role of LaForge, Roddenberry looked up at Burton and exclaimed, "Thanks for making my words come alive." Burton was not only appreciative of the opportunity for steady employment, but also liked all that *Star Trek* stood for. He was excited by the challenge of playing a character who was "living in a time so different from all of the characters I've played. My characters have had to deal with the black experience, [but on *Star Trek*] the issue no longer exists." Finally, Burton was poised to achieve a degree of recognition he had not experienced since *Roots*.

To prepare for the role of the blind Lieutenant (j.g.) Geordi LaForge on *Star Trek: The Next Generation*, Burton took a self-help course designed to teach him to rely on all of his senses. The climax of the course, literally, came when he climbed a thirty-foot pole, blindfolded, and mounted a twelve-inch-square platform at the top. Attached to a harness, he hurled himself off the pole and grabbed a trapeze mounted eight feet away. "I couldn't believe what I'd done. It was the most alive I have ever felt."

During *Star Trek: The Next Generation*'s inaugural season, Geordi LaForge had little to do, stuck behind the navigation console. The amusing premise of "a blind man flying the ship" never really played itself out in any plot lines, especially since everyone quickly realized the *Enterprise* really flies herself. The highlight of the season for LaForge came in the episode "The Arsenal of Freedom," in which he was given his first chance at command. He separated the ship, devised a plan against the defense drone from the planet Minos, and contended with a neophyte bridge crew and a rival officer who vied for command. Burton put in a powerful and effective performance in this episode, his lone opportunity to really shine during *Star Trek*'s first season.

However, Burton was gracious about his lack of screen time and important plots early in the show's run. He acknowledged the constraints of working within the context of an ensemble cast, but still desired more for his character to do. "There's a part of me that thinks, 'LeVar Burton is an important actor,'" he told *People* magazine in 1988. "So it hasn't felt good that my character is not central to all the story lines. But I realize that storming into the producer's office would be maladaptive behavior."

The summer hiatus between the first and second seasons marked two important events—one in the life of LeVar Burton, the other for Geordi LaForge. Geordi was promoted to chief engineer, ending what seemed to be a revolving cast of chief engineers during the first season. Also, LeVar Burton spent his vacation reprising the role of Kunta Kinte for the 1988 Christmas special *Roots: The Gift*.

Burton said, "I'm glad this is the last time I'll play this character. I didn't have any fun. It was hard, for a lot of reasons. First of all, I personally am not a fan of the 1700s. I hate the 1700s. It was not a bright spot in terms of the human condition. It was a time of ignorance, and for Kunta it was an especially bad time. For me, Kunta was always a proud, brave, strong African warrior. And when we first see him in this show, that flame is all but gone. Spiritually and emotionally, he's in pain. And for me to portray that, I'm in pain. I have a strong identification with this character. There are some areas in our lives where we just overlap."

Many fans are aware that two stars from the original cast of *Roots* eventually made prominent appearances on *Star Trek: The Next Generation*. Thalmus Rasulala (Omoro Kinte on *Roots*) played Captain Donald Varley of the *USS Yamato* in the episode "Contagion," and Ben Vereen, also in the original *Roots* cast, portrayed LaForge's father, Commander Edward M. LaForge, Ph.D., in the episode "Interface." However, in a genuinely incredible coincidence, costarring in 1988 with LeVar Burton on *Roots: The Gift* were two accomplished actors who would go on to be cast, years later, as captains headlining their own *Star Trek* series. Avery Brooks, Captain Sisko of *Star Trek: Deep Space Nine* appeared as a freedman abolitionist in *Roots: The Gift*; and Kate Mulgrew, Captain Janeway of *Star Trek: Voyager*, portrayed the historical figure Hattie Carraway, a slave-catching bounty hunter.

While on the set of *Roots: The Gift*, Burton met Stephanie Cozart, a sought-after Hollywood makeup artist who was regularly employed on the hit comedy *In Living Color* and had been nominated for an Emmy award for her efforts on the show. Although he was attracted to her, Burton did not ask her out, since he saw she was wearing a Superbowl ring on a chain around her neck. He assumed that this was akin to an engagement ring. However, after *Roots: The Gift* wrapped shooting, Stephanie asked *him* out. A bit out of practice in the relationship arena, Burton had not been aware she was interested in him. "She asked me what was my favorite food. I told her swordfish and she said she would make it for me. It took me weeks to realize that she was interested in me, because I thought she was unavailable," Burton stated, finding out much later that she had actually broken off her engagement with a star football player but continued to wear his ring around her neck to actively discourage men from making passes at her while she worked. "But when we started dating, I realized that the potential for all my dreams coming true was right there looking at me," Burton exclaimed. After a four-year courtship, Burton and Cozart were married—in a wedding ceremony that included members of the cast of *Star Trek: The Next Generation* as groomsmen and Brent Spiner as best man.

The year 1988 was "the most rewarding financially" for LeVar Burton in twelve years of acting. "I've had a great life. I have the most charmed existence in this life." Referring to his character's impending promotion on *Star Trek*, Burton stated in a 1988 interview published before the second season, "Geordi will have a lot more responsibility. This will give him more of a physical presence. . . . Geordi never had that particular expertise to contribute. It was important to find his niche." The promotion to engineering was also more suited to Burton's personal schedule. "We came up with this promotion and it solves a lot of problems. I now have a better working schedule, for one thing. The first two days of each shooting schedule are bridge days, and since I'm rarely on the bridge now I have those days off."

Continuing the Trek, and Earning a Star

Before the start of the second season, Burton received a call from his good friend Whoopi Goldberg. A longtime *Trek* fan similarly inspired by Nichelle Nichols, and prompted by Denise

Crosby's departure during *The Next Generation*'s first season, Goldberg let Burton know that she would be interested in joining the cast. However, the producers did not believe Burton's message from Goldberg until she took matters into her own hands and called the studio directly. Goldberg's Guinan began a regularly recurring role that would take her through the final six seasons of *Star Trek: The Next Generation*, and she would play a significant role in the feature film *Star Trek: Generations*.

During the second season of *Star Trek: The Next Generation*, LaForge was featured a bit more, but still much of his character was unrealized and his history unexplained. Burton had been campaigning to have Geordi's sight restored so he could, as an actor, use his expressive eyes. Or at the very least he argued to have cloned implants installed, allowing Burton to act with his eyes but LaForge to remain a role model for handicapped people, just as Uhura of *The Next Generation*'s predecessor served as a role model for blacks and women alike. Dr. Pulaski even speaks a line about surgically implanting eyes for Geordi in the episode "Loud as a Whisper," which may have foreshadowed such a change. (Of course, this change was not realized for seven years, until the feature *Star Trek: First Contact*.) Later in the second season, Burton was seen in probably his most significant episode of the year, the fan favorite "Samaritan Snare," in which LaForge was captured by the apparently harmless, slow-witted Pakleds.

During *The Next Generation*'s third season, stories finally began to feature LaForge with some regularity. In "Booby Trap," LaForge conjures up a holographic image of Dr. Leah Brahms, a brilliant starship design theorist. As he finds himself strangely attracted to her, they combine their intellects to save the ship. In the very next episode, "The Enemy," LaForge's unique abilities, shortcomings, and sense of humor are showcased as he is captured by a Romulan spy on the border world of Galorndon Core. As he cannot communicate with the ship or any of his crew, he convinces the Romulan Bochra that they must work together to survive on the inhospitable planet. By this time in the filming of *Star Trek: The Next Generation*, Burton had developed a reputation as the most serious and sober member of the fun-loving cast. "LeVar isn't silly, but we're working on it," Patrick Stewart confided conspiratorially to a 1990 convention audience.

In November of that same year, after the start of the fourth season, LeVar Burton was awarded a star on Hollywood's legendary Walk of Fame in a gala ceremony sponsored by the Hollywood Chamber of Commerce. His star can be found on the sidewalk just west of the Hollywood Roosevelt Hotel. Burton was recognized for his legendary performance in the landmark series *Roots*, his seven years of hosting and producing duties on *Reading Rainbow*, and his role on *Star Trek: The Next Generation*. The ceremony also acknowledged Burton's status as national spokesman for the "Year of the Young Reader," an honor accorded him because of his work on PBS. It would be six years before another member of *The Next Generation* cast was so recognized: it was not until December 1996 that Hollywood bestowed Patrick Stewart with his own star.

During *Star Trek: The Next Generation*'s fourth season, Burton's schedule was quite full. Besides shooting the highest-rated syndicated drama in television history, Burton was juggling his hosting demands on *Reading Rainbow* and the startup of his own production company, Eagle Nation Films, with partner Julia Roberson. The hosting demands of *Reading Rainbow* had grown to at least ten shoots per year in different locales around the country. Also acting as a program producer, Burton worked weekends and over breaks from *The Next Generation* to continue the success of *Reading Rainbow*. In these efforts he even drew sympathy from the powers behind *Star Trek*, especially executive producer Rick Berman, himself a former producer of the children's series *Big Blue Marble*. Berman had a unique understanding of, and appreciation for, what *Reading Rainbow* represented and was trying to accomplish; he was therefore supportive of Burton's efforts.

Star Trek: The Next Generation's fourth season continued the trend of featuring a number of episodes that allowed Burton to stretch his acting muscles, but strangely, Geordi LaForge remained the one character whose history still had not been explored by the show's writers. Geordi still had no family and no past, and remained something of an enigma among the rest of the *Enterprise* crew. This season began particularly poorly for Burton. He was rushed to the hospital for emergency surgery during the filming of "The Best of Both Worlds, Part II," arguably *The Next Generation*'s single most popular episode—as well as the basis for the film *Star Trek: First*

Contact—and was absent for much of the filming of the conclusion to the cliff-hanger. Burton appears in only a few brief close-ups in this pivotal episode. His lines were slightly rewritten for Colm Meaney's Lieutenant O'Brien (yes, he *was* a lieutenant then), who subbed for Burton in several scenes. Burton was all but absent for several episodes following "The Best of Both Worlds, Part II," at home recovering from surgery.

Nonetheless, three episodes during the fourth season stand out as significant Burton/LaForge episodes. "Galaxy's Child" featured the return of Dr. Leah Brahms, played by Susan Gibney, and continued a running character thread dictating that LaForge be unsuccessful with the opposite sex. Appearing "in the flesh" in this episode (as opposed to her previous appearance, in which she was a "mere" holographic image), Gibney exhibited some genuine onscreen chemistry with Burton. Though her character was said to be otherwise attached, fans hoped that Gibney might reappear in Georgi's life should her status change. (It never happened.)

"Identity Crisis," two episodes after "Galaxy's Child," featured LaForge almost entirely transformed into one of the ultraviolet light-beings of Tarchannen III. To create the effect, Burton had to wear a rubber suit that significantly limited his mobility. Performing in the suit for the better part of a week required that Burton enlist the aid of a male costumer whenever he had to go to the bathroom. This both annoyed and embarrassed him. "This is not what I had in mind," he complained, "when I decided to become an actor."

In the fourth season's "The Mind's Eye," Geordi is kidnapped by Romulans in a complicated plot to split the Federation/ Klingon alliance. Under the mind control of the Romulans, who had sabotaged Geordi's VISOR, LaForge demonstrated that his unique and powerful eyewear was also his Achilles heel. This was a *Next Generation* plot device that would surface again in the first feature film starring the new crew, *Star Trek: Generations*.

Meanwhile, at Burton's fledgling Eagle Nation Films, an on-again, off-again project had been the production of the feature *Malidoma*. As screenwriter of this true story of a West African shaman whose destiny is to bridge the gap between his tribe and Western civilization, Burton was set to star in and direct the project himself.

Targeted for shooting during the spring of 1990, it has not yet gotten off the ground years later. However, it remains high on Burton's agenda.

Eagle Nation also secured in 1990 the rights to a series of books, *The Life and Teachings of the Masters of the Far East*, which are the diaries of an explorer named Bear Teeth Spalding and a group of scientists who traveled to the Far East in the 1800s. Other projects at Eagle Nation include *Dancing in the San*, about a black physician who is afflicted with cancer. He must come to terms with himself and his disease before traveling to see the Kalahari bushmen in order to dance in the San and perhaps be cured. Eagle Nation has also been involved, along with other production studios, in an attempt to bring a black western to the screen.

In 1991, between the fourth and fifth seasons of *The Next Generation*, Burton was cast as the voice of Kwame, an African superhero battling ecovillains on the environmental children's cartoon series *The New Adventures of Captain Planet*. Like *Reading Rainbow*, this program has been rated among the best children's programs on television. Burton also provided the voice for the title character—Captain Planet himself, an even stronger superhero who forms when the lesser characters synthesize their powers.

Burton's penchant for accepting roles that are considered morally positive is no accident. "I've really aspired to associate myself with projects that are the best use of the medium, be they television or film, projects that inspire us, cause us to look at ourselves and be awed by that, projects that enable us in some way, that uplift us and carry us forward."

BEHIND THE CAMERA AND UNDER THE COVERS

The fifth season of *The Next Generation* was marked by the episode "I, Borg," in which LaForge befriended the lone Borg Hugh. The two developed a unique relationship that significantly affected the future of the Federation's greatest foes. In the following episode, "The Next Phase," LaForge and Michelle Forbes' Ensign Ro Laren are presumed dead in a transporter accident. It is up to them to warn the crew to save the ship from a Romulan trap. We learn a bit about LaForge's sketchy history during this episode, including these tidbits: LaForge has known Riker the longest of any-

one on board the *Enterprise,* and he and Picard met on an unspecified inspection tour. In "Ethics" and "The Outcast," Burton is seen
sporting a beard—a hirsute change he had rallied for, but one the
producers allowed only for this brief period.

Spearheading the sixth season of *Star Trek: The Next
Generation* was the marriage of Burton and Stephanie Cozart on
October 3, 1992. The week after his wedding, "Relics" aired.
Featuring James Doohan's Scotty from the original series, it premiered as an instant classic. A significant episode for Burton, it
featured him in almost every scene with Doohan. However, it also
showcased one of *Star Trek: The Next Generation's* most egregious
bloopers. It was never explained how Scotty and Geordi were
beamed through the *Jenolen's* shields during the episode's climactic
scene. This event was instantly recognized by fans as a significant
violation of long-established *Star Trek* technology.

In an early sixth-season episode, "The Quality of Life,"
Burton once again sported a beard, despite the protestations of
the producers. They were powerless against Burton's wishes during the filming of this episode, however, as he insisted upon sporting the beard for his wedding nuptials.

"Aquiel," later in the season, was another failed attempt at a
romance for LaForge. Interestingly, the plot twist of revealing the
dog as the murderer in this episode was added late in script rewrites.
In earlier drafts, it had been written that Geordi would keep the dog
after it was revealed that Aquiel herself was the killer.

The sixth season also saw Burton's *Next Generation* directorial debut. "Second Chances" led a reviewer from the *Chicago
Tribune* to comment on Burton's "particular flair for directing."
This unique episode—featuring the transporter-reflection-created
duplicate twin of Commander William Riker, dubbed Lieutenant
Thomas Riker—was considered one of the most difficult special
effects episodes to direct successfully. Burton was also especially well liked by the cast and crew working on "Second Chances,"
reportedly having catered meals brought in for them.

Burton reflected, "For one, it was my first time directing the
show, which was great, but also very challenging. Directing is so
much different than acting. It's a whole different set of skills. For an
actor in the seventh [sic] season of a show, you know your charac-

ter. Basically, you just need to learn your lines. It's more immediate. But for directing, there is more thought, more work. You're responsible for everything: sets, directions, coverage. You use a different aspect of self. I love it and welcome the opportunity to do it again." Burton was confident of his abilities but welcomed suggestions from the experienced *Next Generation* directors. "I got advice from all of them—and different advice from each. They were pretty helpful, especially Jonathan [Frakes]. I couldn't have done it without him. He gives two remarkable performances."

"Second Chances" was also significant because Burton took the opportunity to cast—for a single scene in the transporter room—Dr. Mae Jemison as Ensign Palmer. Dr. Jamison was America's first African American female astronaut and was a member of the seven-person crew of the space shuttle *Endeavor*. Like Burton and Whoopi Goldberg, she cites Nichelle "Uhura" Nichols as one of her greatest inspirations. When asked how he decided to cast Dr. Jemison, Burton commented, "I knew Mae from just being around the planet."

Burton kept busy throughout the hiatus of 1993. Still hosting and producing *Reading Rainbow*, which continued to be showered with praise and awards—including another Emmy, a Peabody Award, and the NAACP Image Award for "Outstanding Performer in a Youth or Children's Series." Burton also continued to voice roles on the cartoon series *Captain Planet*. Looking ahead to the upcoming seventh and final season of *Star Trek: The Next Generation*, the producers and writing staff had promised to finally give Geordi LaForge a background and family. His was the last of the crew members' life histories to be explored in depth. In his personal life, Burton and his wife, Stephanie, also took steps to establish a family of their own.

Following an in vitro fertilization procedure in the fall of 1993, the Burtons' daughter, Michaela Jean, was born on July 8, 1994. The Burtons have spoken publicly about resolving their problems with infertility in efforts to educate patients and others. Burton recorded a national public service announcement for RESOLVE, the national consumer organization that promotes awareness about infertility. Commenting on their success bearing Michaela Jean, and his subsequent work on behalf of promoting infertility awareness, he commented, "We are fortunate that we have the opportunity to reach many people. And we want to make sure that other couples who might experience infertility know that there is help available—from RESOLVE and from professionals in the field. No one has to face infertility alone." At a gala in New York City in October 1996, LeVar and Stephanie Burton were awarded the Barbara Eck Menning Award for their work in promoting infertility awareness.

FEELING GREAT ABOUT MOVING ON

The seventh season's "Interface" finally revealed much about Geordi LaForge's past and his family. Madge Sinclair flew in from Jamaica to portray LaForge's mother, Captain Silva LaForge. Burton had said that Sidney Poitier was "one of the main reasons I'm an actor," and it was he the producers originally hoped to get to play Burton's father, Commander Edward LaForge. However, Poitier had a late schedule conflict and was unavailable, which left the door open for Ben Vereen to step into the role. This episode marked the first time Burton and Vereen had worked together since *Roots*, sixteen years earlier.

The opportunity for Vereen to appear on *Star Trek* was "a dream come true" for the actor. "I always loved the original *Star Trek*, and now I love the new one and *Deep Space Nine*." When he had had a near-fatal accident in 1992, Whoopi Goldberg sent her friend Vereen an autographed picture of herself as Guinan, and Leonard Nimoy sent him his Spock ears from the feature film *Star Trek IV*. "I framed them," exclaimed Vereen. "I believe those ears have magical powers." While "Interface" was due to film, Vereen was appearing on Broadway in *Jelly's Last Jam*. Though LeVar Burton had recruited him to do *Star Trek*, Vereen still had to buy out a day of the Broadway show. There was no question that he would jump at the chance. On the rear of Vereen's *Jelly's Last Jam* dressing room door hung a "Live Long and Prosper" poster, as a testament to his dedication to and enjoyment of the program. Vereen's overwhelming glee at appearing as LaForge's father totally overcame him. "It's crazy," Vereen stated, "but when I put that uniform on, I wept. They had a hard time getting me to take it off."

The seventh season also gave Burton one more opportunity to direct. In the episode "The Pegasus," Burton won praise for directing the story of Admiral Pressman, Riker's first captain, who leads a mission to retrieve their old ship, the *Pegasus*, before the Romulans can get their hands on it. Burton so impressed the Paramount executives with his two directing stints that he has since been asked many times to direct episodes of *Star Trek: Deep Space Nine* and *Star Trek: Voyager*, and is now a familiar name among the opening credits of those programs.

The stress of filming the final episode, "All Good Things . . . ," and preparing to film the first feature, *Star Trek: Generations*, affected Burton a bit differently than it affected his fellow cast members. Despite emotions running high among most of the cast, tears being shed during the filming of the final episode, and general annoyance at all of the media attention given to the filming of the final episode, Burton was nonplussed. He spent his time in his no-frills trailer, burning incense, practicing yoga, and meditating.

Burton was relatively unruffled by *The Next Generation*'s cancellation and move to the big screen. "I actually feel great about it. This has been a very fulfilling seven-year cycle in my life, but I feel in my very being that it's time to move on. Time to do what I've been preparing to do—tell stories that are near and dear to my heart. This has been a great seven years for me and I'm really enthusiastic about having the opportunity and time now to devote to the rest of my career and the rest of my life." However, the exhaustion and aggravation behind creating the show's finale were apparent, as Burton commented on the distractions caused by all of the media frenzy. "What happens is that the most important thing tends to get left behind, and that's the work."

To *Star Trek: The Official Fan Club* magazine, Burton related his favorite episodes over the course of *The Next Generation*'s seven-year run. "Choosing my favorite or most memorable episode is a difficult assignment. For obvious reasons, 'Second Chances' and 'The Pegasus,' the episodes I have directed, occupy a special place in my heart. Most memorable . . . crawling around in the mud pit trying to find the VISOR in the episode called 'The Enemy' comes to mind. All in all, though, I would have to say some of the holodeck shows are among my most favorite episodes."

As for Burton's *Star Trek* movie debut, many of his most exciting and dramatic scenes from *Star Trek: Generations* wound up on the cutting room floor. An extensive scene with Dr. Soran (Malcolm McDowell) torturing LaForge never made it into the final print, thus leaving LaForge with a relatively small role in the finished product. "It was okay," Burton commented on the finished product of *Generations*. "It was ambitious in that it tried to be a *Next Gen* movie, a transition movie, and a two-captains movie—but that's too much going on at the same time." Nonetheless, he put a positive spin on the experience. "I did think the *Enterprise* crash was really good and Geordi had some good stuff to do."

Privately, Burton continued to keep very busy during this period. Among other leisure activities, he spent his time reading the teachings of Far East philosophers. "I don't really understand it all, but I am learning new things. I enjoy finding out about different cultures . . . but I am not studying just any one philosopher."

Burton also took up exercise with a passion, working out with a personal trainer in a quest for a healthier lifestyle. "I love to see my body change and develop as it gets stronger." His workout regimen served another purpose: it pumped him up for his first significant post–*Star Trek* role, the 1994 film *Parallel Lives*, a sequel to the film *Chantilly Lace*. The story of a group of college friends who come together for a reunion weekend, *Parallel Lives* featured Burton's first career nude/sex scene, with actress Ally Sheedy playing his lover. "I have never done anything like this, and I am glad that a woman is directing it because it will bring a different sensitivity to the experience. Right now I am very excited about it. But I am sure that when the day comes, I will be quaking in my boots—not that I will be wearing any!"

In 1994, Burton joined the cast of *Christy*, the acclaimed CBS family drama starring Kellie Martin and Tyne Daly. Burton played Daniel Scott, the first African American to appear in pre–World War I Cutter Gap, Tennessee (the show's setting), arriving in the area to study medicine. CBS declined to renew *Christy* after the season, a decision that disappointed Burton. He commented in a 1995 interview, "*Christy* is a dead issue, which is a shame. In the current landscape of television, they couldn't find a place for it." Also at this time, Burton's Eagle Nation Films signed a "first look" production deal with MTM calling for the development of television and film projects in which he would produce, direct, or act.

Five days before Christmas 1994, Burton found himself back on Paramount's soundstage eight, directing one of the very first episodes of *Star Trek: Voyager*. One of his heaviest chores was helping *Voyager's* chief engineer, Roxann Biggs-Dawson, muddle through some uniquely *Star Trek* technobabble as she struggled with the line "Vent a couple of LN2 exhaust conduits along the dorsal emitters. Make it look like we're in serious trouble."

"Do I miss that?" asked Burton rhetorically between takes. "Nooooo, sir. I don't have to get up at 6 A.M. I don't have to get into a space suit. I don't have to put on that VISOR. Miss it? No." He paused, and emphasized: "No."

A year after *The Next Generation* went off the air, Burton played a psychic killer in *Yesterday's Target* for Showtime television. "It's been great for me because I don't get to play too many villains," Burton exclaimed. Malcolm McDowell's portrayal of the founder of the government agency that employs Burton in *Yesterday's Target* elicited this from Burton: "It's been great to work with him again because we did a whole torture sequence together in *Generations* that didn't make the theatrical version. So we have some unfinished business, and we really take care of it here."

Burton portrayed another villain, The Boss, in a 1995 episode of Leonard Nimoy's United Paramount Network series, *Deadly Games*. "When Leonard's office called I took the offer seriously, even though I don't guest on episodic television. Then I read the script, which was a lot of fun. So, I went and did the show."

Entrenching himself even further with the youth of America, Burton voiced a role in the acclaimed Disney cartoon *Gargoyles*, which had just been cited, along with *Reading Rainbow*, as among the best programs for children's viewing. The significance of Burton's role in the *Gargoyles* episode entitled "Mark of the Panther" was that he "appeared" with role model Nichelle Nichols. *Gargoyles* has a reputation for employing *Star Trek* actors in voice-over roles, and has featured Jonathan Frakes, Marina Sirtis, Brent Spiner, Colm Meaney, Kate Mulgrew, and others.

In the same year, Burton was asked to host the National Business Hall of Fame induction ceremony, as leaders of business met to honor executives who had been particularly active in working to increase the quality of education nationwide. He also portrayed Dr. Truman Fairchild, a scientific genius in the field of biotronics, on the CD-ROM game "Bluestar" from Magnet Interactive Studios. "It's a tribute to LeVar's considerable acting skill that we cast him in the role of Dr. Fairchild," commented a spokesman for Magnet. "In contrast to his legendary role as the helpful, sensitive, and conscientious Lt. Commander Geordi LaForge, Dr. Fairchild is severe, stiff, and very aware of his own genius."

Burton was originally slated to make a guest appearance as Geordi LaForge on the *Star Trek: Voyager* episode "Death Wish" featuring John de Lancie's popular character, Q. However, it was not LaForge but rather Riker who made the appearance as someone whose family lineage is affected by the Q—in this case, by his involvement in the American Civil War. Because Burton at the time of filming was sporting a clean-shaven head—clearly not Geordi LaForge's "look"—Frakes' Riker was substituted at the last minute. (Of course, *Star Trek* aficionados know that Riker's family lineage made little sense in this role, as his roots were in Alaska, which was not even remotely a member of the Union during the Civil War.)

Moving into 1996, Burton continued his hosting stint on the ever-popular *Reading Rainbow*. The series, which had won a Peabody and nine Emmys (and dozens of nominations), began a recurring focus on literature-based mathematics in its mix of featured subjects. Additionally, in an episode that revolved around the juvenile book *Owen*, Burton flashed back to his own childhood in Northern California. He made reference to the title character in *Owen*, a young mouse who has a little trouble giving up his treasured blanket, and discussed aspects of his own childhood. In 1996 *Reading Rainbow* also featured a unique episode with the famous percussion group Stomp. At the conclusion of the segment, Burton got on stage and took his place performing with the unconventional musicians.

Capitalizing on his lengthy relationship with Paramount studios, Burton broke Eagle Nation's loose ties with MTM and signed an exclusive deal with Paramount to produce television as well as feature films. In 1996 he sold his first television series to the

United Paramount Network, a half-hour comedy entitled *Daddy's Little Girl*. "I created the show as an homage to *The Courtship of Eddie's Father*—a show I absolutely loved as a kid." Burton will executive produce as well as star in the program, tentatively scheduled for a 1997 premiere.

Fame, of course, has its price. In 1996, Burton and his wife had to seek a restraining order against their daughter's former nanny. After firing her, the Burtons received continual harassing and threatening phone calls. When they outfitted their home with a call-screening device, the nanny began to dial up LeVar Burton's pager. "She has been making repeated threats to 'get even,'" the Burtons stated in their written request for an injunction. "We fear for the safety of our family and those in our employ."

Despite setbacks such as this, 1996 featured significant high points for Burton. President Clinton nominated Burton to the United States National Commission on Libraries and Information Science, stemming from his work on *Reading Rainbow*. This nomination was later confirmed by the U.S. Senate. Burton also made his feature-film directing debut with *Double Dutch*, a movie described as, "*Rocky* meets *Sister Act* with jump ropes."

After the filming of the first *Star Trek* feature film, Burton commented on the rumors that the next film would feature the dreaded Borg. "As you well know, Geordi has a great relationship with the Borg," Burton said, referring to the sixth-season *Next Generation* episode "I, Borg." "Geordi and Hugh are good friends, so I hope that will come into play." Filmgoers who saw the hit *Star Trek: First Contact* know that the plot line did not involve Geordi's friend Hugh, but it did offer Burton an opportunity for a few good scenes. In particular, Burton as LaForge had extensive scenes with James Cromwell's Zefram Cochrane, and Burton was aboard the *Phoenix* rocket as it made the first warp-powered flight in human "history." Also, and perhaps most important for Burton's happiness and well-being as an actor, LaForge's VISOR was finally replaced with implanted cyber-eyes, which featured some very bioniclike special effects. Burton does not offer much of an explanation for LaForge's significant costume change, and neither does the film. "I just got tired of wearing them," he said.

Asked what he thinks life will be like as we approach the millennium, Burton responded, "My vision for the twenty-fourth century is this: my hope is that we will have evolved to a place where we are much more self-realized, much more aware of what is available to us, what we are capable of as unique individuals. Unique beings. I hope that in the twenty-fourth century we are operating closer to the highest level of potential. We have come to terms with our concept of separation in ourselves, and that we will no longer look across the street, across the block, across town, or across geopolitical borders to see someone who is not like ourselves. I hope to see ourselves reflected in others. We have to align ourselves.

"If we really start maximizing ourselves to the total level, if we have total recall about who we are, we will be able to change the planet before our eyes. We can be effective in making change, in accomplishing what we desire.

"You know that phrase, Love your neighbor as yourself? My hope, as we head toward the millennium, is that we need to take the message to the next level. My neighbor and myself are the same."

LeVAR BURTON

Lieutenant Commander Geordi LaForge
Also directed Star Trek: Deep Space Nine *and* Star Trek: Voyager

TELEVISION:

Billy: Portrait of a Street Kid ('77)
Roots ('77)
Anyone for Tennyson? ('79)
Battered ('78)
One in a Million: The Ron LeFlore Story ('78)
Rebop ('78, '79)
Roots: One Year Later ('78)
The $20,000 Pyramid ('78)
Dummy ('79)
The Muppets Go Hollywood ('79)
The Osmond Family ('79)
American Spectator ('80)
Guyana Tragedy: The Story of Jim Jones ('80)
Fantasy Island ('81)
Grambling's White Tiger ('81)
The Acorn People ('81)
I Love Liberty ('82)
Trapper John, M.D. ('82)
Emergency Room ('83)
Reading Rainbow ('83–present)
The Jesse Owens Story ('84)
The Love Boat ('84)
Wonderworks ('84)
The Midnight Hour ('85)
Liberty ('86)
Murder, She Wrote ('86)
Sesame Street ('86)

A Special Friendship ('87)
Houston Knights ('87)
Star Trek: The Next Generation ('87–'94)
Roots: The Gift ('88)
Central Park ('90)
New Adventures of Captain Planet ('91–present)
Firestorm: 72 Hours in Oakland ('93)
Batman: The Animated Series ('94)
Christy ('95)
Deadly Games ('95)
Gargoyles ('95)
Politically Incorrect ('95)
Star Trek: Deep Space Nine (director) ('95)
Star Trek: Voyager (director) ('95, '96)
Yesterday's Target ('96)

FILM:

Almos' a Man ('76)
Looking for Mr. Goodbar ('77)
The Hunter ('80)
The Supernaturals ('86)
Mountains of the Moon ('90)
Parallel Lives ('94)
Star Trek: Generations ('94)
Double Dutch (director) ('96)
Star Trek: First Contact ('96)

CHAPTER 4

MICHAEL DORN

A Great *Trek* Record

*"When I first started watching the show, I thought it was funny.
Then I realized the nuances . . . race relations, balance of power kind of
stuff. Our new show has gone so far beyond shoot-'em-up—except my
character. He always wants to blast!"*
—MICHAEL DORN, QUOTED ON *THE LATE SHOW* IN 1988

There's something appealing about those raw, uninhibited emotions, desperate to be released from stifling rules and regulations. The constant urge to just throw something, to attack without considering the consequences, to throw your head back and howl. When all the soaring talk of humanism and *Star Trek*'s social agenda gets out of hand, you need someone like Worf to bring you back to earth. Admit it, you love Worf, and therefore you're a fan of Michael Dorn.

THE MAN BEHIND THE FOREHEAD

Besides being the birthplace of Michael Dorn, tiny Luling, Texas—thirty miles east of San Antonio—is famous only for its annual Watermelon Thump. Born there on December 9, 1952, Dorn and his family moved two years later to Pasadena, California, the place he still calls home. Dorn credits his inexhaustible work ethic to his father—a foreman for a road construction crew—and his mother—an East Los Angeles schoolteacher who never took a vacation until she retired. Dorn also holds her responsible for his distinctive voice. "My mother was an English teacher. She would always emphasize pronunciation. I was very conscious of that."

Dorn spent his childhood playing bass guitar and piano. He dreamed of two things: music and flying. A dedicated aerophile, Dorn studied airplane magazines and familiarized himself with every jet: military, commercial, and private. But an early diagnosis of astigmatism prevented him from pursuing a future as a pilot. Instead he focused on music, playing bass guitar and occasionally keyboards in numerous local rock groups. He even skipped his senior prom at Blair High School to play a gig for $70. "That was a lot of money in 1971."

After graduating from high school, Dorn entered Pasadena City College and spent two years studying psychology ("too boring") before switching to a major in radio-television communications. He excelled in front of the camera at Pasadena City, and friendly encouragement prompted him to leave school to explore acting possibilities while pursuing a career as a rock musician. He moved to San Francisco, where he managed to earn a few dollars playing in bands. Because the money he earned making music was not enough to support himself, he supplemented his income by occasional modeling work, including posing as the Viceroy cigarette man. In 1973 he enrolled at San Francisco State College as a drama major and discovered that he "enjoyed doing campus [stage] productions, including some Shakespeare works, but people kept telling me that I belonged in front of a camera. I finally believed them and dropped out of school in 1975 to start work as a film and TV extra in Hollywood."

Dorn began his Hollywood career earning a living as "atmosphere." A friend's father, an assistant director on *The Mary Tyler Moore Show*, offered Dorn both encouragement and a job. While Moore, Ed Asner, Ted Knight, and Betty White got all the laughs, Dorn was "sitting in the background, making $90 a week. [But] I was thrilled about this brilliant, brilliant writing I heard." His role on *Mary Tyler Moore*, listed in the credits as "Sam the Newsman" in the rare episodes he got to utter a line, nonetheless kept Dorn employed through the late 1970s. It also helped him to earn small nonspeaking parts in the 1976 hit feature film *Rocky* (as one of Apollo Creed's bodyguards) and *Demon Seed* (as a physicist), released a year later. It was while filming *Rocky* that he met makeup artist Michael Westmore. They would be reunited eleven years later and spend countless hours together on the set of *Star Trek: The Next Generation*. During the late 1970s, when acting work was slow, Dorn was usually able to find work touring with various rock bands.

Dorn considers his professional acting debut to be the few lines uttered as a furniture mover on the short-lived *W.E.B.*, a 1979 series based on the feature film *Network*. Impressed with Dorn's work, the producer of the series introduced him both to an agent and to noted acting coach Charles Conrad, under whose tutelage Dorn began studying. Six months later (in 1980), he landed the role of Officer Jed Turner on the popular NBC series *CHiPs* and spent the next three years refining it. Although he has claimed that his big moments on *CHiPs* came whenever he got to speak lines as extensive as "Go get 'em, Ponch," Dorn has fond memories of his first notable part. "I loved doing cop roles. . . . I got to drive fast and I never got hurt." And playing a regular character on a successful series meant a steady income. "I had never had that much money in my life. It wasn't even that much, actually, because I was not the lead. But it was a lot for me. I thought, 'Wow, maybe I shouldn't take this, maybe I should give a little bit back.'" When *CHiPs* went off the air, Dorn found he still enjoyed the luxury of a steady income. "The residuals were good. . . . When you're an unemployed actor, if you had $500 in the bank, you were rich! I used to save quarters all week. At the end of two weeks, I would have $60. I could fill my refrigerator or go out on a date."

Following his role on *CHiPs*, Dorn landed numerous bit parts on evening television dramas like *Falcon Crest*, *Hotel*, and *Knot's Landing*. He portrayed a lie-detector expert in the 1985 hit film *The Jagged Edge*. He also appeared as a regular cast member on daytime serials: six-month runs each on *Capital* in 1985 and *Days of Our Lives* in 1986. "Well, I wasn't exactly taxed on those shows. I'd show up every couple of weeks to interrupt somebody's conversation. I played Jimmy Carpenter, a bad, well-dressed yuppie on *Capital*, and clean-cut Senator Ed Lawrence on *Days*. Obviously, I wasn't going anywhere in soaps."

Alongside his acting commitments, Dorn has always found time to perform and write music. During the late 1980s, Dorn performed with a band, The Watch, which he claims was "strictly for fun." In a 1984 interview, he discussed his lifelong musical interests. "[In high school and college] I loved Frank Prestia from Tower of Power, and Bootsy Collins. Now I listen to Stephane Grappelli—

he's a great violinist—Patsy Cline, and a lot of classical." (Dorn's favorite opera is *Carmen*.)

"I'm always playing nice guys, nice cops, nice doctors," Dorn lamented. "I want to show a darker side." In an attempt to change his image, he took up acting classes with Brian Reise and began redefining his look. He took this new image to his next audition: the role of a Klingon officer aboard a Federation starship on the new *Star Trek* series.

A lifelong science fiction fan (*Star Wars* was his favorite movie), Dorn was also a professed trekker from a young age. Growing up, Dorn would sit at home watching the original *Star Trek* series with his brother. The boys were big fans of James Doohan's Scotty and were scolded more than once for suggesting after dinner, "Well, lad, you'll be wantin' some Scotch to wash that down with!"

Dorn noted, "Joining the cast of *Star Trek: The Next Generation* was a dream come true. First, because I'm a trekker; and second, I'm playing a Klingon, a character so totally different from the nice guy roles I've played earlier in my career. I heard about the casting for *The Next Generation* through the trade papers, and so I contacted the studio and said, 'I'd like to be a part of it.' For a whole year, I had tried to get in there to see them about an interview, and finally my agent said, 'Well, they have already cast it; it's too late.' I said, 'Okay, maybe something will come up.' At the last minute they called and said they wanted to see me for a role as a Klingon. It was long after the other characters had been cast. In fact, the day that I got hired, I think they had already started filming."

An Afterthought

Some background: in October 1986, Gene Roddenberry was just formulating plans for the new *Star Trek* series. Initially, he was averse to any retreads of characters or races featured prominently in the original *Star Trek* series. Producer Robert Justman's suggestion for a Klingon marine as a regular character was rejected by Roddenberry. The initial casting call included parts for eight featured characters—all of whom survived relatively unchanged into filming the series—but no Worf. The initial cast portrait that was taken June 1, 1987, did not include Worf, and the first public word of his existence appears to be David Gerrold's column in *Starlog*, published July 6, just two months before the series pilot debuted.

Casting Worf was also terribly difficult for *The Next Generation* producers. Resolved to audition only tall, slim, black actors (black men were exclusively considered in order to simplify the onerous Klingon makeup), dozens of would-be Worfs came and went before the casting crew. The producers were unable to settle on any one of the hopefuls.

What they could not know was that Dorn, scheduled for a late audition, was friendly with another actor who had previously auditioned for a Klingon role in the Leonard Nimoy–directed feature *Star Trek III: The Search for Spock*. Dorn's friend explained to Dorn that when he had walked into the audition for the film, he brazenly asked Nimoy, "So, what's a Klingon?" The result of his naïveté, obviously, was that he did not get cast. This inspired Dorn to come up with a strategy for his own audition. "I did not wear any makeup, but I took on the psychological guise of a Klingon. I walked into Paramount in character. No jokes. No laughing with the other actors. When my turn came, I walked in, didn't smile, did the reading, thanked them, and walked right out." The name of the actor who had failed in his Klingon audition for Leonard Nimoy? The same man who would years later become *Star Trek: Voyager*'s first officer, Robert "Chakotay" Beltran.

When *Star Trek: The Next Generation* began its run, Dorn was living simply in a small Burbank apartment. He drove an inexpensive red Volkswagen Jetta, but had a taste for expensive clothing. In 1988, he reflected, "When *Star Trek* came along, I had already decided to live well within my means for a while. I enjoy feeling like Mr. Liquid. Not into status symbols, I bought an inexpensive new car, cash." (Though in 1990, he purchased a new Porsche Carrera.) "I'm hoarding money to buy myself a house in the next year or so, which will be my most extravagant purchase ever. But I've become a clotheshorse, unfortunately, which means I can drop $1,000 in a nice shop without blinking."

Although the role of Worf was established as a recurring one, with the Klingon slated to appear in only seven of the program's first thirteen episodes, after the filming and editing of "Encounter at Farpoint" the producers were convinced that Worf had presence and decided to expand the role. Perhaps the most imposing and memorable quality in those initial scenes was not the extensive makeup, or Michael Dorn's imposing size (he stands six feet, three inches), but his distinctive voice: louder and lower than his regular speaking voice and garnished with a slight English accent. "Gene Roddenberry wanted me to make him different, so I gave him a different kind of voice."

Dorn realizes that his initial status on board the *Enterprise* was something of a mystery to even the show's writers. "It's hard to tell what people are thinking. When they hired him [Worf], I think it was just so they basically could see how it would turn out. But when they saw how I was portraying him, they realized they could do just about anything. His presence, you're drawn to the size, the makeup, the whole nine yards."

Roddenberry also presented Dorn with a clean slate, placing the onus on Dorn to create and mold the character. Dorn had his own strategy for this as well. "As I was on the set with the other actors I noticed that they were all wonderful people. Their characters were wonderful, charming comrades: 'Let's go out in space and save the universe together. We like each other!' Everybody was bonding. I thought it would be a great idea for this character to be completely opposite. Where he hated everybody. So that's what I did. If somebody even mentioned my name, I'd get mad. That's the way it was. If they said, 'Mr. Worf,' I would just bristle. I got to create it and then I coveted it. Was protective of it."

Nonetheless, Dorn was cognizant of Roddenberry's overarching vision of the world of *Star Trek*. "Roddenberry is saying that even Klingons have redeeming qualities. That everybody has some good. I agree with him."

Dorn was not featured in a significant way until the nineteenth episode of the first season, "Heart of Glory." Fans were finally treated to a long-awaited "Klingon episode," and the seeds were sown for exploring the relationship between the Federation and the Klingon Empire. Worf's heritage is examined, and the story of Khitomer and the Romulan betrayal are introduced in "Heart of Glory." (The treachery is fully explored later in the popular episode "Yesterday's *Enterprise*" and the feature film *Star Trek VI: The*

Undiscovered Country.) Larry Nemecek writes, "This tale of personal conflict does for Worf what 'The Naked Time' did for Spock back in the early days of the first series."

In an earlier first-season episode, "Hide and Q," Michael Dorn was responsible for the description of Klingon foreplay as "rough," a suggestion he made to the writers. Also, in an interesting but little-known homage to the original *Star Trek* series, throughout the first season a Worf wore actual costume accessory sported by a Klingon on the original series: the ceremonial gold sash.

In 1988, at the close of the first season, Dorn described the exhausting process involved in his Klingon transformation: "We usually start with the spiny forehead and hair, both attached to a cap, then glue down an extended bridge for my nose and bushy eyebrows. Fortunately, I won't have to have a beard attached anymore." (In the summer of 1988, Dorn grew his own Worf-style goatee and mustache.) "Last, but not least, a gel is brushed all over my face to give life to the makeup, which dries while I'm getting dressed."

The day-to-day grind of the first season of *The Next Generation* was particularly grueling for Dorn. Required to be at the Paramount studios before 5 A.M. for more than two and a half hours in makeup, he was the first of the cast at the studio every day, and often the last to leave. "The birds aren't even singing yet when the makeup man starts working on me." Although he admits that he was able to catch some sleep in the makeup chair, he developed a rash on his face that lasted well over a year until the makeup artists developed a new glue to apply to his forehead. As if wearing over two pounds of makeup every working day was not difficult enough, the false teeth he was made to wear during the early years of *The Next Generation* were painful, had a tendency to fall out, and impaired his speech.

Additionally, Dorn was not as friendly with his castmates during the first season as they were with each other. Like his character, he found himself something of an outsider. Marina Sirtis has said that because he was always in makeup, costume, and character by the time the rest of the cast arrived, they never saw Dorn as anything but Worf. "As soon as he got in that makeup, he got surly," Sirtis recalls.

Dorn reflected on his character: "You know, it's funny, when I first started I thought I was completely opposite of Worf.

Now, I'm not sure, because I can be gruff, I can be aloof at times, I can be short tempered and serious, too. I've definitely been accused of being serious and intense! So I think there is a lot more of Michael Dorn in Worf than I want to imagine. I think that we all have a bit of that in us—an aggressive side. But that's also why I think Worf's become so popular—because of that aggressive side. I think people would sometimes like to let that side of them out."

However, portraying a Klingon can have its potentially hazardous effects on an actor's psyche, as Dorn observed after the first season had finished filming. "At one point, I got a little carried away. Michael Dorn was an alien and Worf was real because I was in makeup sixteeen hours a day. I only saw my true self when I went to bed and got up in the morning. I've since learned to tone it down."

Reflecting upon the first season, Dorn appreciated the difficulties of successfully portraying Worf and the phenomenon of *Trek*. "Worf is the most challenging part I've ever had because it shows the darker side of me. I played a nice guy for ten years, and now I'm serious, aggressive, and aloof. It's also a major challenge to bring this character to life behind the tons of latex, spirit gum, and hair. Incidentally, I never get recognized by *Star Trek* fans on the street, which is a double edge. It's bad for my ego but great for my career, as no one is going to typecast me from here on."

However, despite a grueling schedule, Dorn still found time for his other passions. Throughout the first season of *The Next Generation*, he played with a band named Druicilla and the Blind Mice. After leaving that group, he spearheaded the formation of Little Wallies, a band made up of actors mostly from his acting class.

At this point, he also rekindled his lifelong desire to fly as a result of a conversation with an aviation enthusiast working on the sets of *The Next Generation*. The airplane buff remarked that aviation regulations had loosened, and that even pilots blind in one eye were permitted to fly small planes. When the five-month-long writers' strike hit Hollywood in 1988 (in effect extending the hiatus between the first and second seasons of filming), Dorn took advantage of the extra free time by taking flying lessons in a single-engine Cessna 172. He even earned a pilot's license. "I feel a lot safer up in the air than driving on a Los Angeles freeway. After my fifth flying lesson, having landed the plane by myself for the first time, I had to fight rush-hour traffic all the way home. Somewhere along the line a guy ran into my car. He got out and started yelling that it wasn't his fault, pointing to a woman in another car nearby. I kept thinking, 'My God, it's nuts down here.'"

As if music, flying, acting, and *Star Trek* publicity appearances weren't enough, Dorn made it a point to keep his body in outstanding shape. He worked out at least three times a week "in the early morning at a gym in Hollywood. It's an intense hour of heavy cardio and free weights where I never stop moving. Throughout it, I'm sweating profusely as I go from one exercise to the next without stopping."

Star Trek: The Next Generation's second season began most significantly for Dorn when Michael Westmore made some slight changes to Worf's look. The forehead ridge piece was simplified, which helped alleviate Dorn's skin rash. The new forehead was glued down only around the edges, and was simpler and quicker to apply, but it lessened the facial expressions that the prosthetic piece could reflect. As for his appearance on screen, Dorn commented, "He made me look meaner, I think. It made the look more streamlined. It's more intense and that's what the producers wanted."

"The Icarus Factor" was one of two second-season episodes in which Worf played a prominent role in the story line. Although the program featured a story about Riker and his father's attempts at reconciliation, the backstory featured an increasingly tense Worf. When Wesley discovers that Worf is perturbed because he missed a ritual marking the tenth anniversary of his Age of Ascension, a reenactment of the ritual is set up on the holodeck. (Two interesting tidbits concerning this scene: (1) Among the Klingons wielding pain sticks during the ceremony is six-foot, six-inch-tall former *Entertainment Tonight* host and popular New Age musician John Tesh; and (2) Because the scene was filmed at the same time that Klingon-heavy scenes were being shot for the feature *Star Trek V: The Final Frontier*, the wardrobe department ran out of boots for the Klingons in Worf's chamber. They had to resort to footwear scavenged from the *Planet of the Apes* costume vaults.) The other significant second-season episode for Dorn, "The Emissary," featured Worf meeting up with an old love, K'Ehleyr (Suzie Plakson). The complications that K'Ehler would bring upon Worf's life were the first in his character's story line that would ultimately span over a decade on two different *Star Trek* series.

Dorn intentionally played Worf more on the edge during the second season than he had throughout the first. Echoing the sentiments he shared with the show's producers, he stated, "They didn't want Worf to be this teddy bear—a warm and endearing sort of person who has lots of relationships and friends and a family. Gene Roddenberry, especially, said that this was just not Worf and it was just not very Klingon. And that was especially true of Worf because he has something that is a little more interesting than the average Klingon . . . the fact that he was raised by humans. So he's always trying to fight the feelings of humanity because he does feel some of the things humans feel. Worf is a big, powerful, aloof, serious, aggressive, complex person. He's like a volcano ready to explode."

As an actor, Dorn was wary about getting too intimate with the role. He feared that too high a comfort level on his part may have dulled Worf's sharp edge. "I never want to nail his character down because I like to have some confusion going on," Dorn stated in 1989. "He's sort of a man without a country. He may not like it but he accepts it. He likes being a loner but sometimes he yearns for his own kind." Little could Dorn possibly have known at the time that he still had over a decade of Worf to portray on two different television series, and it was unavoidable that he would eventually "nail him down" to some extent.

In the third season's "Sins of the Father," Worf is thrust into a life-or-death battle for his family's honor as viewers are treated to the first-ever scenes of the Klingon Homeworld. The ramifications of Worf's dishonor in this episode would color the character for years to come. Though "Sins of the Father" was Dorn's single biggest role of the third season, he actually preferred the ensemble episodes, like "The Enemy." Episodes such as this were significant for the development of Worf's character, but featured the entire cast. "I prefer to have episodes like 'The Enemy,' where I'm not the main focus. The central focus in that show was Geordi down on the planet. But I like to have an episode where we all have something to do, where we all have meaty, interesting scenes. I'll take that any day rather than have my own show. I like the challenge of acting with all kinds of different actors."

Dorn's most important scene in "The Enemy" was one in which he initially resisted a controversial decision producer and scriptwriter Michael Piller had made for Worf. Worf refuses to donate blood to a dying Romulan, ultimately resulting in the Romulan's death. This scene was a real turning point for the entire *Star Trek* franchise—for Gene Roddenberry's vision—because a mainstay of both of the *Star Trek* series thus far had always been a distinct lack of significant conflict among the show's main characters. Here, suddenly, *Enterprise* officers clashed over a genuine moral issue and the decision that was reached was neither easy nor uncontroversial. Despite Picard's and Crusher's protestations, Worf chose to allow the injured Romulan to die rather than dishonor himself by donating his blood to him.

"The writers took a risk with the episode 'The Enemy,' where Worf lets the Romulan die," Dorn recalls. "Worf definitely has very distinct feelings about this Romulan. I called the producer when I first read the script and said, 'Tell me about this. Why are we doing this?' I was afraid that the character may be hurt by his decision to let the Romulan die. Basically, what he told me was that Worf is a soldier and an officer but you can't order somebody to give their blood or any piece of their body to someone else. You can't do that. You can order them to lay down their life for you but you can't order them to give a piece of themselves. If you were in the armed forces and a person was dying, they would have to ask you to give blood. We also have a tendency to forget that Worf is not human. He is an alien so his concepts are different than ours. His concepts of good and evil, right and wrong, when he's on duty are the same, but when he's off duty it may be a different story. He says, 'If you order me, I will do it. If you're asking me, no, I will not do it.' I was a bit afraid of the reaction to that, but it was a challenge to play. After a couple of days of reading the script, I got into ways that I could make it more powerful or more intense. I wanted to leave people thinking about what they would do in a situation like that."

One of Dorn's favorite episodes was the third season's "The Offspring," featuring castmate Jonathan Frakes' directing debut and the creation of a daughter by Brent Spiner's Data. Although this episode had a negligible role for Mr. Worf, "it was a wonderful, wonderful episode. The performances were brilliant. Everyone was just incredible. . . . It doesn't have to be Klingon to be my favorite. I love *Star Trek*, so I love good episodes."

Meanwhile, when the cameras were turned off, the cast of *Star Trek: The Next Generation* was becoming uniquely close. Dorn and Sirtis were becoming, in her words, "best friends," and the behavior on the set was anything but serious. Dorn, a fan of Patrick Stewart well before they met on the *Star Trek* set, would get down on one knee and call Stewart "Your Majesty" or "My Liege" every time Stewart would walk onto the bridge. He would also imitate Stewart's role from *Excalibur*, which always succeeded in breaking the entire cast and crew into uncontrolled laughing fits. Dorn and Spiner would perform dueling Gregory Peck impressions during rehearsals, and Dorn developed a game in which he would come up with new and inventive ways to assassinate Stewart on the set. Stewart claims that he wished Dorn hadn't started it because "he's getting so good at it that it's making me jumpy."

Dorn developed a significant fan following by the hiatus after the third season (the summer of 1990), so the producers at Paramount made an effort to increase his role in the subsequent seasons with more Klingon-based plotlines. Dorn found himself receiving a fair amount of fan mail. (However, as he bemoaned to Pat Sajak on a talk show appearance, "When I was on *CHiPs*, I got cards, letters, and pictures from women. Now, on *Star Trek*, I get mail from kids written in crayon, with misspelled words. . . . They write my name 'W-H-A-R-F.' ") How did Dorn explain this resurgent popularity? "[The fans] love that edge and the fact that they can depend on him to say what everybody wants to say."

The fourth season of *Star Trek: The Next Generation* opened, after the conclusion of the Borg cliff-hanger, with the episode "Family," in which Worf's foster parents visit the ship and reassure him regarding the recent dishonor of his family name. In an important episode for Worf, which aired the following month, his mate K'Ehleyr returns to the *Enterprise*. During the course of this one show, Worf meets the son he never knew he had; the woman he loves is killed; and he takes revenge by killing her murderer, Duras, who is also the source of his family's dishonor. Dorn played a wide range of emotions in this sweeping episode for his character. The concluding scene is touching and sober, when he sends his son Alexander (played by child actor Jon Steuer, but later reprised by Brian Bonsall in a recurring role) to be raised on earth by his foster parents.

The first part of the cliff-hanger "Redemption" concluded the fourth season of *The Next Generation*. Against a backdrop of restoring his family's honor, Worf resigns his Starfleet commission to fight alongside his brother in the Klingon civil war. As the program drew to a close, and fans worldwide were wondering whether Dorn as Worf was being written off the program, they were hit with another shocker: the appearance of a Romulan commander who resembled Denise Crosby's long-dead Tasha Yar. This episode, the last before the 1991 summer break, certainly gave fans a lot to ponder.

The summer between the fourth and fifth seasons was a busy one for Dorn away from *The Next Generation* cameras, but not entirely away from *Star Trek*. Director and screenwriter Nicholas Meyer, polishing the screenplay for *Star Trek VI: The Undiscovered Country*, was a big fan of Dorn's Worf. Meyer approached Dorn on *The Next Generation* set and explained that he had written a role in the film specifically for him. Dorn was pleased, flattered, and extremely excited about the chance to work with the original *Star Trek* cast. "I wish all my jobs had come this easy," he exclaimed. Dorn's small role as defense lawyer Colonel Worf, grandfather of his *Next Generation* character, was acknowledged by the film's publicist as a "convergence between the original and *Next Generation* by virtue of the fact that Michael is in the film."

Dorn stated simply, "It was wonderful to be working with the other cast. It was kind of a fantasy because who would have thought when I was watching the original show that I'd be working in the movie? Beyond that, it's like professionalism takes over and you just kind of do the best you can and not make yourself look bad."

This film, touted at the time as the last with the original cast, was considered to be a subtle bridge between the two series. No one could have known at the time that the captains of the two casts would meet less than three years later on the set of the seventh film in the franchise, *Star Trek: Generations*.

During the summer of 1991, Dorn also began voicing one of the characters on the popular comedy *Dinosaurs*. (Also, coincidentally, voicing a recurring character on the show was Suzie

Plakson, who portrayed Worf's mate on *The Next Generation*.) Nonetheless, as he never appeared in his human persona on that program either, he acknowledged the frustrations of being a Hollywood success but remaining virtually unrecognized in public for his efforts. "Here I am in a hit show and a hit movie and nobody knows who I am. . . . Oh well, I figure things happen for a reason, and these are just my humbling experience days." He also realized that most of Hollywood would be jealous of his status and success, and was not fearful of being typecast. "If what happened to the first cast is called being typecast, then I want to be typecast. Of course, they didn't get the jobs after *Trek*, but they are making their sixth movie. Name me someone else in television who has made six movies!"

Prior to the fifth season of *The Next Generation*, Dorn acknowledged the quandary in which the writing staff had put Worf. The violent conflict of the Klingon civil war had affected Worf in a profound way. "This goes back to the outline I created for him when I first got the job. I always saw him as walking a tightrope," Dorn explained before the premiere of the fifth season. "He has lived and worked with humans, while Klingons are very strong in terms of nationalism, one sided and narrow minded, thinking they're the best creatures in the world. There's a lot tugging at him."

The premiere of season five of *The Next Generation* featured the conclusion of the "Redemption" saga. Dorn's Worf again plays a vital role. It is he among the Klingons who initially suspects Romulan involvement in the civil conflict. Later in the episode, he is kidnapped and tortured. Finally, upon being rescued, Worf is forced to choose between his two cultures: the heritage he was born into, or his adopted home. Ultimately, he chooses his life aboard the *Enterprise*, but the decision is not a simple one.

Worf actually dies in surgery in the fifth season's "Ethics," but a part of the Klingon anatomy thought to be redundant conveniently begins functioning and restores him. However, lying dead on a table, although an important plot occurrence, is a relatively easy acting chore. For this reason, Dorn's photo-double, Al Foster, was actually the one lying on the table for much of the operation.

More significant for Dorn from an acting standpoint was the anguish Worf and his crewmates experienced when he asked Riker to assist him in performing ritual Klingon suicide. It is only because Worf ultimately does not have the heart to put his son, Alexander, through the ceremony that Worf does not follow through with the custom. Klingon fans also learned much about the anatomy of the warrior race in this episode: Worf is discovered to possess twenty-three ribs, two livers, an eight-chambered heart, and the backup synaptic system that revived him.

Later in the fifth season, the episode "Cost of Living" featured Counselor Troi not only dealing with her mother's impending marriage, but also helping Worf deal with his increasingly rebellious son. The conclusion of this episode, ending with the fierce Klingon relaxing in a holo–mud bath with his young son, led long-established *Trek* columnist Ian Spelling to ask, "Has Worf gone soft?"

Between the fifth and sixth seasons Dorn continued to carve out a niche for himself, that of voice-over acting and narration. He found himself quite in demand by studios looking for a "James Earl Jones type." In May 1992, Dorn narrated and hosted the film *Yanomani: Keepers of the Flame*. The film addressed what anthropologists consider the last remaining intact tribe of the Americas, the Yanomani of the Venezuelan rain forest, who call themselves the Children of the Blood Drops of the Moon. The film won best broadcast feature and best of festival at the U.S. Environmental Film Festival in 1992. In a more commercial vein, Dorn also hosted *The Future Is Now—The Sci-Fi Channel Preview*, the show that launched the new network; presented an award at the August 1992 Emmy Awards ceremony; and even judged the September 1992 Miss America Pageant.

Dorn's makeup evolved over the years, and application times got progressively shorter and shorter. When the show began, the makeup process could take three hours, but it was down to no more than an hour and a half by the end of the fifth season. One change Dorn had been lobbying for was a different hairstyle. "After five years of Donna Reed, it's time for a change!" His request was answered and the sixth season featured Worf sporting a ponytail. The season began with Worf being talked into an "Ancient West" holodeck program with Alexander in "A Fistful of Datas." The adventure almost results in deadly consequences until Worf saves both the day and his son.

In the two-part episode "Birthright," Worf learns of a Romulan prison camp that may hold his father, who was presumed killed in the Khitomer massacre. In the second half of the episode, Worf has fallen for the young, presumably Klingon Ba'el (Jennifer Gatti). The resulting plot crisis on screen when he learns she is actually half Romulan was almost as dramatic as what was going on off screen.

This episode featured the first broadcast Klingon kiss. Dorn recalled, "Jennifer and I analyzed it to death. How exactly would Klingons kiss? Would it be tentative? Awkward? Sweet? Sexy? After a week of that, we finally said, 'Hell, let's just film the thing and hope our false teeth don't hook together.'"

Later during the sixth season, Worf feels the ramifications of the events in the "Birthright" saga in the episode "Rightful Heir." Worf seeks spiritual enlightenment in the form of the mystical warrior Kahless, but later exposes him as a clone of the original. Fans are treated to Klingon rites, combat, and more scenes of the Homeworld. The story writer, James Brooks, when he pitched his premise, dubbed his story "Jurassic Worf."

Reflecting on the six years of the successful ensemble program, Dorn acknowledged that some of his castmates were unhappy with the paucity of individual character history that had been explored on screen. "I'm one of the lucky ones because my character has always been developed. Every year Worf just blossoms into something else. I've never had an issue with the writers." Marina Sirtis noted, "For an orphan, Worf has more relatives than everyone else put together on this show." Dorn also reflected that in light of recent episodes depicting Worf taking a mud bath and playing cowboy with his son, and, more significantly, aiding in the birth of Miles and Keiko O'Brien's baby, "He has mellowed quite a bit. He's still gruff, sarcastic, and surly. He's still a Klingon, but he has mellowed some, matured, and become a lot more responsible."

During the break before *The Next Generation*'s seventh and final season, Dorn guest starred as an ex–football player and coach on the situation comedy *Getting By*, opposite Telma Hopkins and Cindy Williams. "It's not Worf, that's the best part," Dorn commented. He read a story about aliens who show up for dinner on *Storytime*, a program and role similar to LeVar Burton's hosting duties on *Reading Rainbow*. "Anything that has to do with kids is for me," Dorn emphasized. "Children are our hope for the future and our country seems to neglect that." He also participated as one of the high-profile celebrities in the Great California Milk Drought, a promotional event sponsored by the California Milk Processor Board aimed at illustrating the importance of milk in everyday life (and, for his participation, gave up milk, one of his favorite beverages, for a week).

BRINGING THE EDGE BACK

"Every year I try to do something different with Worf," Dorn said at the opening of the final season. "This year I'm playing him out on the edge. He's almost more Klingonlike or Worflike than he was the first season. I'm playing him at that fine line between sanity and insanity. He's still wonderful to play, but he's become almost too mellow. I'm going to bring that edge back."

The final season of *Star Trek: The Next Generation* focused primarily on *Enterprise* officers who had yet to be as thoroughly fleshed out as Worf. Nonetheless, Worf was featured prominently in a couple of the season's most popular episodes. One of these, "Parallels," in which Worf is shunted between not-quite-parallel universes, gave the show's writing staff the opportunity to explore the possibility of a Worf/Troi relationship. In rehearsal, Dorn made the most of the kissing scene with Sirtis, insisting that they rehearse it over and over again until eventually Sirtis caught on to what he was up to. "Homeward," the episode in which Worf's foster brother, Nikolai (played by Paul Sorvino), is found to have violated the Prime Directive of the Federation, was significant for Dorn for reasons completely unrelated to the script. Worf, costumed as a human-looking Boraalan, has his head under a hood and only his face exposed. This was the only one of *The Next Generation*'s 176 episodes in which Dorn appeared sans Worf makeup. Finally, "Firstborn," the episode that featured an adult Alexander traveling back from the future to change his own fate and ultimately save his father, was one of Dorn's favorites. "In it I was able to do everything I ever wanted to as Worf. The episode has drama, danger, and sensitivity."

Dorn's feelings regarding the cancellation of *The Next Generation* after seven seasons were mixed. Although angry about the cancellation of the highly rated program in which he had found success, recognition, and many friends among his castmates, Dorn acknowledged that he was prepared to tackle new projects. "I reached the apex of Worf three years ago, and around that time, I— and Patrick [Stewart] too, I think—started counting down." He acknowledged that "it's time to get out there and do other things. . . . I got into the business and I love the business because of the challenges, not because I want it to be easy. You don't become an actor to have a steady job. I believe, to the last person, that we all are ready to go." He also revealed that the success of *The Next Generation* was really a tremendous surprise to the cast and crew. "The success was way beyond anything any of us imagined. The whole cast was realistic about work and stuff. We thought, great, this will go on for a year, make a little money, relax a bit, and that was it. We never dreamed that it would go seven years with conventions and all the hoopla—and a movie."

Dorn also felt that the final season's controversial Worf/Troi romance was his "crowning glory. It's not consummated in the series finale, but we do sort of put a button on the whole thing. We leave you knowing there's something there." Dorn was also realistic about the rewards a role on a successful series can reap, admitting that he "enjoyed the freedom that comes from not having to worry about every penny. But I've now developed such an aversion to material things—I mean, I actually own a pinball machine that I just want to unload. I want to get rid of the house and possessions and get a little apartment somewhere."

However, all was not rosy regarding the ending of the series. When Dorn tried speaking with producer Jeri Taylor about what he considered to be a frustrating lack of closure, "She was [more interested] in talking about going on to *Voyager*. She's on her way and I felt like an old shoe. It's sorta like [they're saying], 'Hey, we've got a new group showing up; it's been wonderful; see ya later, have a good finale.'" On *Larry King Live*, Dorn said, "At first I was really sort of trying to deny it, you know. Fine, seven years, let's get out of here. Let's go, I'm ready to leave. And then on the last day, I was a blithering idiot . . . crying like a baby in this Worf makeup."

Dorn was exhausted from the grueling *Star Trek* schedule. With the few days he had off between the filming of the program's finale, "All Good Things . . .," and the shooting of the big-screen *Star Trek: Generations*, Dorn planned to "go to Hawaii and get massaged within an inch of my life."

At the premiere of *Generations*, Dorn exclaimed, "It's overwhelming—the premiere was the first time I've ever felt like a big star." However, his role in the film was negligible, except for the opening scene, which did little for his character except give him a promotion and humiliate him (he was forced off a gangplank into the holodeck-ocean). "It wasn't what I'd call a *Next Generation* movie, because it didn't involve the crew as we'd come to know them. Worf has nothing to do, and the sequence where he gets promoted was a gag. It was really about Kirk and Picard meeting, and that was tough to accept. It's not secret it would have been nice if it had been more like a regular episode, where we're off saving the galaxy. I actually had more screen time in *Trek VI*, but *Generations* was still a wonderful experience. I'm glad they included me. I'm happy to have worked with my friends and I'm hopeful there'll be more to do next time."

Following *Generations*, Dorn found himself swamped with work opportunities. He voiced a character on the popular Disney animated program *Gargoyles*, alongside *Next Generation* costars Marina Sirtis and Jonathan Frakes, as well as with original series veteran Nichelle Nichols. He appeared in an episode of the television comedy *Parker Lewis Can't Lose*, in which he meets a kid who tries to sell him an "original" model of the *Enterprise*. Dorn challenges him, "But how do I know it has the *original* photon torpedoes?!" Dorn also cohosted *Masters of Illusion*, which revealed the secrets behind many of Hollywood's special effects.

In a potential career move that some might have called questionable had he accepted, Dorn was approached by both the Fox and CBS television networks as their first choice to star in a television movie. He was asked by both networks to portray O. J. Simpson in films about the criminal allegations surrounding the ex–football star. However, given the overwhelming television coverage the trial received, the two networks shelved their immediate plans for the film. Ironically, both networks' producers were actually banking on the fact that Dorn—while an accomplished, talented, and professional actor—was not terribly well recognized. They felt that if he were to be recognized at all, it might be from his role on *CHiPs*. (Then again, it is unclear how many of them were fans of *Star Trek*.)

In August 1994, following the filming of *Generations*, Dorn returned to the stage for the first time since leaving college two decades earlier, and for the first time as a professional. Dorn played the father of a 1957 disintegrating black family in Rodney Nugent's *The Letter* at the Hudson Theatre in Los Angeles. Dorn felt refreshed by the challenges of the stage. He did not share a complaint common among established television actors who then appear on the stage: the constant repetition live theater performances entail. "The best part is that you don't have to do it the same way every time. I love to live in the moment. It is not about ad-libbing. It is about, 'What do you feel?' and going for it—not being afraid to take that risk. The woman who plays my wife and I were rehearsing one day and I did something and she said, 'Boy, I wanted to slap you.' I said, 'You should have.' That's what it's all about."

THE BIGGEST RUSH YOU CAN IMAGINE

The year 1995 was busy for Michael Dorn. He starred in an episode of Showtime's *The Outer Limits* with Matt Craven and Jay O. Sanders. "It's called, of all things, 'The Voyage Home . . . [We] play astronauts who land on Mars and, on our last day, we encounter an alien. The alien takes over our bodies one by one and tries to reach the earth because it can proliferate there. We've got to stop it somehow."

Costarring in the feature film *Timemaster*, alongside Joanna Pacula, Duncan Regehr, and Pat Morita, Dorn played the enigmatic Chairman. The Chairman was the creator of a powerful cosmic virtual-reality game that has determined all human conflict, from the dawn of history to the future. "The characters you control are actually real people. If your person dies, your person really dies and you do too. . . . It's like a futuristic Vegas, and because I'm the house, I never lose."

He also appeared in Showtime's *Amanda and the Alien*, which starred Nicole Eggert. Dorn's character is a detective who "has watched *Pulp Fiction* way too often." The show scored well with critics, but Dorn acknowledged, "Well, *I* won't be in the sequel." (The detective died.) Dorn lent his voice to *Tales of the Serengeti*, shown on PBS stations nationwide, and also appeared in and lent his voice to a number of CD-ROM games, including "Star Trek: A Final Unity" and "Vikings: The Strategy of Ultimate Conquest."

Throughout *The Next Generation*'s run, and through this post–*Star Trek* period, Dorn continued to avidly pursue his aviation hobby. Naturally, the financial rewards from appearing for seven years on a tremendously successful drama contributed to his ability to fulfill his lust for flight. "It is a meditation for me. You are up there just thinking about one thing, keeping it in the air. When you land and go home, you are really tired; you are spent, sweated. But you are really at peace. Really relaxed. The people I meet in the business are wonderful people." However, Dorn admitted, "The money [from *Star Trek*] is great and it is freedom and fun and all that. But the funny thing about the money is that you kind of become a slave to it. Become a slave to the things you have. I love my airplane. But then it's, 'Oh, God, I have to take this job because I have to keep up this airplane.' It can become a vicious circle. But that is minuscule compared to the joy."

During seven years of flying, Dorn had bought and sold five different planes, including a vintage Lockheed T-33 from the 1950s—one of the first used for training jet pilots—which he eventually plans to sell in order to purchase a North American F-86 Sabrejet or a Turbine Commander, a twin-engine turbo prop airplane. "My dream is at some point to have a nice beautiful hangar with two airplanes in it: the F-86 and a transportation airplane, the fun one and the work one—but it will take a lot of work and I'll have to land quite a few parts before that can happen."

Dorn's flying experience has put him in the cockpit of both an F-18 Hornet with the Blue Angels (the navy's precision flying team) and an F-16 Falcon with the air force's exacting flight demonstration team, the Thunderbirds. He copiloted a B-17 on a flight from Pomona to San Jose, and is hoping for an opportunity to fly in a navy F-4 Phantom. Though he continues to smart from lack of public recognition when out of makeup and Starfleet uniform, he is recognized by all of the flight controllers once they hear his distinctive voice requesting clearance to land. "Oh, it's you. Please, land first," is the common refrain, according to Dorn.

Michael Dorn's perfect dream weekend is "a flight from California to Hawaii in a two-seat F-15 fighter jet with a young Sophia Loren in the backseat. That would be great." For those wondering about his obsession with this expensive and uncommon hobby, Dorn explains, "This kind of flying is pure excitement. It is the biggest rush you can imagine. You have to be good at it, which gives a sense of accomplishment. But ultimately, for me, flying is all about freedom."

HE'S BACK

"Way of the Warrior" premiered the week of October 2, 1995, the fourth-season premiere of the third series in the *Star Trek* pantheon, *Deep Space Nine*. "In an exciting, unparalleled step, Captain Sisko and Lieutenant Commander Worf will join forces to face the growing threat from the Klingons," exclaimed executive producer Rick Berman. Yet Dorn's appearance as Worf was neither an attention-getting cameo nor a guest-starring role. Dorn signed a three-year contract to appear on *Star Trek: Deep Space Nine*, again donning the makeup, again assuming the role that won him his first true stardom. "We needed to get viewers to resample the show, and we thought having the Klingons back would do the trick," Berman commented.

Dorn's acceptance of this role solidifies one solid fact. Someday, the trivia question will be posed: "Who has appeared in the greatest number of *Star Trek* episodes and movies?" The answer: Michael Dorn, who was originally appended to the cast of *Next Generation* as an afterthought, appeared in 176 episodes of *The Next Generation*, potentially 78 (or more) episodes of *Deep Space Nine*, and three movies thus far, with more certain to come. (The only other person to come even close is *Deep Space Nine* regular Colm Meaney, though he appeared on less than one-third of *The Next Generation*'s episodes and has not yet been asked to appear in a *Star Trek* feature.)

The move back to the daily grind of a *Star Trek* series after seven years might seem a surefire way to be forever typecast, but Dorn insists it was a necessary career move. He felt it was important to continue working at the same intensity level that *The Next Generation* posed, for that was the only avenue by which his career would continue to propel forward. "When you're on a series for a lot of years and you get off, it's time to work right away. Because you have a tendency to be forgotten [by casting agents] when you're on a series, and when the series is over it's like outta sight, outta mind. It's very important that you start working right away."

Dorn came to salary terms with the producers of *Deep Space Nine* with minimal hassle, and was assured regarding the size of his role. But there was one area in which he was very insistent. "I leave writing and producing and directing and everything like that to the professionals. But the makeup is the one thing that I'm being a real terror about. I told them [the producers] that we had to keep it to no more than an hour." And in fact, in a later interview, Dorn admitted that the process had "evolved from really being a pain to being actually tolerable." It is now down to merely fifty minutes.

The other cast members of *Deep Space Nine* embraced Dorn, but were naturally wary of the role he would play. Armin "Quark" Shimerman said, "We knew him from across the hall for two years. Now, he's part of the ensemble. He'll get his episodes like everyone else." Alexander "Dr. Bashir" Siddig was only fearful that *Deep Space Nine* would lose its distinctive edge. "My suspicion is that Michael is being brought aboard in hopes that he will bring a certain amount of those viewers with him. But I would hope that, as the middle child, we suddenly don't start dressing like the older child to become acceptable."

Dorn himself acknowledged the significant differences between the crew of the *Enterprise-D* and the crew of the *Deep Space Nine* station. He told *TV Guide* in October 1995, "I've just come from Beverly Hills, basically, the best ship in the galaxy. The difference is, there's something in each *[Deep Space Nine]* character, some kind of flaw. It's not about being grouchy. They each do something that strikes my character as odd. He's used to officers feeling for each other. These people are out for themselves in some way. Worf isn't that way. He's gruff and surly because that's who he is, and that's okay. It's not because he has something to prove.

"I do miss the bridge [of the *Enterprise*]. In almost every *TNG* episode, we'd all get together and hang out with our captain, which, for both the actors and the fans, was very interesting psychologically. The bridge was comfortable; it had nice pleasant tones; it was the [emotional] equivalent of the living room in the classic family sitcoms. *DS9* has nothing like that—well, maybe the control room, but nothing really happens there. You can go weeks without interacting with the other characters."

Dorn's first season on *Deep Space Nine* featured Worf in the episodes "The Sword of Kahless," "Sons of Mogh," and "Rules of Engagement," as well as Parts I and II of "Way of the Warrior." Worf's ties to the Klingon Empire were severed in "Sons of Mogh," and he was hit with a court-martial in "Rules of Engagement." However, as for the season as a whole, Dorn was less than satisfied with the extent of his role aboard the station. "I was under the impression that Worf was going to have a lot of stories. That's one of the reasons they brought me back. When that didn't come to fruition, I had discussions with the staff. I understand things don't always turn out like you want them to. I don't have any bad feelings about it. It was basically a good year for the show, but I don't think it really was a good year for Worf."

During the hiatus between seasons in the summer of 1996, Dorn kept working. He starred with Corbin Bernsen in *Menno's Mind*, a science fiction film for Showtime that also featured a cameo by *Star Trek: Voyager's* Robert Picardo. He also hosted *Where Are All the UFO's?*, a serious documentary for the Arts & Entertainment Network.

The fifth season of *Deep Space Nine*, Dorn's second, promised more for him to do. Before the season began, he stated, "They told me they'd open him up as a character. However, they just haven't had the opportunity to do that yet because of the ongoing stories that had to be addressed first. What I'm hoping is that we'll open Worf up more during this season and discover new things about him."

With opportunities early in the season that included tutoring the Ferengi Quark in Klingon mating rituals, and romancing the Trill Dax (which landed them both in the infirmary), Worf was integrated into the season's plot lines. Furthermore, Dorn received the opportunity to direct episodes at the conclusion of this season. After attending the Paramount directing "school"—a path of study that Jonathan Frakes had trailblazed seven years earlier, and that had seen over ten *Star Trek* actors on the three different series successfully complete—Dorn took his turn behind the camera.

It was during Dorn's second season on *Deep Space Nine*, in November 1996, that the feature film *Star Trek: First Contact* was released. "It's an action film. We're in trouble and we're going to lose. But this is what I like. I always thought from the moment the thing started that it should be action. You know, 'Hi, this is *Star Trek* the next movie,' then boom, let's go. I'm glad it turned out that way. Worf's parts are very integral to the scene. There [is] very good solid stuff. I'm very excited. I loved it." The reviewers loved it too, one calling Dorn's scene on the deflector dish "Schwarzeneggerish," when he growls, "Assimilate this!"

The fun was evident, too, as the crew of *The Next Generation* gathered once again on the set of *First Contact*. "If you were any other man," Dorn as Worf growled during one take of a now-famous scene, "I would *kiss* you where you stand." Discussing the bridge of the new *Enterprise*, Dorn told a television reviewer, "We left, and when we returned, Gates [McFadden] had the bridge redecorated. We walked in and she had curtains up and a champagne bucket by the captain's chair."

When he is not toiling under the massive Klingon forehead, flying a jet, or playing or writing music, you can often find Dorn relaxing, albeit with some heavy reading. "I read all the documentaries [sic] and books I can get my hands on about war and about different military things. I'm reading a book right now about the rise and fall of civilization and how it relates to all the wars that have been going on over all the centuries. What I find more interesting than anything else is not in the battles; war is hell and there's nothing pleasant about war and there's nothing that should be glorified. It's a brutal, nonsensical way to settle anything. But what's interesting is how little things make, can turn, the tides of battle, and little circumstances can change the fate of whole countries."

Michael Dorn remains unique among *The Next Generation* cast in that he can still walk down the street virtually unrecognized. Does he lust for the traditional, major stardom that his *Star Trek* cohorts have learned to live with? "If I could take the heart of the stardom. To be perfectly honest, it doesn't have a real lure for me. What I want to be is a working actor. I would love to be where people send me scripts and they say, 'Would you do this?' Then you have a number of projects to choose from. It doesn't have to be the biggest-budgeted movie. It doesn't have to be your name splashed across the marquee. I love getting a script and saying, 'Boy, I would love to do this character.' And if it is successful, then cool!"

Having recently settled down with Stephanie Romanov (of *Models, Inc.*), Dorn's immediate future is comfortable both personally and professionally. He considers mankind's future, and ponders whether we have any chance of achieving the kind of world portrayed on *Star Trek*—whether humans will ever cross the boundaries of space and overcome the apparently insurmountable problems now plaguing earth. "I think there's going to have to be a cataclysmic *something*. A lot of people are trying to do better, but basically something needs to happen, like Martians or God coming down and saying, 'You guys have been f***ing up.' But I think we have to get this chance to see if we're going to make it or not. That's what's going to determine whether we'll go on to the future and go out to the stars."

M I C H A E L   D O R N

Lieutenant Commander Worf
Also appeared on and directed Star Trek: Deep Space Nine

STAGE:
The Letter ('94)

TELEVISION:
The Mary Tyler Moore Show
  ('76–'79)
W.E.B. ('78)
CHiPs ('80–'82)
Knot's Landing ('83)
Webster ('84)
Capital ('85)
Charles in Charge ('85)
Falcon Crest ('85)
Hunter ('85)
227 ('86)
Days of Our Lives ('86)
Hotel ('86)
Star Trek: The Next Generation
  ('87–'94)
Reading Rainbow ('88)
Dinosaurs ('91)
The Future Is Now: The Sci-Fi
  Channel Preview ('92)
Getting By ('93)
Storytime ('93)
Gargoyles ('94)
Masters of Illusion ('94)
Parker Lewis Can't Lose ('94)

Science Fiction: A Journey into
  the Unknown ('94)
Amanda and the Alien ('95)
The Parent 'Hood ('95)
Star Trek: Deep Space Nine
  ('95–present)
Tales of the Serengeti ('95)
The Outer Limits ('95)
Captain Simian and the Space
  Monkeys ('96)
Communication: The Human
  Imperative ('96)
I Am Weasel ('96)
Menno's Mind ('96)
Where Are All the UFO's? ('96)
World of Wonder ('96)

FILM:
Rocky ('76)
Demon Seed ('77)
The Jagged Edge ('85)
Star Trek VI: The Undiscovered
  Country ('91)
Yanomani: Keepers of the Flame
  ('92)
Star Trek: Generations ('94)
Timemaster ('95)
Star Trek: First Contact ('96)

CHAPTER 5

GATES MCFADDEN

The Dancing Doctor

*"I live somewhere in arts-and-crafts land. I wish they had Beverly in charge
of arts and crafts on the ship."*
—GATES MCFADDEN, QUOTED IN THE *ENTERTAINMENT WEEKLY SPECIAL
STAR TREK ISSUE,* JANUARY 1995

A s Dr. Beverly Crusher, she is the caretaker of the crew—an
attractive, brilliant, widowed single mother, who is responsible
for the lives placed in her hands every day. Behind Dr. Crusher's
blue eyes and mane of red hair lies a dancer, a romantic, a theatrical director, and a comedian. These are talents that Dr. Crusher
possesses in addition to her medical knowledge. Gates McFadden,
Crusher's real-life alter ego, has cultivated these same talents since
the earliest days of her childhood in tiny Cuyahoga Falls, Ohio.

As the voice of compassion on the *Enterprise,* Crusher's
sense of justice is often at odds with the other officers in the command structure. Once you understand the character and the person, you realize that Crusher the doctor is often difficult to
distinguish from McFadden the actress. Crusher has the captain's
ear and, perhaps, his heart, and she has the power to relieve him of
duty. McFadden has been called the "earth-mother of the crew,"
holding a unique position among the cast as confidante, friend, and
colleague.

GROWING UP ACTING AND DANCING

"Last night I danced in a bar and I won five bucks!"
McFadden announced to her second-grade classmates during show-
and-tell. Winning this dance contest at the Cuyahoga Falls
American Legion hall at the age of seven remains the defining
moment that launched her show-biz career. Three years later, a
touring Shakespeare company visited her hometown. "When I was

ten, my brother and I attended back-to-back Shakespeare in a musty, nearly empty theater. There were twelve actors who played all the parts. I couldn't get over it—the same people in costumes every day, but playing new characters. It was like visiting somewhere and never wanting to leave."

When she was eight years old, McFadden started taking acting lessons at the local Coachhouse Theater. Although she was slightly disappointed that she was not often cast in the "lead gal roles," she usually landed the supporting comic roles, which sustained her love for the stage. In an interview with Joan Rivers, she explained the possible reason for her failure to land the starring roles. "I was the ugly duckling in school. Huge hands, huge feet—which I still have, but I guess I grew into them."

As a child, McFadden's love of acting was perhaps rivaled by her love of dance. McFadden's earliest dance teachers were not traditional. One had been a ballerina and the other, LaDonna, had spent her life with the circus. "I grew up thinking most ballerinas knew how to ride the unicycle, tap dance, and do handsprings. Consequently, I was a bit of an oddball to other dancers." During her early teens, while her friends were out dating, McFadden spent her time practicing unicycle riding and kick-line dancing. She lied about her age, donned sequined outfits, stuffed her brassiere, and spent evenings playing the Elks and Moose Clubs, and appearing on local television programs in Oil City and Erie City, Pennsylvania. While some of her cohorts from these early days went off to become Rockettes, McFadden's parents enrolled her in prep school, enabling her to pursue academic interests while continuing to study acting and choreography.

(It should be noted here that Gates McFadden's actual age is something of a controversy. During her appearance at a *Star Trek* convention in Sydney, Australia, in March 1995, McFadden confirmed March 2, 1953, as her actual birthday. Paramount "officially" records her birthday as August 26, 1953, a date McFadden simply made up because she was uncomfortable divulging her true birthday. In 1992, the British *Star Trek—The Next Generation Official Poster Magazine* published her birthday as August 28, 1949. At a *Star Trek* convention in the United Kingdom in 1994, a brave fan asked about her exact age, referring to a recent magazine article stating that she was in her late thirties. He was offered the response, "The late thirties follows the late twenties." She would comment no further. It seems most reasonable to accept the March 2, 1953, date as correct, as McFadden admitted to the earlier deceptions when disclosing this date.)

Returning home from acting and dance classes, there was only time for homework, dinner, and bed. What little television she watched "would be old movies, the ones with Fred Astaire and Ginger Rogers that I sneaked down to watch after everyone else went to bed."

McFadden has fond memories of her childhood. She returns to Cuyahoga Falls frequently, refusing to let her fame affect her ties to and her love of her hometown. The mayor presented her with the key to Cuyahoga Falls during her stint on *Star Trek: The Next Generation*; and although her parents come first, it has been said that the things she next most looks forward to upon returning home is Swenson's ice cream and Stoddard's frozen custard.

Reflecting on her childhood, she realizes that the world has changed considerably. "Even the physical layout of [my hometown] is different. Shopping malls have changed a lot of this country. Everything's so generic. You can buy Disney stuff all over the country instead of having to go to a place where it's indigenous. It was a really big deal when I came back [from France]. People in my hometown didn't know what a croissant was. You just didn't hear about them. But now as people have traveled more, the world has become smaller that way. I don't know, it's good and it's bad. There's a loss, in that you can get everything everywhere, but I suppose there's a good side to that too."

Considering the changes recent generations have endured, McFadden continued her sober line of thought. "It's very hard. Life is so fast these days, and we're exposed to so much information. Television makes us a witness to such misery. Also you're a witness if you're driving in certain areas, walking in certain areas. It can be next door, wherever. I think it's hard to actually take action. It's much easier to talk about it. And I have done a lot of talking about it and not much action, so I feel remiss in that. My responsibilities to my job and to my family take just about all of the time available."

Gates McFadden earned her BA *cum laude* in theater arts from Brandeis University in Waltham, Massachusetts. While at Brandeis, McFadden studied with the legendary acting teacher Charles Werner Moore—who, coincidentally, also had as a star pupil Rene Auberjonois (Odo of *Star Trek: Deep Space Nine*) when Moore taught at Carnegie-Mellon University a few years earlier.

During her four years at academically challenging Brandeis, McFadden developed not only her acting talents, but also a love of writing and history. These led her to consider pursuing alternative, scholarly careers. "If I couldn't be an actress, I wanted to be an archaeologist. I've always been fascinated with history. I studied it in school and joined the History Book Club when I graduated. The Civil War, Greek and Roman history, German history, et cetera. I also love to read about historical events. I love dirigibles, the big ocean liners, the story of the *Titanic*, and so on."

On her love of writing, McFadden commented, "I wish I could write more for myself. I wish I could find the time to do that. I just feel it's a wonderful way to clarify my thoughts. I'd love to write for the theater. Writing is something I clearly gravitate toward. You know, theater ties into so many things. Theater ties into history, and architecture into writing." In 1990, only a couple of years after making this statement, McFadden had her first play, *Bottleneck at the Bar*, produced. So that it would stand on its own merits and not be linked to the fame she had achieved on *Star Trek*, McFadden wrote the play under a pseudonym, Jesse Stuart Gates.

Just before graduating from Brandeis, McFadden was introduced to Jacques LeCoq, a meeting that would change her life. "I attended his first workshop in the United States. His theatrical vision and the breadth of its scope were astonishing." She left for France to study at LeCoq's Ecole Mime et Theatre, and while there, also became interested in architecture after taking LeCoq's course on the subject.

Primarily she studied acting. "We worked constantly in juxtapositions. One explored immobility to better understand movement. One explored silence in order to better understand sound and language. It was theatrical research involving many mediums." Speaking to an Australian journalist about this experience, McFadden stated, "Just learning to think in another language allows you to see your own culture in a better viewpoint. The whole experience of going away, not having much money, having to make my way in this new world that was so beautiful and had so much history was quite profound. Any time you spend time in another culture, it's not just a matter of visiting the museums [or] taking a quick week's vacation or something. I mean, that can be wonderful too, but to actually communicate, spend the time and all of that, that can be quite wonderful." In her official Paramount biography, McFadden comments, "It was both terrifying and freeing. Suddenly I was taking more risks in my acting."

France had a profound impact on McFadden's life. She says that her experience there "taught her about an artist's responsibility to herself." However, the world has changed, and McFadden has grown and changed with it. Her views have matured and now reflect the confusion and uncertainty we all face in growing older and in considering the issues of the day. "When I was young, it was very exciting to think that we could change the world if we all collaborated, but I think it's not just an artist's responsibility, as I think we all have responsibilities to different things, whatever we choose in our lives. I feel responsible to my family and also to many other things and people in my life. And then how much responsibility do I have for people in Yugoslavia, and people like that? You start to think, how much do I want to do as an individual? How are you going to live your life? I don't have a short philosophical answer. I just know that this thought informs the way I live my life. I don't know exactly how, but it's something that I consider often. What is my responsibility as a citizen, as an actress, as a mother, and on and on? I will say for one that I don't do nearly as much as I could."

Returning from her studies abroad, McFadden based herself in New York and was cast in a variety of stage, film, mime, dance, and improvisation roles before being cast as chief medical officer aboard the *Enterprise-D*. Her acting credits prior to *Star Trek: The Next Generation* included lead roles in the New York productions *To Gillian on Her 37th Birthday*, *How to Say Goodbye*, and *Cloud Nine*. She also appeared in the popular film *The Muppets Take Manhattan*, in which she played opposite Kermit the Frog. McFadden also had roles in the television series *Another World* and *The Edge of Night*. Her experience in *The Muppets Take Man-*

hattan led to a continuing professional relationship with the Jim Henson studios, and she served as director of choreography and puppet movement for the Henson film *Labyrinth*.

In 1981, McFadden choreographed a production of Shake-speare's *A Midsummer Night's Dream*, which *The New York Times* referred to as "cleverly choreographed." In 1983, *The New York Times* said that McFadden portrayed Gillian (in *To Gillian . . .*) "with enchanting intelligence . . . she's as alive for us as she is for the widower whose mind she relentlessly haunts." As Gillian, the deceased title character, McFadden played opposite a sixteen-year-old Sarah Jessica Parker, who played Gillian's (McFadden's) daughter. *The Christian Science Monitor* reviewed McFadden's difficult performance as Gillian's ghost, writing "Miss McFadden handles the trickiness with a common-sensical blend of the ethereal and the pragmatic." In 1986, McFadden was called both "responsive" and "especially attentive" in a *New York Times* review, in this case for her portrayal of Casey Staiger in *How to Say Goodbye*.

In addition to theater roles, McFadden was cast in one regular role in a television series before *Star Trek: The Next Generation*. However, her character of Darcy Stafford in the 1986 CBS flop *The Wizard*, starring David Rappaport, was replaced with Fran Ryan after the pilot episode. This move, *The Washington Post* commented, "is nice for McFadden, bad for the show." As *Star Trek: The Next Generation* fans know, this was not the last time McFadden was to be replaced in a television series.

McFadden was also cast in 1987 in the feature film *Big*, opposite Robert De Niro. However, De Niro was replaced with Tom Hanks, and any chance she may have had to keep the role was lost when she broke her leg skiing.

Throughout the 1980s, McFadden also served on the faculty of the theater departments at her alma mater, Brandeis, as well as at the New York University Graduate School and the University of Pittsburgh. She specialized in improvisation, commedia dell'arte, clown, and movement. Finally, she had to face the choice between continuing to teach and acting full time. Although she chose acting, she desires to return to teaching someday.

It should be noted that until this point in her career, McFadden used the name Cheryl McFadden. *Star Trek: The Next*

Generation was the first job in which she used her middle name, Gates, as her first name. However, even in some early press releases and articles about the formation of the new *Star Trek* cast, she is still referred to as Cheryl.

The role of Dr. Beverly Crusher on *Star Trek: The Next Generation* was not one that McFadden sought. She was committed to appearing with Linda Hunt in *The Matchmaker* for $400 a week, at the La Jolla Playhouse in Southern California, a job she was very excited about doing. In Los Angeles for a completely different audition, she had a few hours to kill before a flight back to the East Coast. Her agent suggested that she try out for the show—for any of the women's roles. As McFadden only had time to read for one, she read for the role of Dr. Crusher. "I didn't have an understanding of the show," she told Joan Rivers. "It wasn't like 'Oh my God, they're doing another *Star Trek!*'"

McFadden initially turned down the role of Dr. Crusher. She was unwilling to give up *The Matchmaker*, and "at that time, television wasn't in my life. I was teaching and I was performing and directing. Theater was my first love, and I had no time." However, unlike the case of many of her *Enterprise* shipmates, Paramount and the *Star Trek* producers pursued her. They felt that they had found the perfect doctor, and when it came time to shoot the pilot, they returned to her. "What I finally decided was that this wasn't a role that would further my acting career, but that it would allow me to have a baby and bring my baby to work, because I would have a steady income and a steady place to go."

However, the filming of *Star Trek: The Next Generation's* pilot episode, "Encounter at Farpoint," still conflicted with McFadden's performances in La Jolla. Now committed to both projects, the morning after opening night in La Jolla, she was driven over one hundred traffic-snarled miles to the Paramount studios in Hollywood. She shot her first *Star Trek* scenes, and then hopped on a small plane and was flown back to La Jolla to perform that evening.

Given McFadden's limited screen experience yet extensive stage work, she was taken to analyzing her props, her lines, and her motivations a bit differently from her fellow cast members. She has admitted that the toughest thing to get comfortable with in shooting a weekly, hour-long drama was the lack of rehearsal time. The first scene she shot in sickbay, she wondered aloud about the lack of files, pens, and telephones. She was informed by propmaster Alan Sims, "Paper's obsolete. It's in the computer. Everything's in the computer." McFadden was especially intrigued by her medical kit, which in a former life was a Lego box, and its contents.

"I did love the hypospray. It was my idea to do it in the neck because it's the last place I'd want a shot. I wanted to show how much we'd progressed." Her fascination with the medical props led McFadden to insist upon understanding how the tricorder, hypospray, atomic analyzers, and laser surgery equipment operated. Although this desire was seemingly impractical, the producers, cast, and crew learned to respect this unique quality in McFadden. Because of her insistence on using the medical instruments with some semblance of logic and understanding, they dubbed her "The Props Queen." Early in the show's run, McFadden stated, "So far my wardrobe consists of a jumpsuit and a jacket. I seem to be one of the few people in the twenty-fourth century who uses pockets."

However, finding more to do than just administering hyposprays was a point of contention for McFadden throughout most of *Star Trek: The Next Generation*'s run. "I told them that if Beverly Crusher really was the equivalent of the Surgeon General of the galaxy, let's give her that respect. I felt that with species carrying new diseases, there was so much more room for excitement and that the *Enterprise* presented a real research environment."

In 1988, during *The Next Generation*'s first season, McFadden reflected, pragmatically, on her sudden fame after many successful years performing on stage. "It's been quite wonderful, this first year, having just one thing to focus my energies on." Reflecting on all that she was not doing (for instance, teaching and acting on the stage) she relayed, "There are always prices to pay for anything in life, and it becomes a question of whether you want to pay that price or not. You adapt, and you find ways of evaluating what's most important to you."

Basically pleased with the way *The Next Generation* was progressing, there were some concerns: "There are still instances where women have all of the emotional parts, and I would prefer to see us a little more involved in the decision making."

Finally, she reflected on her newfound legion of fans, most of whom sent nice, respectful, genuine fan letters—although some inevitably saw her as a commodity. "Some [letters read] 'I want twelve pictures signed' with no mention of 'thanks for your work.'" Some fans—both teens and even some young doctors—considered Dr. Crusher a role model. One doctor considered Crusher so inspirational, "She wanted my picture in the office." However, McFadden also receives letters from convicts, many of whom have a special request: "Please send me a picture, but not the one of you in your uniform—do you have any 8 × 10s of you in your panties?"

Star Trek: The Next Generation's first season featured few opportunities for McFadden to shine. During that season, a running joke on the set was that Dr. Crusher lost more patients than she saved. "Is Beverly on the ship because she's sleeping with the captain?" McFadden inquired. "The reason there are no medical diplomas on the wall is because she didn't really get them!" Often, when a first-season guest star wound up in sickbay, one of the regular cast members would break up the set by confiding to the guest star, "Listen, sorry you're being treated by Bev—you might not make it!"

Fans loved Dr. Crusher in part because she could get away with challenging Picard's orders. In "Symbiosis," she found herself at odds with both Picard and with Starfleet's Prime Directive when it was uncovered that the inhabitants of Brekka were keeping their neighbors, the Ornarans, unknowingly addicted and dependent on the potent narcotic felicium. Dr. Crusher devised a non-narcotic alternative that would serve to end the situation, but the Prime Directive dictated that she not offer it. In this scenario, perhaps standard *Star Trek* fare for many fans, the line separating actress Gates McFadden and Dr. Beverly Crusher was very fuzzy. McFadden comments on that episode, "That is always the dilemma, noninvolvement versus involvement. We live with that today in Bosnia and Rwanda. But my first duty in the show was to end suffering; my second duty was to the Prime Directive."

Among McFadden's other first-season highlights—and lowlights: the episode "The Big Goodbye," in which she, along with Patrick Stewart and Brent Spiner, was able to display her comedic talents; "The Arsenal of Freedom," in which she and Stewart endured flea-infested sand in Paramount's cave set; and "Skin of Evil," which marked the death of Denise Crosby's Natasha Yar, whom Dr. Crusher failed to save.

However, the most significant event of Gates McFadden's first season on *Star Trek: The Next Generation* was one that happened off screen and away from the cameras and the sets: she got fired.

AN UNEXPECTED AND UNWANTED HIATUS

"There were those who believed at the end of the first season that they didn't like the way the character was developing, vis-à-vis Gates' performance, and managed to convince Mr. Roddenberry of that," executive producer Rick Berman recounted. He added, "I was not a fan of that decision." Patrick Stewart was puzzled by the move, even opposed to it, but was unwilling to propagate dissension. "Gates was offered up somewhat sacrificially, to protect the rest of the show," Stewart commented. Although he liked McFadden's replacement, Diana Muldaur, who was created in the image of crusty Dr. Bones McCoy, Stewart was very glad when the actress returned.

The truths behind McFadden's leave—and subsequent return a season later—are unclear. Paramount officially announced that she had left "to pursue other career options," although McFadden has claimed that the news was a surprise to her. "I got a call from my agent saying that they had decided to go in another direction with the character. And that was literally all I heard."

Another explanation arises from an April/May 1994 story published in *Star Trek: The Official Fan Club* magazine. The story claims that McFadden attempted to renegotiate her contract at the end of *The Next Generation*'s first season. Although this may be a reasonable ploy for an actor on a hit series, Paramount refused to meet her demands, and removed her from the program. The article also claims that when McFadden returned to *Star Trek*, it was at a lower salary than the rest of her costars.

Nonetheless, McFadden was gracious in returning. Surprised to be asked back for the third season, she proclaimed, "I certainly missed working with my fellow cast members!" Fans know that the explanation given for her character's absence was that she was off heading up Starfleet Medical for the year, and McFadden was comfortable that the scriptwriters "are not making too much of a fuss in the story line about my reappearance on board the

Enterprise. I think the decision has been made to just make it seem very normal that I'm coming back."

Some avid fans of *The Next Generation*, and particularly of Gates McFadden, have pointed to the enormous letter-writing campaign as instrumental in reuniting Dr. Crusher with the crew of the *Enterprise*. It is claimed that the flood of letters sent to Paramount protesting McFadden's removal was surpassed only by the 1968 campaign that prolonged the run of Kirk's and Spock's *Enterprise* for a third season.

However, the impact of the fan letters was never acknowledged in the announcement of McFadden's return. "Diana Muldaur is a marvelous actress and it's obvious I think so because I've used her many times," Gene Roddenberry exclaimed. "It's all just chemistry. Beverly had that little something. . . . Somehow the way the captain bounces off her works well. It works with Muldaur, too, but it just seems to work a little more with Crusher. . . . It was always our intention to leave the door open for her to return to the show."

McFadden, however, openly acknowledges the "huge fan support—the hundreds of lovely letters" that clearly had an impact in her being asked back for the third season. During *The Next Generation's* first season, McFadden refused to attend any of the popular *Star Trek* conventions held around the country, noting, "I just thought it was going to be a lot of strange people." However, the flood of mail on her behalf changed McFadden's tune. "The fans wrote such amazing amounts of mail to the studio. . . . It was instrumental in having them ask me back. They suddenly realized that my character was really popular. Since that time, I have felt that maybe I shouldn't be so afraid of going to these conventions. I don't like people to know all about the ins and outs of my private life. But, as I started to do it, I realized that nobody demanded that I share anything I didn't feel like sharing. I used to be a snob about it. But everybody's got their thing. Some people go to rock concerts. Some people do this."

During her hiatus from *Star Trek*, McFadden kept very busy, appearing in *The Hunt for Red October* as Jack Ryan's (Alec Baldwin's) wife, a role that primarily wound up on the cutting room floor, especially, according to McFadden, quite a few hot "kissing scenes." She also had a significant role in *Taking Care of Business*,

Patrick Stewart as Oberon in The Royal Shakespeare Company's 1977 stage production of *A Midsummer Night's Dream.*

Stewart *(left)* played the thug in *Hennessey,* his first feature film. It starred Rod Steiger (1977).

Stewart as the drunken butler Stephano in RSC's 1970 production of
The Tempest. In the right background is Oscar-winner Ben Kingsley.

Stewart in the RSC's 1970
staging of *The Two Gentleman
of Verona.* At the insistence of
his son, he later adopted Crab,
his black Labrador co-star.

In the 1995 feature film *Jeffrey*, Patrick Stewart played a flamboyant gay interior decorator—a role he hoped would "dynamite the Picard image."

Stewart received his Hollywood Walk-of-Fame "star" on December 16, 1996.

Majel Barrett Roddenberry
and Patrick Stewart at
Marina Sirtis' wedding.

Jonathan Frakes *(middle row right)* and the cast of the prime-time soap *Bare Essence* (1983).
He met his wife-to-be, Genie Francis *(front row center)*, on the set.

Frakes as Stanley Hazard in *North and South*, pictured with Mary Crosby, aunt of future *Next Generation* co-star Denise Crosby.

Outside of Mann's Chinese Theatre in November of 1996, Genie Francis and Frakes await the premiere of the box office hit—and his feature film directorial debut—*Star Trek: First Contact*.

The young LeVar Burto
received an Emmy
nomination for his role
as Kunte Kinte in the
highly acclaimed mini-
series *Roots* (1977).

Burton portrayed a deaf-mute accused of murder in the title role of the 1979
television movie *Dummy*.

Burton and his wife,
Stephanie Cozart Burton,
at the September 1996
Roots reunion.

Michael Dorn in an early modeling pose.

Yes, that really is Michael Dorn *(left)* as Officer Jed Turner with *CHiPs* co-stars
Erik Estrada and Larry Wilcox.

Photo: Albert Ortega

Dorn and *Next Generation* son Brian "Alexander" Bonsall outside the
1994 screening of the final episode, "All Good Things..."

Gates McFadden and co-star Richard Grieco in the 1995 TV series *Marker*.

McFadden *(right)* and husband John Talbot at the 1994 wrap party after shooting the final episode of *The Next Generation*.

Marina Sirtis and new husband, musician Michael Lamper, on their wedding day, June 21, 1992.

Marina Sirtis and best friend Michael Dorn at a July 1996 benefit in Beverly Hills.

Sirtis and her Yorkshire Terrier, Skillagi, are inseparable.

Sirtis and McFadden at a 1996 promotional appearance for Paramount.

Photo: Twentieth Century Fox

Brent Spiner *(far left)* as Dr. Okum and
Bill Pullman *(center)* in the 1996 mega-hit
Independence Day. "The wig really made
the part for me," Spiner commented.

Spiner and long-time girlfriend Loree
McBride at an October 1996 celebration
honoring 30 years of *Star Trek.*

Photo: Paramount

Denise Crosby, bruised and battered, in the 1989 feature *Pet Sematary.*

Wil Wheaton *(top)* played Gordie Lachance in the 1986 hit *Stand by Me.* Also pictured are co-stars River Phoenix, Jerry O'Connell, and Corey Feldman.

Whoopi Goldberg played
Terry Doolittle in her first
comedic feature film
Jumpin' Jack Flash (1986).

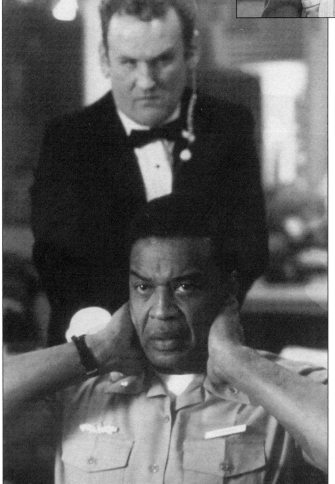

Colm Meaney *(top)* portrayed a
terrorist in the Steven Seagal
vehicle *Under Siege* (1992).

Diana Muldaur starred opposite John Wayne in the 1974 feature film *McQ*.

Fearless (1993) featured Jeff Bridges and a fearful John DeLancie *(background)*.

The groomsmen at Marina Sirtis' wedding: LeVar Burton, Michael Dorn, Patrick Stewart, and Brent Spine

The cast of *Star Trek: First Contact* await the 1996 premiere. *(From left)* Alice Krige ("Borg Queen"), Patrick Stewart, Gates McFadden, Marina Sirtis, Michael Dorn, LeVar Burton, James Cromwell ("Zefram Cochrane"), Executive Producer Rick Berman, Alfre Woodard ("Lily Sloan"), and Jonathan Frakes.

which featured, as her subordinate, actor and good friend John de Lancie, better known to *Star Trek* fans as Q. She also spent time reprising her role, again to critical acclaim, in the off-Broadway play *To Gillian on Her 37th Birthday* and also appeared in the play *Emerald City*. *Variety* wrote of her performance in *Emerald City*, "[McFadden] creates a warmly attractive woman as she shows how the wife matures from lass to lady under the spell of achievement."

BACK ON BOARD—WITH MORE TO DO

Star Trek: The Next Generation's third season, despite McFadden's anxiously awaited return, again lacked feature parts for the good doctor. Other than dealing with her precocious son (and his nanite creations-run-amok in the episode "Evolution"), or being abducted by means of a dangerous dimensional-shift beaming technique in "The High Ground," McFadden remained primarily in the background, tending to the wounded during the year. This lack of quality screen time led her to comment, "I don't think there have been as many scenes for the female characters as there have been for the male characters. I truly am not clear on what the reasons for that are because, as a woman, I find in my life many things that could be explored. . . . I don't think there has been a conscious design not to use the female characters, I just think there perhaps needs to be a more concerted effort to try to explore their characters. . . . I'm sure Dr. Crusher has had more experience in combat. She would have had to have had some training for combat situations, for example. Bev needs a little more James Bond in her life."

Although the *Star Trek* shooting schedule was intense, and the time spent with costars on the set could run into twelve-hour workdays, six or seven days a week, McFadden found the time during the third season not only to appear on the stage, but also to do so with crewmate Patrick Stewart, and in place of another *Enterprise* shipmate, Whoopi Goldberg. The play, titled *So Many People Have Heads*, was a revue featuring skits, songs, poetry, and prose created in the 1970s by the voice coach of the Royal Shakespeare Company, Cicely Berry. Goldberg performed one evening and McFadden the next, her performance hailed as one in which she, drawing upon her training in mime, "literally and figuratively threw her body into the show." Reviewer Ruthanne Devlin noted specifically McFadden's "riveting rendition of the 'Mother Courage' song, an anti-war number, intimate and personal, mocking the male bombast of the Patrick Stewart/Charles Keating song about war's glories." An interesting tidbit of *Trek* trivia: sitting in the front row of the theater during McFadden's performance was actor James Cromwell, who had played the Angosian prime minister in the *Next Generation* episode "The Hunted," and who six years later would star as Zefram Cochrane in *Star Trek: First Contact*.

Without warning, *Star Trek: The Next Generation*'s fourth season featured the emergence of Gates McFadden's Dr. Beverly Crusher as a vital character, with story lines revolving around her and featuring her talents. For fans of Gates McFadden, the 1990–91 season was well worth the wait. The season began with the dramatic conclusion to the most famous *Next Generation* two-parter produced, "The Best of Both Worlds, Part II," which amid all the battle frenzy featured the women of the crew saving humanity. McFadden's Dr. Crusher is the one who discovers the Borg's fatal flaw, and Marina Sirtis' Troi realizes Picard is still a part of Locutus, fighting to break through.

"Remember Me," the fifth episode of the season, featured a McFadden unseen in any other episode previously or subsequently. As Dr. Crusher's universe decayed (due, of course, to a Wesley Crusher science experiment gone awry), McFadden soloed during an estimated 40 percent of the show. McFadden had no stunt double for the swirling-vortex effects sequence at the end of the episode. This incredible stunt—in which she desperately grasps a chair while being sucked out horizontally by the vortex—was achieved by McFadden hanging down from a chair mounted upon a wall, while the editors mounted the footage at a 90-degree angle. Days after filming this episode, the single most strenuous episode of McFadden's six years on the show, she learned that she was pregnant with her first child.

An episode further into the fourth season, "Data's Day," featured a tap-dancing routine between McFadden and Brent Spiner. After rehearsals, McFadden and Spiner actually worked up not only their own choreography, but their own dialogue for the scene as well. Spiner did most of his own tap dancing for the scene, although

McFadden brought in a professional for the final shot. Filming this episode was another small victory for McFadden, as she had complained to the producers on more than one occasion, "I can do all of these things, dance, walk a tightrope, and I am just standing there all the time in my lab coat."

McFadden again got to exhibit her diffuse talents in the episode "Nth Degree," in which the audience is introduced to Crusher's interest in theater and directing. McFadden had been so successful in convincing the producers that Crusher needed to be rounded out with "comedy and hobbies" that executive producer Rick Berman himself is credited with suggesting the *Cyrano de Bergerac* scene between Dwight "Barclay" Shultz and McFadden.

The fourth season also featured the episode that is cited as McFadden's favorite as well as her strangest. "'The Host' introduced a very different species and asked the question 'What is love?' in a very different way," McFadden remarked. The episode not only revealed Crusher as a woman of passion, spending the night with the Trill Odan as he inhabits Riker's body, but also did so in a unique and uncomfortable fashion for McFadden. "The strangest thing I had to do [over the course of *Star Trek: The Next Generation*] was a love scene when I was seven and a half or eight months pregnant." This episode is significant for many fans because it is one of the few that dallies with homosexuality, though ultimately Crusher admits she cannot accept Odan in her new, post-Riker female form.

On June 10, 1991, during *Star Trek*'s summer hiatus, James Cleveland McFadden-Talbot was born. "That's his name, but we call him Jack. Don't ask why. We don't know. There is no reason. Nobody can figure it out. The kid is probably going to call himself Randolph or something," McFadden commented. Throughout the rest of *The Next Generation*'s run, McFadden often brought her son to the set for as much as four hours a day. Jack McFadden-Talbot became so comfortable with the cast that he thinks of the members of the *Enterprise* bridge crew as his aunts and uncles. Actually, this is not entirely untrue, as Brent Spiner is his godfather. Toward the end of *The Next Generation*'s run, when little Jack was three years old, McFadden confessed, "My son hasn't seen the show. He just thinks I have a lot of weird friends—like when Michael Dorn [in Worf makeup] puts his head around the door."

In a holiday card sent out to her castmates, friends, and the crew at the Paramount studios in December 1992, a photo of young Jack McFadden-Talbot was featured. Sitting at the navigation console on the bridge of the *Enterprise*, wearing a black-and-gold Starfleet jumpsuit with ensign's insignia, he was pictured looking up at the view-screen. The card read: "Well, it may be a time warp, Bev, but I know a reindeer when I see one. Happy Holidays. Love, J. C. McFadden-Talbot and Family." The cards were signed by hand, "Love, Gates, John [her husband], and Jack."

Although the fifth season of *The Next Generation* did not provide nearly the highlights for McFadden that the fourth season did, there were other notable events in her career. McFadden was cast as the teacher in the Patrick Stewart–directed *Every Good Boy Deserves Favour*. Her performance, opposite *Next Generation* castmates Stewart, Jonathan Frakes, Brent Spiner, and Colm Meaney, was praised as "convincing" by *Variety*. The two performances in February 1992 led to a short tour with the show the following year, and McFadden's performances were then hailed by reviewers in Atlanta, Chicago, and Los Angeles.

Jeri Taylor became co–executive producer and script supervisor of *Star Trek: The Next Generation* during the sixth season, and credits as one of her achievements improving the roles for women on the *Enterprise*. "I tried to bolster the characters of Troi and Crusher. They had been put in caretaker roles. It's hard to find stories that break them out of that mold. 'Suspicions' was a wonderful vehicle for Dr. Crusher, for it showed her as a charge-ahead kind of aggressive person." ("Suspicions" was the episode in which a scientist was murdered during a test of a new metaphasic shield technology.)

Nonetheless, McFadden continued to be uncomfortable with the limitations of her role as a nurturer and caregiver. "I know that Marina and I always laughed about the fact that both of us can do fencing and that sort of thing, yet we're the ones who bash the pots over the warriors' heads instead of doing our karate or whatever." Perhaps, though, McFadden was equally frustrated with living up to the role-model status she had achieved. "It's most difficult when we have terminally ill children visiting the set. I feel so inadequate. They're looking at the tricorders and hyposprays, and I think, oh, God, if only this wasn't pretend."

By the sixth season, McFadden had fully grown into her role as a sensitive, caring doctor in the highly technical, fictional environment of *Star Trek*, and was able to add her own dynamic to the role. "In the beginning, it was always the same thing. 'Quick, give him a hypospray.' The hypospray became like a panacea for everything that went wrong. I knew we needed to work on things like bedside manner. Now [the sixth season] I always try to touch my patients physically, even if it's not in the script. Sometimes the writers will have me talking to someone else while working on a patient, and I always try to find another way. If I were the patient, I would find that annoying." Fans often remark at conventions about Dr. Crusher's exemplary bedside manner, yet much of what they are really commenting on is the work of McFadden. "I wanted Crusher to be compassionate. I think people can stand pain and uncertainty so much better if doctors give you a moment." In one script, the scene was written so that Crusher spoke to Captain Picard while treating a patient. McFadden spoke up: "I told them, that's rude. Can I at least say 'excuse me' and walk two steps away?" She won her case.

Gates McFadden is an avid reader of books by neurologist Oliver Sacks. Originally, she hoped Dr. Crusher could specialize in neurology, but she lost that fight. Early in the show's run, McFadden suggested (unsuccessfully) to Gene Roddenberry that he develop a script from Sacks' best-seller *Awakenings* (later made into a hit movie starring Robin Williams and Robert De Niro). She repeated this request during the sixth season: "A story like *Awakenings*, where we can reach people who have an unknown disease and revive them, giving them a new level of consciousness." Again it fell on deaf ears. McFadden's failure to get a script based on Sacks' story was the only creative aspect of *The Next Generation* that she was ever "really upset about."

During the sixth season McFadden's Crusher also reached a certain parity with her costars that, in retrospect, seems surprising. It was not until this year, 1992, that there was an official "Dr. Crusher" action figure produced. She was the last of the major *Star Trek* characters made into a toy. "I always thought it was discrimination," she commented on the slight, "because they had dolls of all the men. After all, if we're going to be examples for our kids, we might as well include a doctor!"

During her busy sixth-season schedule, McFadden squeezed in filming an episode of the HBO comedy series *Dream On*, which she relished. "I play a babe, which is something people aren't used to seeing me do."

The sixth season featured a few scripts with substantial roles for McFadden. In "Schisms," the crew is struck with strange symptoms that puzzle Dr. Crusher. In "Chain of Command, Part I," Crusher not only trains for a secret search-and-destroy mission—offering McFadden some much-desired action sequences—but she also gets the opportunity to flirt with a Ferengi, a challenge for any actress. In "Suspicions," McFadden shines in a script about "science diplomacy" dubbed by insiders as "Beverly as Quincy." Interestingly, producer and "Suspicions" scriptwriter Jeri Taylor had been a producer on *Quincy, M.E.*, the Jack Klugman series about a crime-solving medical examiner.

WRAPPING UP, BRANCHING OUT, AND A CHANCE TO DIRECT

During the hiatus between *Star Trek*'s sixth and seventh seasons, McFadden performed as the devil in Stravinsky's *L'Histoire du Soldat (The Soldier's Tale)* at the SummerFest La Jolla 1993. *The San Diego Union-Tribune* raved, "The production relied on Gates McFadden. With winning versatility, she assumed the devilish guises of a sly old man, a woman with a Cockney accent, and a boisterous ex-soldier with a Texas twang." The performance featured seven instrumentalists and only three actors, one of whom was Rene Auberjonois (hailed for his "welcome intensity"). During this time, McFadden also narrated Saint-Saëns' *Carnival des Animaux* with the Cleveland Symphony Orchestra.

"The captain's chair is quite comfortable," McFadden noted to a television reviewer writing an article about the seventh-season premiere episode of *The Next Generation*. She had to command the *Enterprise* and destroy a Borg ship in "Descent, Part II." *The Houston Chronicle* reviewed the episode and noted, "Crusher proves to be a natural, and she gives the center seat her own identity. Unlike Captain Picard, who orders people to 'make it so,' Crusher commands with a crisp 'let's do it' (a line that first came into vogue as the last words of Gary Gilmore before his 1977 execution in Utah)."

The seventh season also featured "Attached," in which Crusher finally explored the romantic spark with Picard. The script for "Attached," by Carl Sagan's twenty-three-year-old son, Nick Sagan, won McFadden's praise for "turning my season around." McFadden's personal acting highlight of the season came in filming "Sub Rosa," dubbed by producer and episode scribe Jeri Taylor "a romance novel in space." Of McFadden's outstanding performance, Taylor noted, "The lovemaking without a partner—this is not easy stuff to do . . . and she committed herself to it completely."

Since the first season, McFadden had been asking for the opportunity to direct, and it came during the last season of *The Next Generation* when she was assigned to direct "Genesis," the episode in which a virus causes the denizens of the *Enterprise* to de-evolve. Her *Star Trek* directing debut, which placed her alongside three other stars-turned-directors (Patrick Stewart, Jonathan Frakes, and LeVar Burton), drew upon her skills garnered while working under the tutelage of Jim Henson as director of choreography and puppet movement for his ambitious 1986 film *Labyrinth*. Leading up to her directing chores, McFadden was "wildly excited" about her opportunity: "Every night in bed, I keep seeing these shots I want to do."

During the filming of "Genesis," the destructive Los Angeles earthquake of 1994 hit. "I was fortunate, but many people on the crew weren't. There was a tremendous amount of loss for some people," McFadden laments. Though the quake caused a two-day delay in production, the episode was ultimately completed and is considered one of the most successful ever. "There are things all over the floor, which you never see. We're usually so pristine on the ship. I had as much fun as I was allowed changing the ship's look. I've used sickbay in a way nobody has ever used sickbay."

The filming of *The Next Generation*'s final episode, "All Good Things . . . ," was a complicated ordeal. Revisions had to be made to the already complex sixteen-day production schedule for the two-hour episode because McFadden had been cast in the whodunit comedy *Mystery Dance*, an ABC pilot with Jane Curtin and Peter Riegert being filmed in Oregon at the same time as "All Good Things . . . " A bizarre coincidence, as seven years earlier the production schedule for *Star Trek*'s two-hour pilot, "Encounter at Farpoint," was also adjusted to account for one of McFadden's other professional commitments.

Ultimately, a seventeenth day of production was added to "All Good Things . . . ," a very expensive decision, though it was not entirely attributable to McFadden's busy schedule. Rather, her skin was the culprit. "The makeup for the future was very difficult," recalled Jeri Taylor. "It took time to put it on and we lost hours because of that. Gates' skin . . . is very fragile and so the prosthetic that is added to her tends to kind of slip. Halfway through each day of shooting we had to completely redo her makeup from scratch."

Filming *Mystery Dance* and commuting back and forth from Oregon did give McFadden a unique perspective on her years in the *Star Trek* cast. "When I was on location in Portland, I wasn't hanging around a studio, like I've been doing for years here, where your trailer opens up to someone else's trailer in the cast and it's just like a coffee klatch. On location, I had a sense of being much more isolated. I'm going to miss this."

In terms of the finished episode, McFadden expressed humorous displeasure at Dr. Crusher's divorce from Jean-Luc Picard, shown as a possible future timeline in "All Good Things . . ." "In the settlement, I would have wanted the fish and the Shakespeare book! I could have had the fish in my Ready Room on the *USS Pasteur*, skewered, or at the very least, I could have his Shakespeare text ripped in half on my desk."

After the close of the final season, McFadden commented wistfully, "This year has been my best, without any doubt. It's been a wonderful period in my life. I didn't have a family when I started the show, and now I do. I've also made very close friends. My life has been enriched by the entire experience, and now I'm excited about the future."

However, McFadden was always pragmatic regarding her role on the show and how it evolved over the course of the life of the program. Despite auditioning for the role with a comedic scene, she remains baffled that "I turned out to be the most serious character." And considering her role as a single mother in a more enlightened world, she commented, "As a mother to the Wesley Crusher character, I also should be the mentor to my son, but it's the men who have the scenes of giving him strong, courageous advice. I've felt that was a cop-out." But McFadden was never shy about her opinions. "Just ask any of the producers," she told *TV Guide*. "Over the years I was always making telephone calls to say, 'Gee . . . couldn't we make Crusher a little stronger on page twenty-three?' or, 'All the men get to say things in the last scene—what happened to the women?!' "

The feature film *Star Trek: Generations* began filming immediately after "All Good Things . . ." had wrapped up. McFadden was "very disappointed in the size of my role. I was hoping to have something more substantial. That's life." A few days after she had finished filming *Generations*, McFadden told a *Star Trek* convention audience in Buffalo, New York, "I'll probably stay home and cry." Nonetheless, McFadden's alma mater, Brandeis University, was fortunate enough to host the world premiere of *Star Trek: Generations*. McFadden chaired the event, the proceeds of which were donated to charity.

It should come as no surprise that Gates McFadden has kept busy since *Star Trek* ceased being a daily part of her life. As soon as *The Next Generation* ended production, McFadden was cast as Kimba Hills Rose, a rich, widowed, antagonistic "bitch" in United Paramount Network's *Marker*, starring Richard Grieco. Although the show only lasted a season, McFadden enjoyed living and working in Hawaii (*Marker*'s locale) and appreciated the free time she was able to spend with Jack. "It's a great place [Hawaii] for a kid to grow up. I love running through coconut groves. It is so beautiful here, and Hawaiians are so lovely."

Additionally, McFadden certainly enjoyed the change in her attire that came with her new television role. "The boots I had to wear [in *Star Trek*] always killed my feet. The spandex uniforms were boiling in the summer and freezing in the winter. It's nice to wear tennis shoes and glamorous outfits. It's great." Although her husband, John Talbot, a contractor, stayed behind in Los Angeles while she was in Hawaii, she often flew back to be together with him, or he would fly out.

While in Hawaii, McFadden needed an emergency appendectomy. She insisted upon having a microsurgery specialist perform the operation, so as to avoid the large scar on her abdomen. The surgeon, it turned out, was a big fan of Dr. Crusher's, and took the time to explain the procedure in detail and answer all of her questions.

While appearing in *Marker*, McFadden also lent her voice to an adaptation of the famous H. G. Wells radio play *War of the Worlds*. It was directed, cast, and produced by John de Lancie and featured Leonard Nimoy, Wil Wheaton, and Brent Spiner. She was also cast as Paul Reiser's boss on the NBC hit *Mad About You*, and has made regular appearances on that sitcom. McFadden has also recorded a number of audio books, and in 1996 participated in *Chicago Theatres on the Air*, annual performances staged and recorded before an audience and later broadcast on radio. She appeared with, among others, Kelsey Grammer, Paul Winfield, Ed Begley Jr., and Brent Spiner.

In March 1996, McFadden traveled to Bosnia and Herzegovina and performed with the USO to boost troop morale. "When I saw the pictures on television of the first troops in all that flooding, my heart went out to them. And besides, there are a lot of *Star Trek* fans in the military." On stage, she told the troops, "I had no idea what a beautiful country this is, or at least could be. I think it's great that you are here."

Returning to the United States, McFadden appeared on stage under the name Cheryl McFadden in Lillian Hellman's classic play about attitudes toward lesbians, *The Children's Hour*. It is interesting to note that she also performed to critical acclaim under the name Cheryl in David Ives' assorted vignettes of modern life, *All in the Timing*, in 1995. Apparently, McFadden has chosen to make a professional distinction between her career on the serious stage and her television fame achieved as a member of the *Star Trek* cast. She has also expressed an interest in someday working with director Jane Campion, and she covets the opportunity to play the role of Beatrice in *Much Ado About Nothing*.

Gates McFadden the actress has kept busy, but she has also pursued many hobbies and interests outside the theater and away from the cameras. She's a fan of old movies, listing *Les Enfants de Paradis* as one of her favorites, and has freelanced as an interior decorator. She dabbles in drawing and sculpture. She is also an avid gardener and collects any books she can find on the subject. Her interest in architecture, rooted in her trip to France while she was in her early twenties, has led her to design her own house. She has claimed that she is into an "Eastern influence" phase, noting that her house utilizes a lot of glass and natural elements, and straight lines, by employing a minimalist approach: bright, open areas, and Japanese glass screens. It survived the earthquake of 1994 intact.

She is undaunted by the possibility of never working again in Hollywood. When asked what she would do if the theatrical and film offers dried up, she commented without hesitation: "I don't know, but I doubt I'd be at a loss as to having other interests and doing other things. I love a lot of things, and I'm pretty much obsessive about most things I do, whether it be gardening, or architecture, or music. I'd be an obsessive hairdresser. With my experience with my wig, I certainly would be."

As Dr. Crusher, McFadden started wearing a wig so she wouldn't have to deal with her hair every morning. However, her real hair is just like her wig, and she stopped wearing the wig midway through the sixth season of *Star Trek: The Next Generation*. A flaming redhead, wig or not, throughout her tenure on board the *Enterprise*, in *Star Trek: First Contact* McFadden is suddenly a *blond*. Despite the attractive and stylistic change, the alteration, obvious to even the most casual viewer, was never explained in the film and has never been discussed by McFadden.

Frustrated that story elements such as the Picard/Crusher relationship were not followed up, and despite limited screen time, McFadden enjoyed her experience on *Star Trek: First Contact*. "When we all hit the bridge, it's like, did we ever leave? It is true, we do all have chemistry," McFadden exclaimed. She enjoyed being teased again by Patrick Stewart for her "midwesternisms," and admitted that it was difficult to get serious while filming the big-budget feature. "We sort of do a set of Monty Python, and after we've done anything we can do to get a laugh, then we do the scene." McFadden had two significant scenes in the film, one on the bridge and the other in sickbay. An audience favorite, it is in this latter scene that McFadden reluctantly calls upon the Emergency Medical Holographic Program, Robert Picardo's "Doctor," to save the day.

Over seven years of the television program, McFadden has one favorite line of *Star Trek* dialogue: "'Jean-Luc, there's something I've been meaning to tell you.' I said it twice on the series, and no one ever did get to hear what I was going to say. I could have been talking about a lovechild or my love for him—who knows?" She finally did complete the sentence when autographing Patrick Stewart's "All Good Things . . ." script. She wrote:

Patrick
There's something I've been meaning to tell you—
I'll love you in the past, present, and the future—
Love, Gates

Reflecting on the television show that has made her famous and financially secure, and has afforded her the opportunity to affect thousands of people while pursuing any number of career options, McFadden stated in 1996, "This show comes directly from Gene and his vision of the world. It's more than just a blending of imagination and technology. He offered a real vision of hope, and he believed in the possibility of humanity. The world is actually a better place to live in."

GATES McFADDEN

(also known as Cheryl McFadden and Jesse Stuart Gates)
Dr. Beverley Crusher

STAGE:
The Bloodletters
Bottleneck at the Bar**
Cloud Nine
The Homecoming
The Matchmaker
A Midsummer Night's Dream*
  ('81)
To Gillian on Her 37th Birthday
  ('83, '84, '90)
How to Say Goodbye ('86)
The Emerald City ('89)
So Many People Have Heads
  ('90)
Viva Detroit ('90)
Every Good Boy Deserves
  Favour ('92, '93)
L'Histoire du Soldat ('93)
All in the Timing ('96)
The Children's Hour ('96)
This Town ('96)

TELEVISION:
The Edge of Night ('83)
Another World ('84)
The Cosby Show ('86)
The Wizard ('86)

Star Trek: The Next Generation
  ('87–'88, '89–'94)
All My Children ('89)
L.A. Law ('89)
Beyond the Groove ('90)
Dream On ('93)
Mad About You ('94, '95, '96)
Mystery Dance ('94)
Marker ('95)
Party of Five ('95)

FILM:
The Dark Crystal* ('83)
The Muppets Take Manhattan
  ('84)
Dreamchild* ('85)
Rustler's Rhapsody ('85)
When Nature Calls ('85)
Labyrinth* ('86)
Legend ('86)
The Hunt for Red October ('90)
Taking Care of Business (a.k.a.
  Filofax) ('90)
Star Trek: Generations ('94)
Star Trek: First Contact ('96)

  * *indicates choreographer*
  ** *indicates playwright, as*
  Jesse Stuart Gates

---- CHAPTER 6 ----

MARINA SIRTIS

From Hoi Polloi to Counselor Troi

"Being an actor to Greek parents is considered one rung up from walking the streets at night."
—MARINA SIRTIS, QUOTED IN THE HARTFORD COURANT, MARCH 16, 1996

"If the show [*Star Trek: The Next Generation*] continues to spit out British actors of this caliber onto the American stage, it deserves its own special Tony," claimed *The New York Times'* 1996 review of Marina Sirtis' performance on the Hartford (Connecticut) Stage in the revival of playwright Joe Orton's witty *Loot*. Giving Sirtis' performance a rave review, as well as implying that her stage presence ranks with the likes of Royal Shakespeare Company veteran Patrick Stewart, is fulfillment of the highest order for Sirtis. It is confirmation that her success and popularity on *Star Trek: The Next Generation* was not a fluke, and that her prospects for future success are bright indeed.

TRADITIONAL UPBRINGING, UNTRADITIONAL CAREER

Marina Sirtis was born March 29, 1959. The elder of two children, her life was marked by genuinely humble beginnings with traditional Greek parents. Her father, John, was a tailor; her mother, Despina, a dressmaker; but, growing up in North London, Sirtis knew from the time she was a young child that she wanted to spend her life acting. "My mother tells me that when I was three, I used to stand on the seat of the bus and sing to the other passengers. . . . I would make my own little plays and climb up on a pile of rocks and sing—it was just something I always did. Maybe I watched too much TV as a kid, I don't know."

Her parents did not feel Sirtis should get involved with the "locals." Fearing that the influence of English children would pollute their daughter and turn her against the strict Greek values in

144

which they believed, they forced Sirtis to spend most of her childhood alone, performing her own little dramas and watching the neighborhood children playing in the street outside her home.

As a young teenager, Sirtis was, in her own words, an "ugly duckling." "My hair was frizzy; I had one large eyebrow across my forehead and, being Greek, I had too much facial hair. Plus I had Edna Everage–style glasses. I looked awful. When I was thirteen, I underwent a transformation. One of my best friends told me she was going to sort me out because I looked so dreadful. She took me to the hairdresser's to have my hair cut short, got out hair removal cream, and plucked my eyebrows. I turned from an ugly duckling into a swan." This trip to the hairdresser's had a more significant impact on Sirtis' life than she foresaw at the time. Her first gainful employment, at age fourteen, was as a shampooist in the shop.

Before her "transformation," Sirtis felt insecure regarding her appearance and had a terrible self-image. She became the class clown to compensate for her looks, but instead of being really funny, she was merely disruptive in class. After the "transformation," Sirtis said, "I became boy-mad. The problem was that my parents didn't give me a lot of freedom. All my friends were going out at night with boyfriends and I had to stay at home watching television."

Sirtis loved *Dr. Who* (her favorite doctor was Tom Baker), and she told a convention audience that she was terrified by the villainous Daleks. "I used to watch *Dr. Who* hiding behind the sofa. Garbage day was very traumatic for me—the Daleks were out. Garbage cans were scary when I was a kid."

Not only did her protective home life lead her to a love of television, it also sparked her passion for football (American soccer). "That was one of the reasons why I became fanatical about football. It was the one place my parents let me go. So every Wednesday night and Saturday I would go to Tottenham Hotspur's games. It was my one escape. I was one of those girls hanging around after the matches. I was totally in love with Joe Kinnear but I ended up going out with Graeme Souness. I was sixteen and he was eighteen and he was my first love. He was *somebody* and the fact that I was going out with him was a big notch in my belt.

"But I had to keep him a secret from my parents. They would never have allowed me to carry on seeing him. I used to tell lies to them to get out to see him and they never found out." In a 1993 article in the *Sunday Times of London*, Kinnear, now the manager of the Wimbledon "football" team, recounted that his players tacked up a picture of Sirtis as Counselor Troi in the team's locker room with a caption reading, "He did not make love to this beautiful woman."

Sirtis' brother, Steve, also a sports fanatic, went on to become a professional soccer player in a Greek league. When he needed knee surgery, big sister Marina was delighted to be able to use a portion of her *Star Trek* earnings to fly him to the United States and have the surgery performed in America by a leading sports surgeon.

In high school Sirtis rebelled against her parents and became involved in the acting club, intent on pursuing a career on the stage. Behind her parents' backs, Sirtis surreptitiously applied to the prestigious Guild Hall School of Drama. She told her parents of her application only after her acceptance had arrived, and they begrudgingly approved of her decision. Years later, she reflected, "I was very bright in school, and my parents had lofty ideas of my becoming a lawyer. I think my father was quietly supportive before he passed away. [John Sirtis died in 1982.] I think with *Star Trek* my mother has finally accepted it."

As Sirtis said on Comedy Central's *Short Attention Span Theater*, Guild Hall was "an old-fashioned kind of drama school. . . . The most modern thing we did was Ibsen." She related her most embarrassing moment on stage: in the role of Ophelia in *Hamlet* her costume was not ready for the production, so instead of wearing a long white dress, she dressed in a long white lacy undergarment. As Ophelia was going mad, the top of the gown loosened up, ". . . and I looked down, and there they were, for all the world to see."

Although in her third year she left Guild Hall in a huff over a teacher's comments, Sirtis landed a position as a member of the Worthington Repertory Theatre. Her first major role with them was Ophelia. A couple of years later, she portrayed Magenta in a European tour of the immensely popular *Rocky Horror Picture Show*, a role that enabled her to reveal her considerable vocal talents.

Old World tradition does not die easily. Sirtis' parents hired a matchmaker to find a suitable mate for her when she was nineteen. "I remember the woman coming by to tell my mother she had found a husband for me: so I asked her if she thought I was attractive. When she said yes, he would be very pleased with me, I told her that if I was pretty then why couldn't I find a husband for myself? She was shocked by my so-called honesty. My mother gave me a thrashing for being rude, but Mother and Father never tried that stunt again."

Sirtis has appeared in supporting roles in three motion pictures, but these she refuses to discuss. She is quite unhappy about the brief nudity she displayed in each, and the illegal still photos that were subsequently created. She considers these movies the low points in her career: *The Wicked Lady* (1983), in which she gets bullwhipped by Faye Dunaway; *Blind Date* (1984), in which she plays a prostitute who gets killed; and *Death Wish III* (1985) with Charles Bronson. However, she did point out that working with Faye Dunaway was "like working with the Queen of England." Besides these forgettable roles, her employment before coming to the United States included a job as a sweater folder at a clothing boutique in a shopping mall, and as a cafeteria worker. Finally, in 1986, Sirtis used the money she had squirreled away to fly to America and embark on a Hollywood dream.

Coming to Hollywood was significant in Sirtis' career not just because L.A. is an entertainment mecca, but also because she felt she was often getting passed over for starring roles in her native England due to her exotic good looks. "I was working a lot, but always the supporting actress, never the girl-next-door. I came over to test the waters."

Her Hollywood career before being cast in *Star Trek: The Next Generation* was marked by fleeting glimpses of success. Ten days after she arrived in the United States with only a six-month visa, she landed a guest role on the series *Hunter*. Other small television roles followed, but no steady work came her way during her short stay. Just before she was due to return home—broke, credit cards "maxed out," and depressed—Sirtis auditioned for the role of the chief security officer aboard the *USS Enterprise*, Lieutenant Macha Hernandez (later changed to Natasha Yar). Meanwhile, Denise Crosby had been auditioning for the role of Lieutenant Commander Deanna Troi, the ship's Betazoid counselor. Both

Sirtis and Crosby came in to audition three times, but series creator and executive producer Gene Roddenberry had them switch roles on the third callback. Three days later, Sirtis' work visa had expired. She was in her Lake Hollywood apartment, crying and packing for a return flight to London, when she received a phone call telling her that she had been cast in the role of Counselor Troi. She was so excited to have gotten the part that she signed her Paramount contract without any knowledge of her pay. Sirtis felt that if she were to look at the salary figure she just might jinx herself.

Landing a role on *Star Trek* was not a complete surprise, however. Astrology and the tarot have played a small part in Sirtis' life, and she claims that tarot cards told her that she would be living and working near water: a sign, she claimed, that she would be able to keep her Lake Hollywood apartment. Besides astrology, Sirtis also believes in the power of dreams and has claimed to have strange, predictive dreams. She dreamed of Laurence Olivier's death the day before he passed away, and she dreamed the birth of London Siamese twins the night before the news hit the papers. Certain dreams, she claims, allow her to know when something bad is going to happen.

She told *People* magazine of an event that foreshadowed her future on *Star Trek*. "I was walking home from the theater one night with someone, and we looked up into the sky, and there was this big orange thing. I wasn't scared. It was just kind of interesting. Other people in the area saw it too. It looked like the size of a Goodyear blimp, but farther away. It was really too far away to be a blimp or a balloon. And it was really bright, it was really shining." In Sirtis' brief biography published in the Paramount press kit for *Star Trek: The Next Generation*, she is quoted as saying, "I do think I've seen a UFO. Actually, I'm convinced I saw a UFO."

In retrospect, Sirtis is glad she did not land the role of the security chief. "They have to spend too much time on 'Planet Hell' [also known as stage 16 on the Paramount lot, where the alien planet sets are constructed]. I don't like stuff that gets me dirty, that gets stuff in my hair, breaks my nails." Although a bit nervous about taking the role of the counselor, never having had any psychology courses in school, Sirtis did what she could to prepare. As soon as she landed the job, she subscribed to *Psychology Today*.

Holding Counsel

Sirtis did not embrace her impending success like a typical Hollywood star. Living within modest means, she slept on a futon in her sparsely furnished two-bedroom apartment until an ex-roommate took her bed shopping, after the first full season of *The Next Generation*. Even though Sirtis still did not see the need for a real bed, her friend insisted, "There are certain things that one expects of a TV person, and one thing is that they should have a bed."

"It's taken me years to become an overnight success," Sirtis exclaimed in a Paramount press release that promoted the cast of its new syndicated program, *Star Trek: The Next Generation*. Yet that first season of the new show had its rough spots, and for Marina Sirtis, her character almost did not survive the season.

After being deemed too "loose" in the pilot episode, "Encounter at Farpoint," with her flowing hair and her cheerleaderlike "scant" uniform, Troi adopted a nonregulation uniform and the famous "bun" hairstyle for the shooting of the first regular episode, "The Naked Now." Her telepathic abilities were also softened to mere empathy, which led to better writing for the character (Sirtis herself cringed over some of her emotional soliloquies in the pilot). However, according to Larry Nemecek's *Star Trek: The Next Generation Companion*, the writing staff would continue to find her character very difficult to write for. After being just about written out of the scripts in four first-season episodes—"Hide and Q," "Datalore," "11001001," and "Heart of Glory"—Troi was almost dropped entirely in November 1987.

However, the first season was not totally without moments for Sirtis. The show's third episode, "Haven," features Majel Barrett as Troi's mother, Lwaxana, who comes onto the ship to fulfill an arranged marriage of her daughter—an odd parallel to an earlier event in Sirtis' own life. In "Skin of Evil," the episode that featured the death of Denise Crosby's character, Tasha Yar, Sirtis' tears were reportedly real as she was bidding good-bye to her good friend. In "The Big Good-bye," Sirtis, in her guise as Troi, is given the opportunity to do some linguistics coaching. (Always very good at accents, Sirtis was initially asked by Gene Roddenberry to develop her own inflections and vocal style for the role of Troi. The actual conversation as Sirtis related it:

Gene Roddenberry: You have to do an accent.
Me: Okay, where do you want the accent to come from?
Roddenberry: Betazed.

Consequently, Sirtis has claimed that Troi speaks in a mix of many nations' accents).

The beginning of the second season saw some very positive changes for Troi. Most noticeable, although not the most important, was that she received a wardrobe and hairstyle change. (She had been known around the *Star Trek* set as "old bunhead" during the first season.) Perhaps the most significant sign that the character had evolved in more than just appearance, however, was evident in the first episode of the second season, "The Child." The episode—recycled from an unused script for the television-series-that-never-was, *Star Trek II*—was necessitated because of the ongoing Hollywood writers' strike. Ilia and Decker, whom Trek fans were introduced to in *Star Trek: The Motion Picture*, were originally conceived of as regular cast members in the aborted series. Troi's role in "The Child" was originally written for Ilia. Sirtis was praised by directors and producers alike for rising to the challenge of a much-expanded role.

However, the second season also saw some significant changes in the roster of female cast members aboard the *Enterprise*. Gone was Gates McFadden's young, single mother Dr. Beverly Crusher; in her place was Diana Muldaur's Dr. Kate Pulaski, created in the mold of DeForest Kelley's Dr. Leonard "Bones" McCoy. Also gone was Denise Crosby, "Skin of Evil" having been the twenty-second episode of the first season (of twenty-six produced), and her last. Joining the cast on a recurring basis was Whoopi Goldberg as a bartender and the captain's confidante, Guinan.

"I was very upset that Gates left the show," Sirtis revealed in an interview published in *Star Trek: The Official Fan Club* magazine at the end of the first season. "I was close to Denise but she was married and had a whole life outside the show. But Gates and I were the two single girls on the show and we used to hang out together. We are very good friends. I was watching the show the other day and I must admit I got a bit of a lump in my throat thinking that she wasn't going to be there for the second season. I'm still dealing on an emotional level with how much I'm going to miss her. Actors do become close friends with the people they're working with very quickly, and they become your family. I've always been very amazed by that. Gates was a wonderful person and I'm going to miss her a lot."

"To be honest, I was never intended to be the vamp of the show," Sirtis told *The Hartford Courant*. "Gene Roddenberry's original intention was that I be the brains of the show. Then . . . I seemed to be the only young woman in the cast. So I had to become that thing. You know that thing—a show like this has to have an attractive woman." She acknowledged to London's *Daily Mail* in 1995, "The producers wanted a chick on the show that the guys fancied because when they weren't watching spaceships being blown up, they needed something nice to look at."

Even after only one season, Sirtis, like Patrick Stewart, was becoming frustrated over the paucity of responsibility given to the women characters on the show. "I think sometimes I feel that the women have to fight a bit harder than the men for more advanced ideas. You know, I might say, 'I know this is how it is now between men and women, but don't you think things would have advanced a bit by the twenty-fourth century?' I would like to see more equality on the show. They gave the women more powerful positions on the ship and then sometimes gave them lines that didn't really match the position that they had. To be honest, I don't think that happened much with my character, but I did see it happening sometimes."

In 1989, two years after *Star Trek: The Next Generation* began airing, Sirtis commented on her life in Hollywood. "I can't imagine living anywhere else. . . . A friend of mine from England told me, 'You know, the reason you didn't fit in England is because you were so L.A. Just look at you. You've been here ten minutes and already you've got the acrylic nails.' L.A. has the lifestyle I'd been searching for but can't have in England because it's so gloomy [there]. I think a lot of the Brits are going to be mad at me for saying that, but it is. I used to think I had three weeks of PMS every month. It's ludicrous. Here, I have my normal two days of PMS like any normal person and I'm happy the rest of the time.

"Every working-class person loves L.A. Everyone is welcomed because of who they are and try to achieve, not because of how much money they make. Until you've lived in England and experienced the wrong end of the class system, you don't know this." Sirtis has exclaimed that she loves the old studios; she loves driving to work in the morning (she drives a white Chrysler Le Baron convertible); and she absolutely loves the weather. Although not fond of the Hollywood party scene, where people were more interested in looking over her shoulder to see who *else* was walking into the room, she enjoys the appreciation that the devotion of one's life to show business can bring. In England, she would minimize her extensive credits. "I'd put it down as some little thing. Over here, you can have a walk-on and say you were costarring. It's a different kind of mindset. People here realize it's hard to be in show business. Even if you just have two lines in a film they know that probably one hundred girls tried out for it.

"L.A. is a positive city. It's hard to describe. You have to be an actor in England and then come here to see the difference. I was reading an article about Ken Branagh who just did *Henry V*. He said you get to a certain point in England while you're building your success and people are encouraging you. Then once you've made it, they try to tear you down, saying, 'Who does he think he is?'"

Star Trek: The Next Generation's third season had a few notable moments for Sirtis. "Who Watches the Watchers" was filmed almost entirely on location at Vasquez Rocks, a county park that was used for some location shoots during the original series. Filming this episode was one of the most uncomfortable for Sirtis and the cast. The temperature was over 100 degrees. However, the actors were forbidden to wear any deodorant or perfumes during the long days of filming because Vasquez is home to snakes, bees, and scorpions.

"The Price" is a notable episode for its infamous bed scene between Troi and Devinoni Ral, the first such scene in any *Star Trek* episode. "It's the first time you ever see two people in bed together, talking postcoitally. . . . You know they've 'done it,'" Sirtis related to *Drama-Logue*. "It was nice to do the love scene because I had never let my hair down before, either figuratively or literally. I liked the way the hair represented what was going on inside me. Once I decided to reject him, the hair went back up."

The very next episode, "The Vengeance Factor," featured a nonspeaking cameo by Sirtis' real-life boyfriend, later her husband, musician Michael Lamper. He played the role of Mallon, the blond

Gatherer placed in charge of the group after their leader leaves with Picard. "Ménage à Troi," toward the end of the third season, was the season's Lwaxana episode. Featuring Sirtis, and revealing much of her backstory, this episode did not unveil as much of Sirtis as many fans might like to think. Body doubles were used for Sirtis' and Majel Barrett's nude scenes.

During *The Next Generation*'s third season, Sirtis caused a bit of a stir by putting up DON'T EAT TUNA stickers around the studio. She found her efforts unappreciated. "What really pisses me off is that people took them down! I thought, I don't understand you people. I'm putting up stickers to inform you that dolphins get caught in nets and drown and they use dolphins as bait, by dynamiting them. Six million have been killed since 1960: a dolphin dies every four minutes. Now, why does it hurt you to know the facts? They're just so pig ignorant."

In addition to her dolphin crusade, Sirtis is also very concerned about the damage being done to the environment. "We're poisoning ourselves. I don't think people realize how, by upsetting the natural order of things, they're messing up irreparably. Not just by chopping down trees in the rain forest but even the way we're killing animals." She admits that, although she's not as knowledgeable as professionals, her presence at events brings people out to listen. "It's stupid, but that's the way it is. People listen to celebrities, even if they're wondering what color your lipstick is."

Other relevant issues occupy Sirtis' time and energy as well. In 1994, she participated in a Hollywood star-laden plea to Congress to cover women's reproductive health services in the impending health care reform then under consideration.

By the end of *Star Trek: The Next Generation*'s third season, it was acknowledged that the show had come into its own, escaping the shadow of the original 1966–69 series. However, a show with such a large ensemble cast always risks underdeveloping certain characters, a fate Sirtis feared had befallen Troi after three seasons. In a 1990 interview, she stated, "I think they've been sort of bound up in her telepathic capabilities. We don't really know what she does when she's just being herself. We don't really know much about her planet. Unfortunately, Hollywood still has its formulas for what women do."

However, Sirtis insisted that she loved the turn her life had taken, as well as the constant employment and fame popular episodic television brought her. "I love the whole Hollywood studio thing. It's wonderful to actually drive onto the Paramount lot and be recognized when you go out. Brent Spiner and Michael Dorn are my best friends, and I think we spend 10 percent to 20 percent of our time together talking about being recognized. And to be honest with you, I like getting paid all the time."

During the hiatus between the third and fourth seasons (over the summer of 1990), Sirtis went home to London and stayed with her mother while filming the BBC film *One Last Chance*. Since her move to Hollywood and the death of her father, the lingering tensions from her earlier rebellious period and the distance she may have felt from her mother were resolved. Sirtis had a terrific summer working in her native England and staying home with "Mum." "It's a wonderful family feeling of togetherness. It was lovely being so spoilt. Mum fed me so much I put on ten pounds. . . . But she doesn't really approve of *Star Trek*. Greek movies are all about love and death and are very melodramatic. She thinks *Star Trek*'s a bit flighty and lightweight." Sirtis' mother used to ask her when her job [on *Star Trek*] would be over. Her mother thought that she must be lying to her so she would have an excuse not to return to England.

ACTION, ADVENTURE, AND MARRIAGE

Star Trek: The Next Generation's fourth and fifth seasons had more opportunities for Sirtis to shine. In "The Loss," Sirtis was able to stretch her acting muscles, losing her empathic sense and grappling with the implications of her "loss." This episode opens with a scene in which we see Troi counseling an adult crew member, the first time such a scene had been written for someone who was, after all, the ship's psychologist. At the time the episode was being written, producer Michael Piller revealed that the writers toyed with the idea of not giving Troi back her lost empathic sense. Sirtis found her fan mail very favorable after the first airing of "The Loss," and though Troi regained her abilities at the conclusion of the story, she received a particularly large number of favorable missives from fans with disabilities.

Sirtis had long requested more action scenes for Troi, and her wish was fulfilled in "Night Terrors." However, the scenes in which she "flies" (wearing a suspended harness) took an entire day of filming and were not what Sirtis had in mind: she is deathly afraid of heights.

In the season-five episode "Hero Worship," Troi had one of the longest and most realistic counseling sessions yet. In Larry Nemecek's *Star Trek: The Next Generation Companion*, Michael Piller is quoted as saying, "Since Jeri Taylor and I have been here, the counseling scenes have become much more numerous and realistic. But that experience does not come from practicing—it comes from being a patron!"

Also in season five, "Power Play" saw Sirtis in some action sequences. Troi, Data (Brent Spiner), and O'Brien (Colm Meaney) are all possessed by alien entities. The three invent the nicknames Slugger, Buzz, and Slash for their possessed personae. Sirtis got so dirty from the blowing sand on the Planet Hell set, Nemecek recalls, that she had to take a midday shower and get made up again before filming could continue.

The 1992–1993 *Star Trek: The Next Generation Writers/ Directors Guide* identifies and summarizes a character who, over five seasons, has finally been fleshed out. The counselor is an expert in "human engineering," dealing with the shipboard community in much the same way as the ship's chief engineer is an expert in the ship's mechanics. Her ability to read emotions—unlike full-blooded Betazoids, who are fully telepathic, Troi is half Betazoid, half human—led her into becoming an expert psychologist and ultimately a Starfleet counselor. The guide, often referred to as the writers' and directors' "bible," states that not only is Troi responsible for watching over the emotional condition of the crew, but she is also an expert "at recommending to Picard the right action to take when interpersonal conflicts arise among the various civilians and Starfleet personnel who populate the ship, and the differing cultures and beliefs they represent." This detailed and vital description of a senior officer on board the *Enterprise* is a far cry from the state of the character four years earlier, when she was almost written off the show.

During the hiatus between the fifth and sixth seasons of *Star Trek: The Next Generation*, Sirtis and her boyfriend of three years, Michael Lamper, were married. Their relationship had been a tempestuous one for quite some time. Admitting that she may not be the easiest person to live with, Sirtis attributed much of their difficulty at the time to her moodiness.

She was introduced to Lamper when he came to dinner with her good friend Ann Turkel, of the rock band Turk. "He never left," Sirtis said. As she had previously been in a long, committed relationship that ended on a bad note, Sirtis felt it was important to show Lamper, who had been married before, that her feelings for him were serious. She did not want a repeat of her previous romantic experience, and was dedicated to exploring a deep, emotional commitment with Lamper that would stand the test of time. In her previous relationship, Sirtis' ex-boyfriend (whom she refers to as Peter "May-He-Rot-In-Hell") sold an exclusive story to the London tabloid *News of the World* in which he refers to her role on *Star Trek* thus: "I hope she's playing a Klingon, because that's what she is, a Kling-on." However, Sirtis was quick to point out that what the tabloid press published was nothing but sour grapes, as it was *she* who broke off the relationship with *him*.

The wedding between Sirtis and Lamper on June 21, 1992, was fraught with disaster. Reportedly, the wedding photographer dropped the camera, ruining an entire role of film. Sirtis' seven-foot-long wedding train got caught in the lobby doors. The best man forgot the rings and had to race to the rear of the church to retrieve them. The flower girl, who was supposed to gracefully toss flower petals as she walked down the aisle, instead raced down the aisle, ran in circles around the altar, and screamed during the ceremony. Also, friend and castmate Whoopi Goldberg, who was to participate in the ceremony, had to cancel at the last minute due to her filming schedule on the movie *Made in America*. (However, Patrick Stewart, LeVar Burton, Michael Dorn, and Brent Spiner were all in attendance and served as ushers and groomsmen. Gates McFadden, Majel Barrett Roddenberry, and others from *The Next Generation* family were also there.) Sirtis was saddened by her friend's cancellation and overwhelmed by the problems that plagued the day, but has still referred to it as the happiest day of both her and her husband's lives.

The couple honeymooned in Cabo San Lucas. Lamper, an avid surfer, tried twice to teach Sirtis. Both times she ended up

". . . on the beach, completely covered in sand, with my bikini around my ankles."

Reflecting upon married life, Sirtis is very happy and content. Three years into the marriage, Sirtis was quoted as saying, "As soon as I was married I felt different. Probably because of my insecurities I felt the fact that he married me meant that he really must love me. I think I'm a great wife. I do all the cooking and I suppose I spoil Michael. I know it sounds terribly Victorian but I think that one of the ways of showing Michael how much he means to me is by making nice meals for him and being there for him. I'm comfortable with that because I'm a nurturing kind of person."

And as for the future? "As far as children go, my feeling is that if it happens, it happens, and if it doesn't, it doesn't. And both scenarios are okay. My biological alarm clock is not ringing. If we did have a child, either my husband or myself would stay at home. I feel that if you bring a child into the world it should be your first priority. Otherwise, don't have it."

Now Sirtis and Lamper are what she describes as a "Hollywood couple." They ride their Harley-Davidson motorcycles and take equal delight in listening to Bon Jovi (Jon Bon-Jovi was "her heartthrob") and the *Les Miserables* soundtrack.

Sixth-season episodes of *Star Trek: The Next Generation* fulfilled much of the richness that Sirtis had brought to the role, as well as much of the character development that the writers, directors, and producers had built into Troi over the course of five seasons. In "Man of the People," Troi ages rapidly following the sudden death of a visiting mediator's mother. Although the episode itself was not notable—except in that it was rushed into production due to delays in filming "Relics" (with James Doohan)—Sirtis had some excellent "scenery-chewing" moments in a performance that Nemecek quotes producers Michael Piller and Ron Moore praising as "sexy and scary." Later this season, "Chain of Command, Part I" began an event that many fans, and Sirtis herself, cheered. Following replacement-captain Jellico's order, Counselor Troi reverted to wearing standard Starfleet-issue uniforms when on duty, a change that remained in effect during the rest of the series.

Off camera, for the filming of "Man of the People" Sirtis had to have her face waxed to take care of a bit of "peach fuzz."

Consequently, the heavy makeup she wore for this episode burned her face and she was in agony for two days.

Season six's "Face of the Enemy" is the episode Sirtis points to as her all-time favorite episode of *Star Trek: The Next Generation.* "It was not a 'girlie' episode. Any of the crew could have been transformed into a Romulan. Troi was chosen because she was an empath, not because she was female." *The Hunt for Red October*–style premise of espionage, danger, and intrigue featured in "Face of the Enemy" had originally been proposed as a story line revolving around Dr. Crusher, and actually evolved in meetings with the writers once they realized that the story worked better with Sirtis' empathic character in the lead role. Sirtis noted with some pleasure that this is the first episode in her recollection in which Troi got angry. In a sillier moment, she revealed that after the long days of filming on the set of Romulus, the Romulan homeworld, she had renamed it the bad hair/bad clothes planet.

By the sixth season of filming, the *Star Trek: The Next Generation* cast was known as one of the most comfortable, friendly, and lively on television. Practical jokes on the set were the rule, not the exception. During the filming day, Sirtis would often leave her beloved toy Yorkshire terrier, Skillagi ("little dog" in Greek), in her trailer. As she related on *The Joan Rivers Show,* the cast loved to play jokes with her little dog, which Michael Dorn called a "hairy cockroach." Once when she left the dog with Brent Spiner while she was off shooting a scene, she came back to the trailer to find Spiner stuffing her Skillagi into the microwave oven. Another time, when Spiner had the dog, he told Jonathan Frakes to "take it long," and mocked a long football pass. However, not all the cast members were particularly mean regarding Sirtis' pet. Patrick Stewart was very fond of Skillagi, and spoke to him in his rarely used native Yorkshire accent. Joan Rivers was particularly sympathetic to Sirtis' stories, as she owns the same breed of dog, the famous-in-his-own-right Spike. Once Rivers realized she and Sirtis shared an affection for the same breed, the subject of discussion never left their dogs.

Despite all of the teasing Skillagi took from her castmates, Sirtis was a bit miffed that the *Star Trek* producers kept passing her up whenever they used a dog on the show, and that they did not want to use either of her two cats for Spot. However, Skillagi does

have his own place in *Next Generation* history. He became terribly
confused during the filming of the seventh-season episode "Sub
Rosa," in which a lot of live plants and shrubbery were used to dec-
orate the cemetery scenes featuring Gates McFadden. Skillagi
"christened" each shrub, and then defecated right where
McFadden was to stand during the filming of the scene. Sirtis left
Skillagi in her trailer during most of the subsequent weeks.

During filming in the sixth season, Sirtis had the ubiquitous
line, "Captain, he's hiding something." On one occasion, Stewart
looked at her and blurted, "We know that, you stupid cow! You waste
of space!" Then the strong fearless captain ran and hid behind Michael
Dorn. Sirtis could only look up at Stewart and exclaim, "Well, excuse
me, Your Majesty! I don't write the lines, I just say them!"

As relationships progressed among the cast, it should be
noted that Sirtis and costar Jonathan Frakes had always been very
close to Gene Roddenberry. Following Roddenberry's death, Sirtis
began regularly having dinner with his widow, and her television
mother, Majel Barrett. They remain close today, and Sirtis has commented that Barrett is like a substitute mother to her, as she doesn't
see nearly enough of her real mother back in London.

Star Trek: The Next Generation's seventh season resolved
many of the story arcs that had been introduced over the years. In
Data's dream sequence in the episode "Phantasms," Troi appeared
as a cake. Sirtis had to play her scene stuffed in a box that was worse
than uncomfortable. "If you put a prisoner of war in there you'd be
put on trial for war crimes. Marina was a trooper about it," stated
visual effects coordinator Dan Curry. This scene also featured a
controversial sequence where Data stabs Troi, a scene that writer
Brannon Braga described as "a very shocking moment, very dis-
turbing." In the very next episode, "Dark Page," Sirtis performed her
own stunts, notably the "jump into space" shot, which was created
by having the actress leap off a large blue-screened platform onto air
mattresses.

Season seven's "Parallels" featured the first kiss between
Troi and Worf. ("I think the writers had seen one too many episodes
of *Beauty and the Beast*," she said.) During the rehearsals for the
kissing scene, Sirtis and Dorn did not actually kiss, they merely said,
"Okay, then we kiss." Finally, during the filming of the scene, they

actually kissed. Dorn stopped acting after the kiss and said, "Something seems wrong, let's do another take." After another take, Dorn stopped again and said, "No, it still doesn't seem right. Let's do it again." They went through this routine about four times until Sirtis finally realized what Dorn was up to. On the final shot for the scene, Dorn made growling noises in Sirtis' ear. When asked if it was Worf or Dorn doing the growling, the actor just smiled and walked away.

REFLECTIVE AND SAD . . . AND A MOVIE CAREER

The final episode of *Star Trek: The Next Generation*, the two-hour "All Good Things . . . ," left Marina Sirtis in a state of sad disbelief that the series was over. On the set, she cried and was angry: angry at Paramount for canceling the hit series for no apparent reason; and angry at her castmates, who did not seem to be as upset as she over the cancellation. "I am really quite hurt that they are not going to miss me as much as I am going to miss them. These people around here and my husband are all I have in this country. Every time I think about it I start crying."

However, with the prospect of a movie career (the filming of *Star Trek: Generations* was only days away), Sirtis quickly became reflective. At a convention right after the filming of "All Good Things . . . ," Sirtis told the crowded audience of fans, "You have to believe me when I tell you these have been the happiest seven years of my life. Everything I have, everything I own, I owe to you, the fans. . . . I'm trying to get through this without crying."

On the script for "All Good Things . . . ," and particularly regarding the final scene around the poker table, Sirtis finally expressed a concern that she had hid for years. In a newspaper interview, Sirtis said that she never understood how the writers allowed her character to play poker. "How stupid can they be? It's like, I'd wait until a really good hand came up and say, 'No, Geordi, honey, I can't tell if you're bluffing.'"

Right after the final episode was shot, Sirtis had her long hair—so recognizable as Counselor Troi's—cut. "It was a symbolic move when the series was canceled. I thought, 'Let's leave that character in space.'" She wore a wig throughout the first film featuring *The Next Generation* cast.

In a very candid 1994 discussion published after *Star Trek: The Next Generation* ended its seven-year run, Sirtis admitted to a very difficult time during the early period of her career. "I used to have an eating disorder. I can't diet, because it sets the madness off again. As soon as I start counting calories, I start becoming obsessive about it. So I don't count calories, nor do I weigh myself. I haven't weighed myself in years." She goes on to say that she has an "anorexic personality," and was still suffering the effects of her disorder— starving and binging—when she began working on *Star Trek: The Next Generation*. She maintains her figure by grinding workouts and states that she can now eat "anything, everything. . . . Food isn't the enemy anymore." Sirtis' recovery from this problem is one that may be looked upon by young people as a heroic victory worthy of emulation, but she warns, "If one has an eating disorder, one has to treat it the way a recovering alcoholic treats alcoholism. You take it one day at a time."

As an adult, Sirtis continues to be insecure regarding her body image. "I still think of myself as an ugly duckling," she told the *Daily Mail* in 1995. "I feel okay when I'm dressed up, but when I'm not wearing any makeup and schlepping around in jeans and a T-shirt I don't feel particularly attractive. I don't have enough hair, my nose is too big, and my body always needs working on—my waist is too thick. I'm 5'3" tall and I would like to be three or four inches taller. . . . I think I've never had a good body image because I grew up in an era when if you didn't look like Twiggy there was something wrong with you, and God forbid that we had breasts!"

Three days after shooting had wrapped on "All Good Things . . . ," Sirtis began filming her scenes for the big-screen *Star Trek: Generations*. Initially, she almost turned down participating in the film because her role was so minuscule. She ultimately relented, however, and hoped for increased roles in the future movies starring *The Next Generation* cast. "I was excited about becoming this movie person," Sirtis reflected. "There's a kind of hierarchy in Hollywood and movies are at the top of the ladder. . . . We had more time, bigger trailers, all the frills. We came to this film after working seven years together and so things were very comfortable and there were no surprises."

The most memorable scene in *Generations* for Sirtis was on the sailing ship, when the holo-simulation is interrupted after

Captain Picard is informed that his brother and nephew have been killed. Troi had to provide emotional support for her distraught captain in a scene that was hailed by critics as powerful. "Patrick and I have worked together for seven years and so we have a really good relationship. Actually when we finished the scene Patrick was really sweet. He came up and thanked me. He felt confident enough and trusted me enough to let go like that, and he felt that he couldn't have played it with any other person. I take that as a huge compliment from Patrick Stewart."

Of course, fans most remember Sirtis' role in *Generations* as being the person who crashed the *Enterprise*. The scene was jinxed from the start: Sirtis' chair caught on fire due to an on-set special effects explosion and she quite unintentionally sat on burning embers. The butt of many jokes, Sirtis was not pleased about her role in crashing the Federation's flagship. "A teenager flew the *Enterprise*—no problems. A blind man flew the *Enterprise*—no problems. An android and various ensigns flew the *Enterprise*—no problems. Troi finally gets a chance to fly the *Enterprise*, so what happens—she crashes and destroys the ship!" Patrick Stewart has commented, "That woman shall never drive my ship again." For advice on how to fly the ship and what buttons to press—something she had never done over the course of seven seasons—she asked Brent Spiner. He replied, "Marina, you're not playing the piano. You don't have to press a million buttons."

Sirtis kept busy between the filming of the first and second *Next Generation* movies. She lent her voice to the popular *Gargoyles* animated series and performed Sabine in the audio version of Nick Bantock's best-seller *Griffin and Sabine: An Extraordinary Correspondence*. She filmed a television pilot with Michael Dorn and hopes to launch a stage production of *Othello* with him. Sirtis' first experience on the American stage, the Hartford Stage production of Joe Orton's *Loot*, won her the previously noted rave reviews from both the local press and the national media (such as *The New York Times*). She also completed filming the feature-length psychological thriller *The Bet*, with Ann Turkel, her friend and former bandmate of her husband.

Sirtis was much more pleased with the size of her role in *Star Trek: First Contact* than that in *Star Trek: Generations*. "I never thought I'd hear the words coming out of my mouth that 'Deanna Troi is the comic relief in a Star Trek movie'—and I'm thrilled!" she exclaimed in a television interview. Sirtis feels that the tremendous success the film has enjoyed is something of a vindication. The cast knew that some critics questioned whether The Next Generation would successfully translate to feature films, and the disappointing showing of Star Trek: Generations did little to alleviate those reservations. "We've always kind of had the feeling that, yeah, they were successful on TV, but they can't cut the mustard on the big screen."

On one of the first days of filming on the bridge of the new Enterprise-E, Sirtis turned to Patrick Stewart and exclaimed, "It's like we were never gone. The bridge is different, but we pick up where we left off." Her role in First Contact was highlighted by probably the most comic scene in the film, in which she gets drunk with James "Zefram Cochrane" Cromwell. Sirtis related that she regained her confidence in performing comedy after performing on stage in Loot. "I had tried to make Troi funny in the past and it never worked. I used to think that Troi couldn't be funny but I realized I had just sort of lost my timing. I had a scene in which we see a side of Troi we've never seen before. She's drunk and quite belligerent about it."

Sirtis hopes for a future with The Next Generation cast on the big screen. "We have two shows [Voyager and Deep Space Nine] snapping at our heels. There's a whole slew of actors anxious to get on the big screen. I'll be happy if we do another one. I'll be very happy," she stated.

For future projects out of her Starfleet uniform, Sirtis' dream is to work with Robert De Niro. She'd also like to work with "the brilliant" David Caruso. "I've told my agent to put me up for anything he's doing. I think he's a really wonderful actor." She takes her future film career seriously, and claims she has a place already set aside on the mantel for "the Oscar Award I'm going to win someday." While she considers the trajectory of her professional career, she is content taking care of her home, her husband, Skillagi, and her cats. (Their number has swelled to five: Knack, Little Dee, Sluggo, Tigger, and Data, who received his name in honor of his yellow eyes.)

"If I live to be one hundred years old, to certain people on some level I will always be Deanna. And that's not something I'm in any way ashamed of. All of us on the show worked very hard. We were young, and we knew we would have to work again after it was over. We knew it behooved us to make it the best it could be, and we did. It's just that I didn't become an actor to play one role."

Perhaps the prospects for Sirtis' future career can be best summed up by a line she spoke, as Troi, on the sound effects track of the most popular pinball machine of the early 1990s. After players lose their last ball and are about to walk away from the machine dejected, they hear the familiar voice of Counselor Troi intone, "I believe you want to continue." Undoubtedly, given her drive to succeed and her unbridled energy, unrivaled enthusiasm, and tremendous talent, Marina Sirtis will indeed continue.

MARINA SIRTIS

Counselor Deanna Troi

STAGE:
Hamlet
The Rocky Horror Picture Show
Loot ('96)

TELEVISION:
The Thief of Baghdad ('78)
Raffles ('80)
The Adventures of Sherlock
  Holmes ('81)
Call Me Mister ('82)
Masterpiece Theatre ('84)
Hazel ('85)
Hunter ('86)
Star Trek: The Next Generation
  ('87–'94)

Reading Rainbow ('88)
Gargoyles ('94)
Heaven Help Us ('94)
Science Fiction: A Journey into
  the Unknown ('94)
Minder ('96)

FILM:
The Wicked Lady ('83)
Blind Date ('84)
Death Wish III ('85)
One Last Chance ('90)
Waxwork II: Lost in Time ('92)
Star Trek: Generations ('94)
Star Trek: First Contact ('96)
Gadget Man ('97)

CHAPTER 7

BRENT SPINER

Handy Android, Versatile Actor

"I don't understand why anyone would build an android that resembles a middle-aged Jewish man."
—BRENT SPINER, QUOTED AT A NEW YORK CITY STAR TREK CONVENTION

Brent Jay Spiner Mintz has led the life of a successful Broadway stage actor, popular television star, "hot" feature-film commodity, and even recording artist. Emerging from the ensemble cast of *Star Trek: The Next Generation* as both a fan and a critical favorite, Spiner molded a role that other actors may have found confining. He turned what easily could have been an emotionless and humorless machine into one exuding innocent humor, warmth, and ironic introspection. Data reflects on life's moral dilemmas and the nature of humanity while never ceasing to ask the questions that we pose to ourselves every day. He is not Spock. Nor is he merely a superstrong, supersmart accessory, a computer with a grip. His continual quest to achieve what everyone around him takes for granted is one of the defining successes of *The Next Generation*, and one of the reasons the program is so endearing. In fact, the character is in many ways the most human on the show.

GO OUT AND PLAY? NOPE, THREE MOVIES A DAY

Born in Houston, Texas, on February 2, 1949, Brent Spiner is the younger of two brothers. Brent and his brother, Ron (two years older), were raised exclusively for several years by their mother, Sylvia. (His father, Jack, a furniture store owner, died of kidney failure at the age of twenty-nine when Brent was but a ten-month-old infant.) Sylvia took full control of the furniture store, as well as of her two boys' upbringing. "She was phenomenal," Brent told Tom Snyder. "She played ball with us, and even put on boxing gloves. I decked her a couple of times, [but she] could have taken me if she'd wanted to."

When Brent was six, Sylvia married Sol Mintz, a salesman and former record store owner. Their seven-year marriage was "unhappy for everyone," Spiner recalls, since Mintz ran the household "like a military school." However, Mintz left two lasting impressions upon young Brent. The first was the voluminous pop music collection he brought into the household, forcing Brent to listen every night ("whether we wanted to or not") to the strains of Frank Sinatra, Judy Garland, Nat "King" Cole, Rosemary Clooney, and others. This musical feast led him to love and appreciate these pop standards, and even resulted in his recording his own album of pop tunes in 1991. Second, Sol Mintz, now deceased, left Spiner his name. Although legally still Brent Jay Spiner Mintz, Spiner has dropped Mintz for his life on stage and in front of the camera.

Spiner claims that from the time he was eleven years old he watched as many as three movies a day. "At fifteen I was already a major film buff. I could quote lines from movies, tell you who was in it and in what year it was made. I always fantasized about being an actor." His favorite film was *The Searchers*, starring John Wayne, though he watched every movie, in every genre, that he had access to, "except *The African Queen*, which I'm saving for my deathbed." Not content to lose himself solely in the exploits of screen actors, Spiner was also an avid reader of science fiction, engrossing himself in stories by the likes of H. G. Wells, Jules Verne, Ray Bradbury, and Isaac Asimov. In the sixth grade, when he was twelve years old, Spiner wrote his first play.

Entranced by both television and the cinema, Spiner fell particularly hard for comedy. He spent countless hours watching, studying, and memorizing the routines of Stan Laurel, Buster Keaton, Jack Benny, Jerry Lewis, Dick Van Dyke, and Lucille Ball. To this day, his second favorite television program remains *I Love Lucy* (his first is *Candid Camera*). "Is there a sitcom that has been done since *I Love Lucy* that is better?" he asks. "It's not until about the eleventh viewing that you can stop watching Lucy and start focusing on Desi. He's one of my favorite actors of all time. He's brilliant. When I watch sitcoms today, I find myself going, 'Oh, yeah, Lucy did that,' or 'Oh, yeah, Lucy and Desi did such and such.' I think my impetus for being an actor began somewhere in the middle of the *Lucy* episode in Hollywood with

William Holden. I watched that and said to my mother, 'I gotta do that one day.'"

As a child, he and his older brother received a Dean Martin and Jerry Lewis puppet set with "a little red record" containing a comedy routine as a gift from their grandparents. The brothers spent hours acting out the routines contained on the record. Calling Jerry Lewis "a god," he claimed that he took "many a fall down the stairs at great injury just to be like Jerry." To this day Spiner treats Labor Day and the annual telecast of the *Jerry Lewis Muscular Dystrophy Association Telethon* as a "religious holiday." Spiner often watches the telethon with good friend and Lewis-ophile Mark "Luke Skywalker" Hamill, who has an extensive collection of Jerry Lewis memorabilia. In 1992, while watching the telethon, Hamill showed Spiner his most recent acquisition—Lewis and Martin puppets and "a little red record." That day at Mark Hamill's home, Spiner remembered every joke on the album.

Spiner grew up without the benefit of a strong and support-ive father figure in the household, and suffered the squabbles and torture that a younger sibling often endures at the hands of an older one. For his portrayal of Lore, Data's evil twin on *Star Trek: The Next Generation,* Spiner stated that his "initial impulse was to call upon the anger I once had toward my older brother, Ron. We've become very close, [but once] Ron had me convinced we'd had a middle brother he'd done away with. I was about five and Ron was about seven. My mother had just pulled out of the driveway to go somewhere, and he was telling me this story—with butcher knife in hand—about this older brother in a cave somewhere with a knife in his back. I swear my mother heard me screaming ten miles away in her car."

However, Spiner was and remains close to his extended family. His grandfather once owned Frosty Root Beer; his uncle Dr. Nathan Cottler taught him, Ron, and his cousins pre-med courses every other Sunday while Spiner was still in junior high school; and his aunt Beverly is one of alter-ego Data's biggest fans.

Thinking medicine might be a good career choice for young Brent, as he knew "everything there was to know about the human body," his uncle landed him a job as an orderly at St. Luke's Hospital in Houston when Brent was sixteen. Spiner worked in the recovery room under the noted heart surgeon Michael DeBakey.

Upon putting on the green scrubs for the first time and seeing himself in the mirror, he blurted, "Hey Lady!" (a famous line from Jerry Lewis' *The Disorderly Orderly*). When a severely ill patient woke from his unconscious state and looked up at Spiner to ask, "Am I dead?" Brent replied, "Not yet." This was the first serious black mark on Spiner's short-lived medical career. Not long afterward, he was in the emergency room taking the temperature of another unconscious patient. The patient woke up and rolled onto his back before Spiner could stop him. The rectal thermometer broke, and Spiner was caught red-handed removing the broken bits of glass from the unfortunate patient's backside. Teenage Spiner was fired from the hospital that day.

While at Houston's Bellaire High School, from which he graduated in 1967, Spiner studied drama under renowned teacher and drama coach Cecil Pickett—"He was Mr. Chips"—along with classmates Dennis and Randy Quaid, Robert Wuhl, Cindy Pickett, and New Age guru Marianne Williamson (among others who later found success and fame). "I later went to the Lee Strasberg School in New York, but I know more fine actors, directors, and writers from high school classes than I do from that professional acting class." Pickett left Bellaire in 1968 to teach first at Houston Baptist University then at the University of Houston, and Spiner followed. A few credits short of a degree, four years later Spiner left the Univesity of Houston to pursue acting full time, and ultimately completed his formal education at Trinity College and Strasberg in New York. His college years offered Spiner his only chance to play a variety of Shakespeare roles, his favorite being Shylock from *The Merchant of Venice*.

At nineteen years old, while still in school, Spiner got his "first real job," at the Houston Music Theatre. At this time he also got his actor's equity card, allowing him to work in most productions. With him while he applied for his card was friend and fellow Houstonian Charlie Robinson, with whom he would later work in six episodes of the network comedy *Night Court*.

Spiner spent 1973 performing in regional theater in places as diverse as Fort Wayne and Chicago, in plays that included *Cabaret*; *Promises, Promises*; and "one of the worst plays ever written," *The Portable Pioneer and Prairie Show*. He moved to New York

City in 1974 and supported himself for the first six months by driving a taxicab. "In those days, if you ever wanted to be on Broadway, you went to New York, not Hollywood," Spiner explained, discussing the recent phenomenon of big-name Hollywood stars headlining the marquees of Broadway. Spiner would spend over a decade performing on and off Broadway in plays and musicals, and appearing in New York–based films (even headlining an obscure one), before moving to Hollywood and pursuing his future on the small screen.

While renting a small apartment in New York City on Eightieth Street between Amsterdam and Broadway, Spiner landed his first two New York stage roles in the off-Broadway productions *Polly* and *The Crazy Locomotive*. Shortly thereafter, he was praised by *New York Times* drama critic Clive Barnes as "admirably nutty" for his 1975 role in *The Family*. In 1976 he played an interpreter, a mime, a dragon, a giant, a henchman, and a Chinese girl—all in one production: *Marco Polo*. Many more plays followed, including *Table Settings*, *A History of American Film*, *Leave It to Beaver Is Dead*, and a two-man production of *Émigrés*, on which *New York Times* critic Mel Gussow commented, "Spiner enlivens his performance with a whiplash nervous energy and physical limberness. Scarcely missing a beat, he swerves from good fellowship to wounding abrasiveness. He makes his character unpredictable."

Most notably during his years on the New York stage, Spiner landed roles in Joseph Papp's 1980 production of Chekhov's *The Seagull* (which also starred a young Christopher Walken) and the original 1983 production of *Sunday in the Park with George*. His role in *The Seagull*, that of suicidal playwright Konstantin Treplev, was "the one that finally pushed me over into the serious actor category." He stated in 1996, "I played Konstantin. I remember the famous [theater critic] John Simon saying that I was too comically homely, even for that part. It didn't hurt my feelings because if John Simon didn't say something nasty about me, I wouldn't really be in the theater."

Unfortunately, Spiner injured his back during the opening night of the production and was out of commission (and the show) for several weeks. The injury persists to this day, most recently flaring up while Spiner was filming the fifth-season *Star Trek: The Next Generation* episode, "Silicon Avatar."

Spiner was with the production of *Sunday in the Park with George* from the beginning of its run, singing with original cast members Kelsey Grammer and Mary Elizabeth Mastrantonio when the show was presented as part of the Playwrights Horizon Workshop. He remained with the show and its Pulitzer Prize–winning Broadway cast, which starred Mandy Patinkin and Bernadette Peters, and stayed through the final version, featuring Charles Kimbrough (of *Murphy Brown*).

Off stage but in front of the camera, Spiner was cast in the television movie *The Dain Curse* (1978) and in Woody Allen's 1980 autobiographical feature *Stardust Memories*. In 1981, Spiner was chosen for the starring role in the low-budget comedy *Rent Control*. Veteran Italian film director Gian Polidoro wrote the screenplay and wanted to prove he could make an American comedy.

The plot revolved around small-time writer Leonard Junger (Spiner) who is desperately seeking a $400-a-month two-bedroom apartment in New York City to lure his departed wife and child back to the city. Spiner relates that director Polidoro had seen him in a couple of plays and had sent him the script. "I thought it was horrible. I begged him to let me do it," was Spiner's reaction, not an untypical one from a struggling actor looking to make it big. And though the budget on *Rent Control* was all of $100,000, Spiner jokes, "To the director's credit, it looked like a $200,000 movie. The filming of the movie was better than the movie itself. We shot it in seven weeks in the streets of New York, with no permits. We'd grab a shot and then run because we were doing everything illegally."

The film opened locally in art-house theaters to mixed reviews. "The model for *Rent Control* . . . is a certain type of Woody Allen comedy," wrote *Village Voice* reviewer Michael Musto. "Not since *Stardust Memories* has there been such a distasteful parade of freaks, caricatures, and trolls (but here they're in leading roles, and are supposed to be sympathetic)." On Spiner's performance, Musto wrote that he was "winningly ordinary," which in context was a compliment. *The New York Times* reviewer Vincent Canby also praised Spiner's acting.

Spiner's two final roles on the Broadway stage before relocating permanently to Hollywood were notable, albeit for distinctly different reasons. He was cast as Aramis, one of the Three Musketeers in the 1984 musical of the same name, but the show was doomed from the start. Spiner "knew we were in trouble from day one," when the director explained his concept for the show was to combine the seventeenth-century story with the year the play was written (1927) and the year of the production (1984). Spiner thought to himself, "We're dead. It's over." Despite the death of the producer on the second day of rehearsal, his son decided to carry on the production without him. The play closed after one week, eight performances, losing a record $12 million. *The New York Times* theater critic Frank Rich called the performances "professional," but stated that the production made the three main characters "often seem like interchangeable stand-ins for the Three Stooges." Spiner has called it "maybe the worst Broadway show of all time."

Spiner relocated to Hollywood in 1985 ("I had been a serious actor long enough, it was time to make a living"), and immediately took the stage as Seymour in the 1985 Westside Playhouse production of *Little Shop of Horrors*. A slew of television guest appearances throughout 1985 and 1986 followed, including roles on the popular dramas *Hill Street Blues*, *Hunter*, and *Paper Chase*, and in the television movies *Manhunt for Claude Dallas* and *Robert Kennedy and His Times* (in which he portrayed Allard Lowenstein, a political supporter of the senator during his presidential campaign). Despite the failure of *The Three Musketeers* a year earlier on Broadway, Spiner briefly returned to New York to take on the costarring role of The Duke in *Big River*, an enormously successful Broadway musical. He replaced another actor, who had originated the role of The Duke to critical acclaim, Rene Auberjonois (who years later would be cast as Odo on *Star Trek: Deep Space Nine*).

In 1987, Spiner solidified his status as a television actor. He was cast in an episode of *Cheers*, and had some significant scenes in the television film *Family Sins*. He agreed to appear in a recurring role in the situation comedy *Mama's Family* (the *Carol Burnett Show* spinoff starring Vicki Lawrence) as long as he was promised a larger role: West Virginian hillbilly Bob Wheeler on *Night Court*. The *Night Court* producers enjoyed his performance and, although the role was originally slated for only a one-shot appearance, brought him back when the governor of West Virginia complained to the network regarding its portrayal of "hicks." Wheeler was reintroduced as an immigrant from Yugoslavia who purchased the courthouse snack bar with his wife (played by Annie O'Donnell). Spiner as Wheeler appeared on a total of six episodes and was intended to be written in as a regular character for the 1987–88 season, but Spiner landed a better role: one that would have him hurtling through space and capturing millions of viewers' hearts.

A STREAM OF DATA

Star Trek II, the aborted 1979 sequel series to the original *Star Trek*, featured as one of its main characters a young Vulcan lieutenant commander named Xon. *The Questor Tapes*, a 1974 television pilot penned by Roddenberry (though never picked up as a series), featured Questor, a brilliant and strong yet innocent and childlike android seeking his creator. Combining the strengths of each of these characters, Roddenberry developed the role of Data.

In approaching the role, Spiner looked no farther than the script to the pilot episode of *Star Trek: The Next Generation*, "Encounter at Farpoint." "It's really quite simple. In the pilot episode, Commander Riker calls me Pinocchio. That was the jumping-off point for the character. I was looking for a hook of something to hang the character on. It seems to me that Pinocchio was as clear a call as I could have gotten. So it was basically given to me as a gift from [writer and producer] Gene Roddenberry."

Spiner had six auditions before finally landing the role of Data (briefly, Patrick Stewart was penciled into it, and Eric "The Traveler" Menyuk was also seriously considered). However, Spiner's *Star Trek* audition experience paled before the dozens of makeup tests. He was forced to endure three grueling days before the camera in every shade of makeup. Spiner wanted to play the role "straight" (no colored makeup) but executive producer Roddenberry insisted that Data be visually unique and "he's already used ears." Skin colors tested included bubble-gum pink, green, blue, and virtually every metallic shade. Ultimately, the decision was down to between battleship gray and the pale gold/yellow that eventually won out. Though Roddenberry liked the gray tone, producer Rick Berman and makeup designer Michael Westmore preferred the golden yellowish skin color.

The application of the colored makeup, gold contact lenses, gold powder, and dyed black hair with a penciled-in hairline required Spiner to be "in at 5:45 A.M., out of makeup one hour, fifteen minutes later." The contact lenses were the worst part of the costume for Spiner. He occasionally had difficulty getting the lenses out, and complained, "It took about a year to get used to the contacts—for a long time, it felt like I had Elvira's fingernails in my eyes." In discussing the makeup appearance with producer Roddenberry, Spiner recalls the conversation they had. "'Look, don't you think by the twenty-fourth century, they would have figured out how to make skin? If they can make my face move and my body move and my brain work, can't they do skin?' Roddenberry's reply was, 'What makes you think what you have is not better than skin?' which is the way Gene thinks. And it's hard to argue with, you know?" As for Data's slightly stilted speech patterns, Spiner explained that just wearing the uncomfortable contact lenses "gives me the impulse to use no contractions as I talk."

Spiner used a kerosene-based cleanser to remove the extensive makeup. "I must swallow a gallon of kerosene a week. One day I suppose they'll find all my organs have been pickled."

The respect the core cast of *Star Trek: The Next Generation* felt for one another was always genuine, but that first season, perhaps no single actor was hailed by his castmates quite like Brent Spiner was. His range of acting talent, honed from years on Broadway and in a wide variety of television roles, made his experience invaluable among the troupe, many of whom possessed significantly less experience than he did. One example of the admiration the cast held for Spiner is evident in the acting technique they came to call "Spining." Simply, Spining is the act of acting, or reacting, to an event that is not really there. The center of the view-screen on the *Enterprise* bridge, for example, is nothing more than an X made of masking tape, often with spectators or crew visible through the other side. Nonetheless, Spiner modestly explained the bridge scenarios the actors would find themselves in before the special effects were put in place (in postproduction). "We talk to the X, the X talks to us. We are afraid of the X, the X is afraid of us. We negotiate with the X, the X negotiates with us."

The most significant episode for Spiner in *Star Trek: The Next Generation*'s first season was "Datalore." This episode, which featured Data's evil brother, Lore, and the *Enterprise* being threatened by the appearance of the Crystalline Entity, showcased Spiner in the dual role of Data and Lore. Larry Nemecek notes that in its original conception, Lore was originally a non-look-alike love interest for Data. However, extensive rewrites and Spiner's suggestion of the "evil twin" concept molded the episode into one of the highlights of the first season and introduced a nemesis who would plague the *Enterprise* many times to come. Patrick Stewart commented on "Datalore," "[Brent] was so good that I was excited to be watching it. You know, here's a man that I've worked with for eight or nine months who continues to go on impressing and surprising me."

Also during the first season, the episode "The Big Goodbye" allowed Spiner to showcase his comedic talents in one of his first extended holodeck sequences. In an homage to the original *Trek*, the explanation of Data's skin color ("he's from South America") is reminiscent of the famous "Chinese rice picker" line explaining Spock's ears in "City on the Edge of Forever."

After only a short period of time filming *The Next Generation*, the cast felt so comfortable with one another that their antics on the set and their undisciplined behavior were extreme enough to cause one first-season director to walk off. In "The Battle," as Data is exploring the darkened corridors of the starship *Stargazer*, Spiner shined his light across the ship's dedication plaque and stammered in his best Jimmy "It's a Wonderful Life" Stewart voice, "For God's sake, Mary, they built this thing in Bedford Falls." Late the first season, during the filming of Tasha Yar's holographic farewell message in "Skin of Evil," Patrick Stewart was dancing around the green hills, twirling his arms and singing. Spiner has said that he was enjoying himself so much that he didn't want to leave, and it took LeVar Burton to come onto the set and drag him off with a long hooked pole.

Whoopi Goldberg joined *The Next Generation* cast on a recurring basis at the beginning of the second season, and Spiner insightfully acknowledged the impact her arrival had. "I think Whoopi was instrumental in the success of the show even though she wasn't there that often. They built the set of Ten-Forward [the

Enterprise's bar and off-duty lounge] especially for her. I think she validated the show for everybody when she said she wanted to be on it." As for his own character, it "will evolve during the course of the show. If we run six years, by the end of the six years I will be almost human. I think the difference between me and everyone else will be negligible by the end of six years except that I've got superhuman strength. But in terms of my behavior, I'm assimilating human behavior right now."

Five episodes of *The Next Generation's* second season featured Spiner's Data in significant story lines, including three episodes filmed and aired back to back in December 1988 and January 1989—a scheduling oddity. The first, "Elementary, Dear Data," explores Data's fascination with Sherlock Holmes, his apparent friction with Dr. Pulaski (meant to simulate the original *Trek's* McCoy-Spock friction), and his friendship with LaForge, while allowing Spiner to stretch his acting muscles on a period set resembling Victorian London. In the very next episode, "The Outrageous Okona," Data explores comedy and is coached in a holo-comedy club by a comic played by Joe Piscopo. Originally, Spiner idol Jerry Lewis was to play the part, but the plan was thwarted by a last-minute scheduling conflict. The episode that aired immediately following the Christmas holiday break was "The Schizoid Man," in which Dr. Noonien Soong's mentor falls ill and dies, but somehow transfers his consciousness into Data's android body and is reluctant to release control (Dr. Soong was Data's creator).

A month later, "The Measure of a Man" brought to trial Data's rights as a sentient being when a Starfleet commander, without the requisite knowledge to do so, attempts to gain permission to disassemble him to make duplicates. It is one of Spiner's favorite episodes, and he commented that it "is not just a great *Star Trek* episode, it's great television." For trivia buffs, in this episode Data's personnel file can be viewed, his full name being revealed as 'NFN NMI [No First Name, No Middle Initial] Data.' Toward the end of the season, in the episode "Pen Pals," Data admits to having been carrying on a pen-pal relationship with a lonely girl on a world with dangerous geological storms. Data and Captain Picard conclude that though they must offer assistance, Data's actions constitute a violation of the Prime Directive.

Often during the filming of an episode, members of the cast—especially Spiner and Michael Dorn—would try to make the actors laugh during the filming of a serious scene. They would often succeed, yet the other actors found it very frustrating when trying to turn the table on Spiner, who rarely broke out laughing. During a scene in the second-season episode "Contagion," Michael Dorn's Worf was supposed to carry a seriously damaged Data across the bridge into the turbolift, which he accomplished by hoisting him over his shoulder. While there, Spiner tried to make Dorn laugh by making strange gurgling sounds in his throat. After having to reshoot the scene several times because of Spiner's behavior (and, of course, Klingons are not supposed to laugh), Dorn decided to take revenge. During the final take Dorn marched across the set with Spiner flung over his shoulder. When he reached the turbolift, he turned and slammed Spiner's head into the doorjamb. The expression on Spiner's face never changed, however, and that take can actually be seen in the episode.

The second season of *The Next Generation* was a very full one that nicely fleshed out Data's character and endeared him to most of *Star Trek*'s loyal fans. The wide range of stories and plots offered Spiner opportunities to make the most of his role. At the end of the season he reflected, "I think Data's appeal is, number one, he's an accessible character. He doesn't possess any real negative human qualities. He's innocent, he's not egotistical, never mean or unpleasant. He's a very pure character. As the show goes on, he'll become less innocent and less sophisticated. He'll have more human traits, but he'll never really be human. That's another reason people identify with him: he's the outsider and wants to be part of everything that's going on. He's sort of the Greek chorus and watches humanity and comments on it. I think that's his real function on the show."

After two years, Spiner assured an interviewer that "the charm hasn't worn off doing *Star Trek*, even with doing the same character. You have different lines, different problems—particularly this character, which, so far, is open to limitless possibilities. Initially I thought it was going to be a trap [being] locked into a mechanical man. But it's been just the opposite. It's been the loosest character on the show in terms of what he can and cannot do."

And in terms of his extensive makeup, "I still have a degree of anonymity, though that's becoming less and less all the time. But that's also the appeal of Data. There's a mystery about the fact that he doesn't look ordinary. It's a benefit when there are eight people on a stage and one of them shines—well, that's who your eyes are going to go to!"

Though even in 1989, when the program was but two years old, Spiner admitted that he could not realistically play Data forever. "There's something really youthful about Data, and increasingly I'm becoming less and less so."

During the 1989 hiatus, longtime friend and former Bellaire High schoolmate Tommy Schlamme offered Spiner the opportunity to appear as Preacher Man in the film *Miss Firecracker*, starring Holly Hunter. Two years later, Schlamme again put Spiner to work during his vacation, casting him as a school-board member in the made-for-television movie *Crazy from the Heart*.

It should come as no surprise, given his upbringing and his love of classic television, that Spiner's favorite hobby is watching it. "I'll tell you the truth. When I'm not on TV, I'm watching it. I watch television. I love television. I don't care what anybody says— they all watch television. No one in North America does not watch television. If they tell you they don't, they're lying. Television is comforting. Particularly when you live alone. It gives you the illusion that you actually have friends and family, which I don't," he jokes. "Except for Tom Selleck; we're very close." On vacation in an expensive and exclusive resort in Bora Bora, Spiner checked out after one day. "They didn't have cable," he lamented.

Star Trek: The Next Generation's third season continued to offer Spiner opportunities to "flesh out" the nuances of Data's life and existence. Four episodes featured notable Data story lines. In "The Ensigns of Command," Data is sent on a mission to announce the evacuation of a colony that is being bathed in dangerous radiation.

Spiner realized during the filming of this episode the extent of his character's popularity and of the global impact of *Star Trek*. On the schedule of visitors to the set for this episode was a listing for "twenty Tibetan monks." They all thought it was a joke, until, during filming, Tibet's exiled Dalai Lama and his entourage of monks appeared. "My God, those really are monks!" Spiner remembers thinking. Not only were the monks big fans of the program, they adored Data in particular. They insisted on having a photo taken on the set, they in their robes and Spiner in his Data makeup and uniform. Spiner kept the monks company and befriended them, and he recalls, "When the bells rang out for 'quiet on the set,' these people did professional quiet."

In the third season's "Deja Q," Data is assigned to watch over a supposedly powerless Q and inflicts himself with a severe electrical shock to protect Q from the angry Calamarain. The episode concludes with a restored-to-power Q presenting Data with a special gift: a lesson in humanity in the form of a good laugh. "The Most Toys" pushed Data to the brink of murder in a well-received episode in which he is kidnapped to become part of a collection of galactic treasures and curiosities. After the actor who was originally signed to play the story's protagonist, collector Kivas Fajo, was hospitalized two days into filming, all previously shot footage was rendered unusable. A new Fajo (Saul Rubinek) was quickly cast and costumed, and the filming of his scenes, most of which were opposite Spiner, had to begin all over again.

"The Offspring" featured Data attempting to further his creator's work by fashioning a daughter, Lal. This episode, which marked Jonathan Frakes' directorial debut, was praised by critics and fans. It is also the single favorite of both Patrick Stewart and Jonathan Frakes. Spiner credits actress Hallie Todd as Lal. "Hallie was incredible. She's a fine actress," and in keeping with his knowledge of classic television minutiae, he added, "Did you know that her mother played the next door neighbor Millie Helper in the old *Dick Van Dyke* series?"

One of the most challenging things about portraying Data was his extensive vocabulary, which Spiner felt required memorization, since Data spoke without pauses. "Rarely on *Star Trek* did I have a clue what I was talking about. We had some really brilliant guys who were on the set all the time. [They] filled us all in on what we were actually talking about." Pronunciation was another matter entirely. "We just had one rule on the set, and that was basically whoever said a word first, that was the pronunciation. And we always hoped it wasn't Patrick [Stewart], because he pronounces words in such a bizarre way. I mean, the word 'temporarily' he says 'temp-ra-ly'—and swears that's correct."

During the hiatus between the third and fourth seasons, over the summer of 1990, Spiner recorded an album of pop standards. "I needed to do something over the hiatus and it seemed the most accessible thing to be doing in my own time." Called *Ol' Yellow Eyes Is Back*, and featuring Spiner made up as Data on the album cover, the album received national release in June 1991. One tune, "It's a Sin to Tell a Lie," featured backup vocals by The Sunspots, comprised of *Next Generation* costars LeVar Burton, Michael Dorn, Jonathan Frakes, and Patrick Stewart. The record also featured classics like "Embraceable You" and "Zing Went the Strings of My Heart," as well as Randy Newman's dramatic "Marie," which Spiner chose because "I love the song. If anyone today is writing 'pop standards,' it's Randy Newman." The album was produced by *Next Generation* associate producer Wendy Neuss (who later became a producer on *Star Trek: Voyager*, and Patrick Stewart's steady girlfriend). "Some people might think I got off the android assembly line yesterday, but these songs were sung by the singers that I grew up with, that I love and respect."

Early in the fourth season, *Star Trek: The Next Generation* surpassed the original *Star Trek* for number of episodes produced. (The original cast produced seventy-nine episodes. *The Next Generation* crew made 176 episodes, and aired number 80 in October 1990.) Unlike others who may have claimed their certainty of success, Spiner acknowledged that he was as surprised as anyone about the longevity of the program. "When I took the role four years ago, it was just another job. I figured we'd do a pilot and then go home. I really thought the odds were against us because people were initially reluctant to accept a new *Star Trek*. Now here we are eighty episodes in."

He reflected on the direction his character had taken through the run of the series. "When I was initially cast as Data, my biggest fear was that he has a very small canvas to paint on. I thought I was going to get locked into playing something very restrictive. But as it's turned out over the years I wind up doing something other than Data—or doing Data playing at being something else—at least once or twice a year."

Spiner, single and available in 1990, did "get a lot of romantic mail. They're just curious about my availability or they're telling me about themselves, their problems, and how difficult life is for them. But the letters are really written to Data. [The fascination lies in that] he's a really accessible personality. He's vulnerable and innocent and there's a feeling that he's somebody to tell your troubles to." Is Spiner Data? "Marina [Sirtis] says of all the characters on the show I'm the closest to my character. But I do think I'm as innocent as Data. I think I'm as big a sap as Data is. I tend to believe everything that's told to me."

For Brent Spiner fans, the highlight of *The Next Generation*'s fourth season was the episode "Brothers," in which Spiner portrayed Data, Lore, and his geriatric creator, Dr. Noonien Soong. Spiner would shoot one day as Lore and Data, and the next as Soong, after a four-hour makeup application. "It was difficult," Spiner recalled. "I had to hear dialogue that I hadn't read yet coming out of somebody else's mouth before I would get into it. [I had] to remember where I was when I was Data, and so on."

Other fourth-season highlights featuring Spiner include "Data's Day," in which Data's understanding of human behavior is sorely tested on the day of Keiko and Miles O'Brien's wedding. Spiner worked long hours practicing the tap-dance routine with costar and professional choreographer Gates McFadden. He performed most of his own dancing, only relying on his double for a brief scene that viewers will notice is shot from either overhead or below knee level. In "In Theory," Data pursues a relationship with an ensign who is on the rebound from an unemotional boyfriend and falls for him. This episode featured Michele "Alien Nation" Scarabelli in the role of love interest Ensign Jenna D'Sora. It was Patrick Stewart's directorial debut as well.

It is hard to describe in print the unique closeness the cast had with one another: the enduring friendships that formed, the undisciplined horseplay on the set, the professional and personal support with which they provided one another. Brent Spiner, Marina Sirtis, and Michael Dorn remain close friends and often go out together. Spiner was the best man at LeVar Burton's wedding, and during the run of *The Next Generation* the two would travel weekly to a Korean health spa for a massage and steam bath. Spiner was also named the godfather of Gates McFadden's son in 1991.

Over the summer of 1991, Spiner personally commissioned famed entertainment artist and caricaturist Al Hirschfeld to create a portrait of *The Next Generation* cast, which included the core seven cast members, departed member Wil Wheaton, regulars Colm Meaney and Whoopi Goldberg, and "deceased" Denise Crosby (depicted as a ghost). The portrait was made into a limited-edition lithograph of 375, of which Spiner bought many and gave them as gifts to the cast and many of the crew and producers of *The Next Generation*. The remaining copies were sold at retail, with an initial valuation of $1,200, a figure that has since increased substantially.

Three more episodes marked the fifth season's focus on Spiner's increasingly popular Data. The season opened with the conclusion of the two-part "Redemption" saga, in which Data faces his first true test of command and apparently violates Picard's orders, while dealing with an unfamiliar crew skeptical of the android's abilities. "Hero Worship" featured young Timothy, the lone survivor of the wrecked *SS Vico*, who takes to imitating Data's personality and mannerisms. In "Time's Arrow, Part I," the concluding episode of the fifth season, the *Enterprise* crew discovers Data's head among artifacts dating back to the late 1800s found in San Francisco. The cliff-hanger concludes with Data trapped in old San Francisco and Captain Picard leading an away team to rescue him.

Much earlier in the season, Leonard Nimoy made an appearance on *The Next Generation* as Mr. Spock. "We have a raucous set," Spiner recalls. "We all regard the bridge of the ship as one big nightclub and do a long improv that goes on all day—only to be interrupted by having to do scenes from the show. But we were on our best behavior when Leonard was on the set. It was kind of like we were working with a visiting dignitary." The first thing Nimoy asked Spiner, upon meeting him, was "How do you remember these lines?" and acknowledged that by the third year of *Star Trek* (1969), he was losing brain cells. Spiner replied, "I had the advantage of starting this series with no brain cells." In this same vein, Spiner has emphasized on a number of occasions, "I'm just a dumb actor who memorizes brilliant dialogue."

In February 1992, Spiner costarred with Patrick Stewart, Jonathan Frakes, Gates McFadden, and Colm Meaney in the Stewart-directed, Los Angeles stage production of *Every Good Boy*

Deserves Favour. (The following year, they took the show on the road to Chicago and Atlanta.) He portrayed Russian mental patient Alexander Ivanov, a man obsessed with the notion that there is a full symphony orchestra playing inside his cell. (The production is staged with a full orchestra in view of the audience.) The *Los Angeles Times'* Timothy Madigan called him "the perfect lunatic." *Variety's* Jim Farber wrote, "Spiner proves ideal. . . . Like a crazed marionette, he twitches and writhes to an internal succession of phantom pizzicatos and crushing crescendos. His critical opinions about music and his frenetic behavior provide the play with its dominant comic spark." Patrick Stewart said of his friend and colleague, "He happens to be one of the funniest men I've ever known."

The sixth season began with the conclusion of "Time's Arrow," as Picard and his away team attempt to retrieve Data and save him from apparent destruction. "A Fistful of Datas" followed shortly thereafter, in which Data's memory gets crossed with the *Enterprise's* holodeck database, and Spiner broadens his repertoire once again, playing numerous characters in the Old West holodeck scenes. Joked Spiner, "It's certainly the most fun episode I've ever had to do. I'd like to do a show next season called 'For a Few Datas More.'" "The Quality of Life" followed, in which Data makes a case for and stakes his career on the rights of apparently "alive" machines, the exocomps. In "Birthright," Dr. Bashir (Siddig El Fadil, a.k.a. Alexander Siddig) of *Deep Space Nine* brings aboard the *Enterprise* an alien device that accidentally jolts Data, causing him to experience something akin to dreaming. "I thought that was a wonderful idea and really stretched the boundaries of the character." Spiner, meanwhile, not only was able to take Data in yet another new direction, but he also had the opportunity to reprise the role of Dr. Noonien Soong, albeit that in this episode Soong appeared to be in his forties (which significantly reduced Spiner's time spent in the makeup chair).

The sixth season concluded with the first part of the episode "Descent," a popular cliff-hanger featuring the Borg and introducing Data's emotion chip (which was later to be an integral part of *The Next Generation* feature films). However, though the episode featured exciting action scenes and the return of the program's most popular villains, the show ranks as Brent Spiner's most memorable episode for an entirely different reason. It began with a thirty-second teaser, a holographic poker game that featured Data, Albert Einstein, Sir Isaac Newton, and physicist Stephen Hawking playing himself. "I think it's a very clever scene. The juxtaposition of these players discussing reality and playing poker simultaneously creates a very amusing moment, I think, and a very memorable moment in the history of TV. I just can't imagine that a moment like this will ever occur again."

Leonard Nimoy had met Hawking at the video premiere party for the documentary about his life, A Brief History of Time, and Hawking expressed his interest in appearing on Next Generation. Nimoy then relayed the message to the show's producers, who pounced on the chance to feature the famed physicist in an episode. "The Hawk [Hawking] is really a fabulous actor in his own right," Spiner exclaimed. "I don't know anybody that could have portrayed him as believably as he did. He was terrific and he was excited about being here. I was more nervous than I've been all year just because I'm unused to playing scenes with the brightest man in the universe. He's easily the smartest actor I've ever worked with—not to say my costars aren't bright, but none of them, including myself, are the most brilliant person in the world—and Stephen Hawking happens to be."

Fans have often wondered why, given his obvious talent in front of the camera, Brent Spiner never stepped behind it, joining the ranks of Star Trek directors that included Jonathan Frakes, Patrick Stewart, LeVar Burton, and Gates McFadden. Spiner explained, "I did the same research as [Jonathan Frakes] did: I went to the dailies every day, and talked to the editors every day, and learned about lenses and such. And I thought it would be really special to direct. But by the time it could have actually happened for me, our director of photography had directed. So had one of our editors. And even one of the special effects guys directed." He jokingly continued, "We even had a caterer direct. . . . One of the Teamsters directed. So finally, by then, I just didn't think it was that special."

Star Trek: The Next Generation's final season began with the conclusion of the "Descent" cliff-hanger, again featuring Spiner as both Data and Lore. "Phantasms" featured Spiner in a frightening episode in which nightmares begin creeping into Data's dream program, introduced the previous season. In "Inheritance," Data meets a woman who claims that she was once married to Dr. Soong and considers herself Data's mother. In fact, the woman is yet another android built by Soong, but this episode is more significant in that it wraps up many threads and unresolved facts surrounding Data's backstory. "Thine Own Self" featured Data losing his memory and getting "killed" by an angry mob that considers him a monster after he unwittingly infects their village with radiation sickness. The very next episode, "Masks," forced Spiner to don various characters as the ship begins to assimilate an entire Mayan-like culture. Spiner embodies a woman, a child, an old man, and others speaking from the ancient culture. "Dustin Hoffman took a year to figure out how to play a woman in *Tootsie*—how am I supposed to do it in two days?" Nonetheless, the episode was considered a success, partially as a result of the producers granting Spiner's request for some revoicing of some of the characters in post-production.

As *The Next Generation* wrapped up its seven-year run and headed to the movie screen, Spiner was reflective regarding his career up to that point as well as what the future might hold. "Coming out of a long series like *Next Generation*, either people know me or it's one big chill factor. You know, Fitzgerald once said, 'There are no second acts in American lives,' and I'm sitting here praying for a third act. Maybe I could do spaghetti westerns or something. It didn't hurt Clint." He was reconciled to the fact that, in much of the public's mind, he would always be remembered as Data. "I'm sort of philosophical about it, and I . . . You know, Data's a nice character to be remembered for, if that's what I'm known for. And it could be much, much worse. And I think if I'm lucky, if I'm very, very lucky, it'll translate somehow like, for me, an actor like Art Carney will always be Ed Norton from *The Honeymooners*. Every time I hear the name Art Carney, I think Ed Norton. He was brilliant as Ed Norton. But after playing Ed Norton, Art Carney went on to win an Academy Award and play about, you know, thirty, forty excellent roles in films. So if I'm stuck with Data forever, that's fine with me."

Though he does not watch many *Next Generation* episodes, nor does he take in the other *Star Trek* series, he has taken something of great value from his seven years as Data: strong friendships with his castmates. "Science fiction is not a genre that particularly interests me. Since *Blade Runner*, I haven't seen any sci-fi that I thought was remarkable. It's the friendships. Work is work. I've done a lot of jobs I enjoyed and a lot of jobs I didn't particularly enjoy. I've done episodes as Data that I've enjoyed and episodes I haven't enjoyed. The one constant on this show has been the relationships with the cast. We've developed some really rich friendships, and I expect those will go on forever."

HAS-BEEN CITY

What did Brent Spiner have planned following the end of *The Next Generation*'s run? "If the history of hit TV shows tells us anything, I'll most likely be on the first train to Has-Been City, and that's just a quick stop on the way to oblivion," Spiner laughed. "There's no getting around it—for the rest of my life I'm Data. I would love to think the audience will instantly accept me as another character. But, in reality, the best I can hope for is that they'll see me in future parts and say, 'Oh my God, that's Data!' and then forget about it ten minutes later." Spiner has landed the future parts he hoped for, and audiences have been able to look past his recognizable Data veneer. However, before he could move on to other roles, in 1994, he still had to be adorned in gold makeup to portray Data in the first film with *The Next Generation* cast, *Star Trek: Generations*.

Among the plot lines in *Star Trek: Generations*, some critics did not like the inclusion of Data's emotion chip, which afforded him an aggressive sense of humor. Though derided by some reviewers as "juvenile and cheap," Spiner defended the move. "I thought Data's evolution with humor started at the right place. We've got to have room to grow here—we've got more movies to make. Now I'm looking forward to the lust chip." He was pleased that, unlike some plots in *Star Trek* that simply seemed to have been dropped (the Worf/Troi relationship, for instance), his behavior followed a nice continuity. "It was always a gradual journey toward being more human and understanding humanity and human behavior a little better. So it kinda arced—and in this picture it arced even further—but I'm just glad the evolution continued and it didn't stop cold."

But the dramatic change in Data portrayed in *Generations* was not an obvious development and Spiner was initially concerned. "For a long time, I had been sort of euphemistically painting on a very narrow palette in muted colors. So the film was a real opportunity to cut loose and be wild. When I first read the script, I was a little concerned because it was so different, even though it represented the natural evolution of the character. Thinking about it, I finally came to the conclusion that, in a worst-case scenario, at least they'd love me in France."

During the shooting of *Generations*, the cast was on a boat for six days for the filming of the opening scene. They placed bets on who would get seasick first, and most bets were on Spiner. (They remembered that in the episode "Data's Day," he couldn't accomplish the twirls in the tap-dancing routine because he would vomit.) However, Spiner was armed with seasickness medication, which he took for a week before setting sail, and he was not the first to get ill—Gates McFadden was.

However, Spiner has an aversion to heights, and the new Stellar Cartography room of the *Enterprise* (featured in the film) caused him some consternation. "We'd been on the ship for seven years. But obviously there were a lot of rooms I'd never been in and it was necessary that I see the room prior to the movie. It was a huge platform that was fifteen feet in the air; it was like a diving board surrounded from the floor to the ceiling by a blue screen that they projected all these images on. But I'm not great with heights—this is from someone who has traveled the galaxy. And it moved too. It was not stationary, and as you got closer to the edge it started to move. We were up there for two starlit days. [Roller-coaster aficionado] Patrick loves heights, of course, and I explained to him when we first got there that I'm really nervous right now and I don't care for heights at all, and for the next two days he started doing this [at this point, Spiner started jumping up and down] and it would start bouncing—it really would! We had no problem with it, but I was terrified the entire time."

As a memento from the *Generations* shoot, Spiner got one of the "prop guys" to give him the clapboard from the last scene of the movie. He also went through the tedious process of obtaining approval to keep one of Data's uniforms. (About ten were used in the film.) Though he finally got the requisite approvals, no one ever gave him the uniform. Yet if he had followed in the footsteps of two of his castmates it would have been his: after the last shoot, he met Jonathan Frakes, Gates McFadden, and Michael Dorn at a restaurant for dinner. He discovered Frakes had simply worn his uniform off the lot (and still had it on under his jacket) and McFadden had worn her lab coat off the set over her street clothes.

In a comment that would foreshadow his next few years, Spiner told a reporter upon the wrap of *Generations*, "It feels good. I feel I've arrived. I've waited my whole life to be on the big screen, and here it comes." His next few years would find him in demand as both a television and a screen actor, and afford him the luxury of choosing among high-profile projects.

Since *The Next Generation* left production as a weekly series, Spiner has had roles in television programs ranging from *Mad About You* (as a talent scout) and *Gargoyles* (as recurring character Puck) to *Deadly Games* (as a systems analyst) and *Dream On* (as a repairman). Fans were treated to his "famous" Jimmy Stewart impersonation when he hosted the Hitchcock classic *Rear Window* on TNT's Our Favorite Movies series. He participated in John de Lancie's revival of the radio play *War of the Worlds* and worked with Gates McFadden in *Chicago Theatres on the Air*, an annual play staged for a radio audience listening at home.

In 1996, Spiner was ubiquitous at the cineplex, appearing in two of the summer's biggest hits, *Independence Day* and *Phenomenon*, which, coincidentally, opened on the same day. "I kind of like the idea that people going to the movies over the Fourth of July weekend and knowing that they're pretty much bound to see me." As Dr. Okun, the scientist who heads the government's alien research program in *Independence Day*, Spiner donned a wig of long gray frizzy hair. ("The wig really made the part for me.") He was thrilled to have the chance to work with Jeff Goldblum, whom he had admired for some time, and was reunited on the movie with Randy Quaid. "We hadn't worked together since college and it was magic to be on the same set together."

In *Phenomenon*, Spiner worked for only one day on the film as Dr. Nierdorf, a psychologist who puts star John Travolta through a battery of tests. "It's really only one scene. Travolta was great to work with."

Spiner rounded out 1996 in his familiar role as Data, in the box-office smash and critically acclaimed *Star Trek: First Contact.* "It's a continuation of the last film's story because the emotion chip is still an ingredient. But the story in *Generations* was more about Data's ability to control emotions because of its newness and his lack of experience. He was like a child in the first film. A lot of people didn't care for that but to me it seemed the only place to go. You have to have a point of departure and Data was new. You couldn't start with maturity. I think this film is about Data's growth experience in a way. He's much, much more in control of his emotions and when he's not, he can turn off the chip. The story in this movie takes him one step farther toward humanity as he confronts the Queen trying to seduce him into the hive by offering Data real human flesh."

Variety reviewer Joe Leydon singled out Spiner's acting performance, writing, "Credit Spiner and the scriptwriters for finding brave new ways to make a familiar character unsettlingly unpredictable." Costar Alice "Borg Queen" Krige, with whom Spiner shared many scenes, commented that "Brent was tireless in his attempts to flesh out the relationship, fill in any gaps for me, and explore the resonances of the relationship." On filming the action sequences and being spritzed with artificial Hollywood sweat, Spiner commented simply to *TV Guide,* "God I love this stuff." The only scene that was not thrilling for Spiner was the one shot in the missile silo. Director Frakes intended to use a stunt double for Data's "jump" down the missile silo to confront Alfre Woodard's character Lily Sloan. However, the stunt double simply did not resemble Spiner to Frakes' liking, so Spiner had to perform the stunt himself. Given his fear of heights, being lowered down a missile shaft on a line was not his idea of a happy experience.

"Playing an android is pretty easy because you have the advantage of [your work] not being comparable to somebody else's work. It's pretty unlikely that anyone says, 'Hey, I don't believe an android would do that.' So I can pretty much do whatever I want. However, there aren't that many good android parts around, so I'm working on my human portrayals now," Spiner proclaimed in an online forum.

Spiner's next big-screen project is as a costar with Jack Lemmon and Walter Matthau in the 1997 feature *Out to Sea,* in which he plays fastidious cruise director Gil Godwyn, who clashes with the duo.

When he's not working, his only hobbies remain sleeping and watching television. "I love *Picket Fences*; I just can't believe it's not an American habit to watch. I prefer *Chicago Hope* to *ER*, maybe because Mandy Patinkin is a friend of mine." He claims that, even given reruns, he has only seen about forty episodes of *Next Generation*. "My feeling is, it's going to be on the rest of my life in reruns and when I'm in the Old Actor's Home I'd rather watch episodes I've never seen."

Though Spiner exudes a very lonely guy existence and is very tight lipped about his personal life, he is romantically involved. He has dated publicist Loree McBride for a number of years and enjoys spending extensive time alone with both her and her two golden retrievers, Saks and Taylor. After initially settling in California, Spiner had been romantically linked with fashion model and *Deep Space Nine* star Terry "Jadzia Dax" Farrell. "No longer," insists Farrell. "The fact that it didn't work out had nothing to do with him: it had to do with me. I was too young. I think he's a *fantastic* man. He's really a very special person."

Spiner is bemused by fans who are fascinated with his life story, not to mention his sex life. "That's such a boring topic, frankly. Why do people care who people sleep with? I met Judy Garland when I was sixteen, and had a photo taken with her that's in *Ol' Yellow Eyes*, and I think that's enough to make people think I'm gay. I'm not, but if people want to think so, it's fine. That's part of the mystery. Some people think I'm gay, some people think I'm straight, some people think I'm a eunuch—it's all fine. 'Cause in the end, none of it matters."

Brent Spiner's future under the gold makeup at the helm of the *Enterprise* is uncertain. "I really do think I'm getting too old for the part. He's a machine. How much can he age? Unfortunately, I'm getting older every day. They need a young android," Spiner concludes. "Somebody they'll have a good twenty years with." Nonetheless, Spiner is realistic regarding how lucky he has been to portray Data, and his future as the character. "My feeling is that the character for nine years now has been ever evolving. If they can continue to find new possibilities for the character, I'll be glad to play it again. It's been the best thing that ever happened to me."

BRENT SPINER

Lieutenant Commander Data*

STAGE:

The Portable Pioneer and
  Prairie Show ('72)
Cabaret ('73)
Promises, Promises ('73)
Polly ('74)
The Crazy Locomotive ('75)
The Family ('75)
Marco Polo ('76)
A History of American Film
  ('78)
The Cotton Patch Gospel ('79)
Émigrés ('79)
Leave It to Beaver Is Dead ('79)
New Jerusalem ('80)
The Seagull ('80)
Table Settings ('80)
No End of Blame ('81–'82)
Marvelous Gray ('82)
The Philanthropist ('83)
Sunday in the Park with George
  ('83–'84)
The Three Musketeers ('84)
Big River ('85–'86)
The Cherry Orchard ('85)
Little Shop of Horrors ('85)
Every Good Boy Deserves
  Favour ('92, '93)

TELEVISION:

The Dain Curse ('78)
Tales from the Darkside ('84)
Crime of Innocence ('85)
The Paper Chase ('85)
Robert Kennedy and His Times
  ('85)
Sylvan in Paradise ('85)
Hill Street Blues ('86)
Hunter ('86)
Manhunt for Claude Dallas ('86)
The Twilight Zone ('86)
Cheers ('87)
Family Sins ('87)
Mama's Family ('87)
Night Court ('87)
Star Trek: The Next Generation
  ('87–'94)
Reading Rainbow ('88)
Crazy from the Heart ('91)
Sessions ('91)
Sunday in the Park with George
  ('91)
What's Allen Watching? ('91)
Dream On ('94)
Kingfish: The Huey Long Story
  ('94)
Science Fiction: A Journey into
  the Unknown ('94)
Deadly Games ('95)
Mad About You ('95)
Gargoyles ('96)
The Outer Limits ('96)

FILM:

Stardust Memories ('80)
Rent Control ('81)
Miss Firecracker ('89)
Corrina, Corrina ('94)
Star Trek: Generations ('94)
Pie in the Sky ('95)
Independence Day ('96)
Phenomenon ('96)
Star Trek: First Contact ('96)
Out to Sea ('97)

**Also Lore, Dr. Noonien Soong,
and numerous characters in the
episode "A Fistful of Datas"*

CHAPTER 8

WIL WHEATON

Stand by Him

*"I tend to sympathize with some of the people who said
Wesley was annoying. As I watched reruns of the first couple of years,
I could see where he was annoying."*
—WHEATON, IN A 1994 INTERVIEW

When *Star Trek: The Next Generation* was first cast in 1987, Richard William "Wil" Wheaton III was considered to be one of the two "recognizable" stars (the other was LeVar Burton) in the ensemble cast. Born July 29, 1972, upon *The Next Generation*'s premiere in 1987 Wheaton already had a résumé as a professional actor that had spanned eight of his fifteen years. He was a genuine Hollywood veteran among a cast of relative newcomers.

Though he only stayed with the show for half of its seven-year run, his role changed dramatically through the course of the first four seasons. It is no secret that many fans genuinely disliked his character, Wesley Crusher, and many reacted negatively whenever young Ensign Crusher made an appearance. Teenage Wheaton took much of this criticism personally, and despite the continued encouragement of his fellow cast members, especially Patrick Stewart, he chose to leave the show to pursue other opportunities.

What is often overlooked, however, is that Wheaton was extremely popular with many fans as well. During his time on *Star Trek*, Wheaton received the second highest volume of fan mail on the Paramount lot, following only Michael J. Fox. More mail than Patrick Stewart. More mail than any other *Star Trek* cast member.

A CHILD STAR

At the age of seven, Wil Wheaton accompanied his mother, Debbie O'Connor—an actress with more than twenty small film roles to her credit—to an audition for a Jell-O Pudding Pops commercial with Bill Cosby. Both Debbie and son Wil landed parts. After a children's agent spotted Wil in this commercial and told him he had a "good face," he began working regularly in commercials.

Wil Wheaton's early employment was not without precedent from members of his extended family. Debbie O'Connor is the daughter of Frank O'Connor, who had also worked steadily in Hollywood, including a notable part in *Citizen Kane*. Wheaton is not entirely a child of Hollywood, however. His father is a doctor, a cardiopulmonary proufionist.

By the time Wheaton had reached the age of nine, he "got tired of them [commercials]. They got fake to me. I could never understand how you could smile while eating. I wanted to get into theatrics." Wheaton auditioned for, and was accepted into, the Company of Angels Theater in Los Angeles, the first child actor ever to be made a regular member of the company.

He was cast in the play *All My Sons*, but found the nightly work grueling. "It was hard to do that every single night," Wheaton explained, "so I decided to try for TV." In 1982, he landed his first dramatic television role, in *A Long Way Home*, an NBC movie-of-the-week starring Timothy Hutton. Small parts followed on *Highway to Heaven*, *St. Elsewhere*, *The Defiant Ones*, and *The Shooting* (a CBS *Schoolbreak Special*). Each role had a unique flavor. Wheaton relished the diversity: "That's the fun of acting. You can stray from your normal personality and be different people."

Despite his early fame, Wheaton attended a public school up until his high school years. At fourteen, he told an interviewer that he had few problems with his classmates. "One or two jerks might treat me as an object to show off, which is upsetting. But most treat me like a regular, old, normal person. Kids are more sophisticated than they get credit for. Some even ask me, 'How can I get into movies?'"

Wheaton's feature-film debut came in 1984 in *The Buddy System*, opposite Susan Sarandon and Richard Dreyfuss (who, coincidentally, played Wheaton's adult persona in *Stand by Me* two years later). He also had roles in the features *Hambone and Hillie* and *The Last Starfighter*, and a voice-over in *The Secret of NIMH*, before receiving his big break in the hit Rob Reiner–directed *Stand by Me* in 1986.

As Gordie, the brains of a group of four young friends, Wheaton starred with Corey Feldman, Jerry O'Connell, and River Phoenix. Director Reiner won tremendous praise for his handling of the story—as well as of the young actors—from reviewers and moviegoers nationwide. Reiner kept the four boys together during the filming of *Stand by Me*, on camera and off. They attended carnivals together and even went river rafting. They stayed in the same hotels, and Wheaton is said to have fixed the video games in one hotel so the four boys had access to unlimited free games. "When you saw the four of us being comrades, that was real life, not acting," Wheaton said.

His single favorite scene in *Stand by Me* is the one in which the boys are sitting around the campfire discussing cherry-flavored Pez and Goofy's status as a dog: fourteen-year-old Wheaton and his mother actually wrote some of the dialogue for that scene.

Wheaton and River Phoenix maintained a close friendship after filming *Stand by Me*, and when Wheaton lost a role in *The Mosquito Coast* (starring Harrison Ford) to Phoenix, he waxed, with no apparent hard feelings, "Maybe he was the better actor, or maybe we were equal and he matched what they wanted better." However, in later years leading up to River Phoenix's death by drug overdose, Wheaton spoke significantly less about his friend, answering questions about him curtly and commenting only that he had become "weird." It should be noted that throughout his later teen years, Wheaton has been very outspoken against illicit drug use.

THE SPOILS OF SUCCESS

Following his overwhelming success in *Stand by Me*, Wheaton was cast in the title role in Disney's television movie *Young Harry Houdini*. He was thrilled to land the role, having had a childhood interest in magic. Wheaton had always admired the famed escape artist, and portraying him was yet another highlight on the young star's acting résumé. "You'll see the determination Houdini had to get what he wanted," Wheaton exclaimed, "which was to become the greatest magician in the world."

Not only did Wheaton's success in *Stand by Me* help land him subsequent acting roles, but it also earned him the brief status as a teen idol. He was featured in *Tiger Beat, Teen Beat All-Stars,* and other teen magazines. He hosted the *Kids' Choice Awards,* and was cast as Tina Yothers' love interest on a 1987 episode of the top-rated *Family Ties.*

Some might argue that Wheaton's childhood was extremely blessed, while others might view him as nothing more than a typical teenager of the 1980s. With plans to attend USC film school, he was an MTV addict favoring the bands Depeche Mode, the Smiths, LL Cool J, Oingo Boingo, Cameo, U-2, and INXS. He was also a politically aware Republican, and was an avid surfer and "boogie boarder" who claimed to receive his greatest motivation to succeed from his grandmother. There was little socially to set Wheaton apart from his peers. The time he had spent on stage and in front of the camera had not marred an otherwise happy and positive childhood. The trappings of fame had not overwhelmed young Wheaton. Only a menagerie of pets, including a ten-and-a-half-foot python, three cats, a chameleon, a Brazilian parrot, fish, and two yellow Labrador retrievers seemed to set him apart from a "typical" California teen. "I guess there are some child actors who will only hang out with people in the business, which I think is kind of stupid," Wheaton claimed, "but you got to do what you got to do, what makes you happy. I can hang around with just about anyone."

The role of Wesley Crusher was originally intended in the December 1986 casting call as a role for acting-ensign *Leslie* Crusher. She was to be the brilliant teenage *daughter* of the *Enterprise's* widowed chief medical officer, and would possess a remarkable mind and a photographic memory. Gene Roddenberry made the character switch from a female to a male because he felt that there would be a wider range of stories available. Roddenberry is quoted as having stated, "Although I identify with every character [on *The Next Generation*], I identify probably more with Wesley Crusher because he is me at seventeen. He is the things I dreamed of being and doing."

There remains a significant amount of debate about how the character was handled during Wheaton's three and a half seasons as a regular cast member and recurring guest spots. However, it is important to note that many young viewers tuned in to *Star Trek: The Next Generation* because of Wil Wheaton's character.

Wesley Crusher embodied the value of education, was treated as an equal among adults, and showed the younger generation that there was a place for them in the future.

Wheaton almost did not land the role of Wesley Crusher. After a terrible first callback, he was convinced that he had lost the part. On his way home from the audition, he realized that Gene Roddenberry had commented on the fact that he had worn his shoes untied. "Now I'll let my fourteen-year-old wear his shoes untied!" Roddenberry had told Wheaton during the audition. During the ride home, Wheaton realized the significance of this exchange. "Wait a minute, don't you see the hidden meaning there?" he asked himself. "He likes you, you've gotten the role!"

Of the entire *Next Generation* cast, Wheaton was the real "trekker"—along with Michael Dorn. "I've always had a lot of questions," Wheaton told *Entertainment Tonight*. "What kind of music do they listen to? What kind of currency do they use? What does it feel like to be transported? Now I have access to all of the answers, and I can live the stuff I've been watching for so many years."

Wheaton admits that as a teen, he read the novelizations and the comic books, and watched the "old series" on television every night. He has also since bought all of the original series episodes on videotape. "Of all the old series that are on, [*Star Trek*] is the most believable for me because they set everything in the future. What they set for the future then, is what we're living now. We've made a lot of progress in twenty years," Wheaton stated in the Paramount press kit introducing *The Next Generation*.

WESLEY SAVES THE DAY

"When I heard, 'They want you to play a teenager on *Star Trek*,' I thought, 'Okay, but I hope it isn't kid gets in trouble, crew gets kid out of trouble . . .' But it's not like that at all. The kid on the show is like an equal with the rest of the crew. And I think that's great."

During the first season of *Star Trek: The Next Generation*, Wheaton was reunited with director Michael Rhodes during the filming of the episode "Angel One." It was Rhodes who gave Wheaton his first starring role, in a 1981 ABC *Afterschool Special*.

Later that same season, Wheaton's younger siblings, Jeremy and Amy, made nonspeaking appearances as young hostages in "When the Bough Breaks," ultimately saved by their real-life older brother and Captain Picard.

However, one fact emerged as most significant for fans of *The Next Generation's* first season. These were fans who had hoped to embrace the successor to Jim Kirk and his crew. One of the things that made viewers of the new show uncomfortable and annoyed was that of the twenty-five first-season episodes, Wesley Crusher "saved the day" in six of them and was featured much more prominently over the season than many of his castmates. When asked about her "son's" prowess, intelligence, and good fortune in saving the starship time and again, Gates McFadden exclaimed at a *Star Trek* convention, "Well, let's face it. The guy is a genius. Everyone should listen to him and we would have five-minute episodes."

Wheaton, however, wishes to set the record straight. He insists that Wesley "directly saved the ship only one and a half times, and had a hand in contributing to the solution of the problem two times! That's it!"

Some fans count the "Wesley episodes" differently, listing ten total times over the run of the show he saved the ship, as well as five occasions in which he seriously "screwed up," resulting in a major story line for the episode. Each fan may, of course, keep his or her own Wesley scorecard. For the record, the ten episodes that fans most often point to as "Wesley saves the day episodes" are: "The Naked Now," "Where No One Has Gone Before," "The Battle," "The Big Goodbye," "Datalore," "Peak Performance," "The High Ground," "Ménage à Troi," "Final Mission," and "The Game." Wesley's five "screwups" are considered to be found in "Justice," "Evolution," "Remember Me," "The First Duty," and "Journey's End." No matter what the final count is—an issue fans are sure to debate for decades to come—the reality is that Wil Wheaton had many vital plot points and story lines on *Star Trek: The Next Generation* that revolved around his character. Certainly there were more during the first season than those centered around LeVar Burton, Michael Dorn, Gates McFadden, or Marina Sirtis.

The animosity that many fans held toward Wheaton, particularly after the first season, was no secret to him. "You know, I want to be liked. I want people to like Wesley," he stated in 1990. "I was ready to leave the show the first year just because everyone was so negative. I felt very badly. I was very confused. I was only fifteen years old at the time." In a 1996 interview, Patrick Stewart noted thoughtfully, "There was probably envy and resentment [among older fans]. . . . In the early episodes you often saw a child being smarter than the senior crew members."

Star Trek's writers significantly played down Wesley Crusher's role after the first season, but many fans continued to scorn the character. In his final regular appearance—he was to appear a number of subsequent times as a guest star—in the episode "Final Mission," Wheaton gives what is considered perhaps his finest performance on the series. Patrick Stewart, a big fan of Wheaton's, has stated that the farewell scene with Wheaton during this episode was the most "emotionally challenging" for him during the run of *The Next Generation*. The appreciation was mutual, for as much as Stewart respected Wheaton's talent as a young actor, Wheaton idolized Stewart. "Patrick, I really want to impress. I want to show him I can do good," he stated in a televised interview early on in the show's run.

Wheaton feels that, although his character was something of a miracle worker during the first season, aspects of Wesley were never appropriately developed in the subsequent years, such as the relationship between him and his mother. "When Dr. Crusher came back after being away for a year [the show's second season], the writers really focused on a negative aspect of their relationship, which disappointed me a little bit," Wheaton said in a 1990 interview. "They really focused on his mother saying, 'Do this and this and that,' and Wesley saying, 'To hell with you, Mom! I'm doing it my way!' And that's not the way it should have been portrayed at all! I think that Beverly and Wesley have known each other long enough and are close enough that he would come back and say, 'Wow, you've taken care of yourself for a year! I'm pleased with that.'"

Despite the frustrations with the pace at which his character developed, Wheaton still marveled at his treatment by the rest of the cast. "They treat me not like a kid, but like they would anyone else. It's really rad." He developed a unique relationship with each of the cast although he found there were some topics his fellow cast members had difficulty relating to, such as surfing and music. (These were topics he could really only discuss with Denise Crosby, who left the show halfway through the first season but remains a close friend of Wheaton's.) "Whenever I had a really nasty problem, I would go to Jonathan Frakes and Brent Spiner because they really understand me and I could really talk with them. I had a terrible crush on Marina Sirtis all through the show. . . . Michael Dorn and I both play bass guitar, so I talked to him about my music. LeVar Burton, I talked to about anything spiritual plus he's just easy to talk to about anything. Gates McFadden and I just kicked back and had a good time together. Patrick Stewart is great to work with. We had a lot of fun together. Patrick has a very brilliant sense of humor that no one ever sees. I had a wonderful time working with him because of that. He takes a lot of the edge off the day."

Naturally, the writers and producers of *Star Trek: The Next Generation* were neither unaware of nor ambivalent regarding the fans' feelings toward Wesley Crusher, and they utilized his guest appearances to humanize the character. Perhaps most notably, "The First Duty" brought Wesley Crusher down to earth. (This episode also brought the *Enterprise* to earth—to Starfleet Academy—the first time the academy had been shown in an episode.) Writer Naren Shankar, who cowrote "The First Duty," admitted, "We wanted to get away from 'Wesley Saves the Universe.' Wesley was a character that I always felt was a bit underused. He was a difficult character because of the way he was set up in the series. He was always a brilliant prodigy, very innocent and essentially very perfect. When you do that to a character, the writers are completely hamstrung. Where do you take that?" By writing an episode where Wesley made a serious error and suffered the consequences, the writers made the character stronger and more interesting.

This was a major guest appearance for Wil Wheaton as well as for Robert Duncan McNeill. Cast as Wesley Crusher's squadron leader, Nick Locarno, McNeill would eventually play Lieutenant Tom Paris on *Star Trek: Voyager*.

Unlike many of the other cast members, Wheaton's favorite episode is *not* one in which he had a substantial role. "My favorite episode is "Brothers," the one with Data and Lore and Dr. Noonien

Soong. I've watched it three times. Brent Spiner is brilliant. If he doesn't get an Emmy then the Emmys are as lame as the Oscars. I think Brent is phenomenal. Never once did I think it was the same actor playing all the roles. I thought it was different actors. Unfortunately, they cut tons of stuff to make the show fit into an hour. I wish they would have cut my stuff and everybody else's and given it all to Brent because he was so good."

While a regular on *Star Trek*, Wheaton found himself in demand as an actor, and did manage to squeeze in a couple of professional engagements off the *Enterprise*. Paula Abdul, Mike Tyson, and Wil Wheaton were an unlikely trio to make a joint cameo appearance on Arsenio Hall's album and video, *Large and in Charge*. Wheaton also appeared on the television series *Monsters*, which he filmed during the hiatus between the third and fourth seasons of *The Next Generation*.

To Boldly Leave

Over the summer of 1990, Wheaton graduated from Valley Professional High School—where he had served as senior class president. "Final Mission" (Wheaton's last episode as a regular member of *The Next Generation* cast) was broadcast in November 1990. "It had been sitting in my mind for about a year. I was a little disappointed that they weren't giving me anything to do. I was offered a few features that were just too good to pass up and I couldn't do them because I was married to the series. I decided that I really wanted to move on to features and stage and really do some serious acting. I wasn't getting to do any acting on the show, I was only getting to say, 'Aye aye, sir.' Maybe, occasionally, every three or four weeks, I would have one little scene. It was very frustrating." At the age of eighteen, Wil Wheaton left the cast of *Star Trek: The Next Generation*.

Wheaton kept busy off the set of *The Next Generation*. He played goalie for the L.A. Hawks, a traveling celebrity hockey team that included such stars as Michael J. Fox on its roster. He continued to stay in touch with the cast of *Star Trek*, attending performances of *Every Good Boy Deserves Favour* (which starred five *Next Generation*

200 THE FINEST CREW IN THE FLEET

cast members) and Patrick Stewart's *A Christmas Carol.* "Whenever any of us can break out of our *Star Trek* mold, we're always there to support each other. I must have seen *Christmas Carol* six times. . . . It's so important for us to prove that there's life beyond *Star Trek.*"

Wheaton's acting career continued to flourish post-*Trek*, with a critically acclaimed role in the feature film *Toy Soldiers* and another in HBO's *Deadly Secrets.* After leaving *The Next Generation,* "I got in the trenches, went to auditions and acting school. I worked real hard just to make bill payments. I never had to do that before. Being in the industry, especially on a series, tends to shelter you from reality. You never worry about money or your job. Being in the real world has helped me grow immensely," he stated in 1994.

Wheaton left Hollywood briefly in 1992 to live and work in Kansas. He was employed with a high-tech computer company, NewTek, in its product development division. He also worked as the in-house producer for NewTek's video products. "I loved it," he exclaimed, "I enjoyed the anonymity. No one was able to scrutinize me over whether or not I was doing the right career thing."

However, after returning as a guest star in the seventh-season *Next Generation* episode "Journey's End," Wheaton realized how much he missed Hollywood. In January 1994, he resigned from NewTek and returned to Los Angeles. He realized that fans who were once very negative toward Wesley had softened up a bit; and that much of the derision that was launched in his direction was not solely his fault, but also attributable to both the scriptwriters and the short fuse of the fans. "Wesley had his place, and I think the writers screwed up here and there, but I definitely think the fans overreacted," he claimed.

WHATEVER HAPPENED TO . . .?

After Paramount stopped producing new television episodes of *The Next Generation,* Wheaton was not asked to appear in either *Star Trek: Generations* or *Star Trek: First Contact.* This is probably less an indictment of Wheaton's acting, and more in keeping with the fate of Wesley Crusher—whom we learned in "Journey's End" is off being tutored by the entity known as the Traveler and thereby fulfilling Wesley's "unique destiny." He would have liked to have been included in one of the *Next Generation* movies. Upon the release of *Star Trek: First Contact*, he told an interviewer that he felt some residual hard feelings toward his having left the program. "The folks in charge gave me the feeling I turned my back on them. They had me back a couple of times, then shipped me off to the Island of Misfit Toys."

Nonetheless, Wheaton has managed to escape Wesley. He even dyed his hair white for a period in 1995. He has been keeping busy with other projects, appearing in *Mr. Stitch*, a direct-to-video thriller with Rutger Hauer, and the obscure 1995 feature *Pie in the Sky*. He has also made television appearances on the syndicated *Sirens* and on the television film *It Was Him or Us*. Wheaton also joined Leonard Nimoy, Gates McFadden, Brent Spiner, and John de Lancie in the radio drama *War of the Worlds*, as well as a 1994 sequel written by de Lancie, entitled *When Worlds Collide*. Currently, Wheaton is filming *The Absent-Minded Professor* starring Robin Williams, due to be released in 1997. "I play a really nasty, arrogant college kid," Wheaton told *Entertainment Weekly*, adding triumphantly, "and he's dumb as a post."

Despite some lingering negativity regarding his role on *The Next Generation* and his subsequent treatment by the producers, Wheaton remains philosophical about the impact of *Star Trek*, and is genuinely happy that he was an integral part of the phenomenon. "What I really like about *Star Trek* is that it says that there is a future. If society could talk, it would say, 'Now, you've got Mr. Bomb here, and Mr. Disease here, and here's our friend Gadhafi right here.' People are wondering, 'Will there be a future?' *Star Trek* says, 'Yes, there is a future. This is it.'"

As Wil Wheaton is now proving, there is in fact a future beyond *Star Trek*. Whether or not he is ever again asked to participate in the pantheon that is *Trek*, he is at peace with his decision to leave, the fans have forgiven him, and his career is on track. He may not be an integral part of the evolving *Star Trek* universe, but Wil Wheaton is content.

WIL WHEATON

Wesley Crusher

STAGE:
All My Sons ('80)

TELEVISION:
A Long Way Home ('81)
ABC Afterschool Special ('81)
My Dad Can't Be Crazy, Can He? ('82)
The Shooting ('82)
13 Thirteenth Avenue ('83)
The Defiant Ones ('85)
Highway to Heaven ('86)
Long Time Gone ('86)
St. Elsewhere ('86)
Family Ties ('87)
The Man Who Fell to Earth ('87)
Star Trek: The Next Generation ('87–'90, '91, '92, '93, '94)
Young Harry Houdini ('87)
Monsters ('90)
The Last Prostitute ('91)
Deadly Secrets ('93)

A Deadly Secret: The Robert Bierer Story ('94)
Prince Valiant ('94)
Tales from the Crypt ('94)
It Was Him or Us ('95)
Sirens ('95)
Light Brigade ('96)

FILM:
The Secret of NIMH ('82)
The Buddy System ('84)
Hambone and Hillie ('84)
The Last Starfighter ('84)
Stand by Me ('86)
The Curse (a.k.a. The Farm) ('87)
She's Having a Baby ('88)
December ('91)
Toy Soldiers ('91)
The Liar's Club ('93)
Mr. Stitch ('95) (direct-to-video)
Pie in the Sky ('95)
The Absent-Minded Professor ('97)

CHAPTER 9

REGULAR PLAYERS

DENISE CROSBY

"I had the best roles after my character died."
—DENISE CROSBY, DISCUSSING HER APPEARANCES ON STAR TREK:
THE NEXT GENERATION AFTER HER CHARACTER HAD BEEN WRITTEN
OUT OF THE SHOW

When Denise Crosby chose to leave her post aboard the *Enterprise* toward the end of the first season of *Star Trek: The Next Generation*, fans—and particularly female fans—felt the loss of the program's strongest female character. Crosby's Tasha Yar typified how far society had come in raising the status of women from the miniskirted set dressings of the original 1960s *Star Trek* series. Her departure changed the dynamic of the entire program. It raised the status of Worf, which led to the show's writers focusing on his life and Klingon culture and resulted in some of the most popular episodes in *The Next Generation*'s seven-year run. Yet no regular female character was ever introduced who matched Yar's strength and obsessive devotion to protecting the ship and her crew. Yar toiled without equal (in an atypical role for a woman) as the ship's tactical and weapons officer.

Born November 24, 1957, in Hollywood, California, Denise Crosby did not know her famous kin while growing up. She never met her crooner grandfather, Bing, and only met her father, Dennis Crosby (Bing's son), once. Denise's father abandoned her mother, Marilyn Scott, before Denise was born. The only time young Denise ever laid eyes on her now-deceased father was during a bitter paternity suit that came to trial in 1960 when she was three years old. In a courtroom packed with paparazzi, Dennis Crosby was told he must pay child support. Denise remembers it as a surreal experience. "It's very strange. To have a child is a wonderful experience, and he unfortunately missed out."

It was only by chance that in 1984 she ran across Mary Crosby, one of Bing's three children by his second wife, Kathryn. The encounter led to a lasting friendship. "I'm really glad I met her. I think she's terrific."

Although she grew up in a middle-class household, Crosby suffered the stigma of her famous grandfather. It was an albatross around her neck, but one that she felt helped her to understand her *Next Generation* character. "My grandfather was a Hollywood legend. Growing up in Hollywood sort of creates its own Hell Planet! You know, it's not like growing up in the farmlands of Wisconsin. I think you kind of learn certain survival instincts and certain things to get along in this crazy city as a young girl. I was an only child raised by my mother until I was six, when she married my stepfather. So a lot of my time was spent alone, which, I think, is a lot like Tasha's background."

As a teenager, Crosby envisioned herself as something of a rebel. "To this day, I'm probably the only person who was voted Homecoming Princess in eleventh grade at Hollywood High and refused it." She enrolled in the drama program at Cabrillo College in Santa Cruz, but dropped out in 1978 when she was twenty years old after a local paper interviewed her. "They interviewed me because I was in a production at school and I was from this famous family. One of the drama teachers used the story to illustrate to the class that this crap is what Hollywood's all about, using people's names to get somewhere. I was very, very hurt by it. So I just checked out."

Crosby left California. She spent the next six months exploring the mountains and villages of Guatemala and Mexico. She then flew to Europe and spent a year modeling on the runways of London and Paris, going through her "European runway thing. I hated modeling, but I was taken to Europe by three California designers who were trying to launch their fashions there. I loved London, so I just stayed on."

Upon returning to Hollywood at Christmas to see her mother, she was contacted by a casting agent. "Toni Howard was casting a movie and had seen my picture in a magazine. I looked wild. My hair was about a quarter of an inch all the way around. I wore army fatigues and no makeup." Although Crosby did not get a role in the film Howard was casting for (Diary of a Teenage Hitchhiker), Howard encouraged her to enroll in acting classes. Meanwhile, in 1979 she posed nude for an extensive *Playboy* pictorial in which photos of a punked-out Denise were displayed under a headline labeling her "a different kind of Crosby." It was, she admits, "some kind of rebellion on my part, some way of saying screw you to the family image."

Geoff Edwards, game show host, rock-music video director, and son of director Blake Edwards, was shown the *Playboy* spread by his girlfriend at the time, who also sported really short hair. "One day, she said, 'Want to see what's really hip?' and showed me the *Playboy* pictures," Edwards said. The photos left a lasting impression on him. Months later, Edwards (who was by then unattached) and Crosby were invited to dinner at a mutual friend's home. It was a blind date. (Well, mostly blind; he had seen the *Playboy* pictures, after all.) Edwards claimed that she had walked off the *Playboy* pages and turned out to be "statuesque and smart."

"It was love at first sight," Crosby exclaimed. "I had one other blind date in my life, and it was a nightmare. I ended up puking in the guy's car. But Geoff had it—he turned me on. Four days later we were living together." Four years later, the two were married, uniting two famous Hollywood bloodlines. More important, Crosby finally had an extended family to call her own, Blake Edwards and his wife, Julie Andrews.

Throughout the early part of her career during the early 1980s, Crosby found work in theater, television, and the movies. She appeared on stage in Los Angeles in such parts as the title role in the critically acclaimed *Tamara* and the lead in *Stops Along the Way*, a controversial one-act play directed by Richard Dreyfuss. She landed roles on *Days of Our Lives*, *L.A. Law*, and in several made-for-television movies. Big-screen credits include *Arizona Heat*, *48 Hours*, *Trail of the Pink Panther*, and *Miracle Mile*. If you look carefully, she is also recognizable in a very brief uncredited cameo in the 1979 Blake Edwards–directed Bo Derek hit *10* (filmed right after she had met Geoff Edwards).

In December 1986, a casting call was issued for the new syndicated series *Star Trek: The Next Generation*. Among the list of characters was Lieutenant Macha Hernandez, a "twenty-six-year-old woman of unspecified Latin descent who serves as the starship's security chief." Also being cast was Counselor Deanna Troi, the starship's "chief psychologist." Denise Crosby was auditioning for the role of Troi, and Marina Sirtis for that of Yar (then Hernandez). Although producers Rick Berman and Bob Justman liked them in those roles, Gene Roddenberry switched them. "He thought I was an American Golden Girl. I reminded him too much of Grace Kelly. Gene wanted an exotic for the part of Troi." Once Crosby was cast as Hernandez, the character's name was changed to Natasha Yar, and she was given a Ukrainian background to match Crosby's blond hair.

The early episodes of the first season saw Crosby in a number of different situations. Following the pilot episode, the first regular show of the season, "The Naked Now," featured the now-infamous scene between Yar and Data in which we learn that Data is indeed "fully functional." "I really liked 'The Naked Now' because it showed humor in all the characters and it took us out of our ordinary elements and showed different colors of our characters," Crosby recalls. The next episode, "Code of Honor," had an extensive fight scene between Yar and an alien woman whose honor has been challenged. The fight, which harkened back to the original *Trek* battle between Kirk and Spock in "Amok Time," was considered an homage to that scene. However, since many on *The Next Generation*'s staff felt that it was important to make a sharp distinction between the new and old *Treks*, not everyone on the staff of the new program was comfortable with the tribute.

At the time, Crosby was still excited about serving on the new *Enterprise*. "The most enjoyable thing has been acting out this wonderful fantasy. It's like a fairy tale to me. It's fun and it's really challenging to make it real. This is all science fiction. It hasn't happened yet, so you're kind of creating it as you go, and that's a challenge to make all that very real. However, it's also very specific as to what you can do and can't do. I find it really challenging to say, 'Arm the photon torpedoes' and 'Phasers on stun!' That's real stuff and yet not real! That's what's fun about being an actress."

Unfortunately, the next dozen or so episodes featured little in the way of character development for Crosby. She wanted out. "It was so great to see a woman take the job traditionally held by a man." However, she added, "Often, they just wanted me to stick my chest out, wear a tight uniform, and shake my butt! I could do that, but I wanted some substance, too. I couldn't see doing that for six years. It was my choice to leave. It really was a thought-out, difficult decision to make but completely with the blessings of everyone."

Gene Roddenberry did not try to entice her to stay by promising her bigger roles. While her castmates patiently awaited their turns in the spotlight, Denise Crosby was gracefully written out of the show. Roddenberry made it clear that her leaving was in no way his choice, nor the decision of the studio executives. "She was very well liked," he stated.

"Skin of Evil," the episode in which Yar died, had as its protagonist Armus, who resembled a living tar pit. (Insiders dubbed the episode "Yar and Tar.") In devising the first-ever "permanent death" of a *Star Trek* cast member, Roddenberry insisted on a "senseless" but typically sudden death befitting a security chief. The moving scenes of the crew reacting to Yar's death were not just attributed to fine acting. Marina Sirtis was actually crying at the departure of her friend, an event that Larry Nemecek calls "one of the most moving scenes shot for the young series." Filming the scene in which Yar dies, however, was a physical challenge. "I was wired, yanked, and flipped," she claims. "I whiplashed my neck and pulled ligaments getting killed."

Crosby later noted that had she been written scenes like the one between her and Worf throughout the season, she would not have asked to leave. She also felt the monologue she delivered in the final "hologram tape" was the single best scene she had over the course of the first year on the show. "I do a four-page monologue. Ironically, I had to die to get the show I wanted." Of course, *Star Trek* fans know that though she left the show vowing never to look back, she would in fact return in some of *The Next Generation*'s best and most popular episodes.

Incidentally, *Star Trek* trivia buffs will note that the episodes "The Big Goodbye" and "The Arsenal of Freedom" aired before "Skin of Evil," although they actually took place on stardates *after* that of "Skin of Evil." This means that Tasha Yar appeared in two shows *after* her death. Additionally, "Symbiosis" was filmed after "Skin of Evil" but was scheduled to air before it. Therefore, Crosby's true final scene as a regular member of *The Next Generation* cast was in *this* episode, waving good-bye from behind a console as corridor doors close behind Picard and Crusher.

It is easy for *Next Generation* fans to forget that Denise Crosby was a regular member of the cast during the first season and was not originally intended to be killed. She appeared in twenty-three of the premier season's twenty-five episodes and would later appear seven additional times as both Yar and Sela. She was interviewed as a regular member of the cast for news reports and publicity appearances promoting the new *Trek*. On her first day on the job she exclaimed, "I get to drive onto the Paramount lot without any problems. That's been the best part so far." She was also photographed for one of the first sets of *Star Trek: The Next Generation* toys. "That first year we were made to take a series of thousands of photographs from every angle. I thought, wow, cool, I'm going to be this action figure. When it finally came out, I was horrified. It looked like this horrible frightening transsexual. I had a meeting with a director [years later], and he had the Tasha doll sitting on his mantel next to a John Travolta *Saturday Night Fever* action figure. I picked them up and did a little *Saturday Night Fever* dance with Tasha and John."

Though she left her post aboard the *Enterprise* in 1988 without any firm job prospects, Crosby quickly found work. She costarred in the feature film *Miracle Mile* (1989) alongside Mare Winningham and Anthony Edwards, and she headlined the critically reviled chiller *Pet Sematary* (1989). She continued to land roles on television, appearing on such shows as *WIOU*, *The Flash*, and *Dark Justice*.

Crosby made the first of seven return appearances in the third season's very popular "Yesterday's *Enterprise*." In this alternate timeline story, Yar is still alive and concludes the episode by returning with the out-of-time *Enterprise-C* twenty-two years into the past, restoring the appropriate timeline. However, the events portrayed in this episode would prove to have lasting repercussions for the fate of the entire *Star Trek* universe. Unaware of it at the time, though, fans were enthralled by the episode, which has become a favorite, and Crosby was pleased at the chance to die "with meaning."

The repercussions began to be felt as fans received a shocker at the conclusion of *The Next Generation*'s fourth season. In the season-finale cliff-hanger "Redemption," the Klingon civil war is revealed to be backed by a faction of Romulans. In the episode's final scene, the Romulan commander is revealed to look amazingly like Tasha Yar.

Fans and reviewers alike considered this conclusion on a par with *Dallas'* famous "Who Killed J. R.?" plot. Who was this Romulan who so resembled the slain *Enterprise* chief of security? Theories abounded. One reviewer listed the "Evil Twin" theory; the "Pure Coincidence" theory; the "Anti-Tasha" theory (in which the black ooze that killed her turned himself into an evil Romulan version of Yar); the "Tasha Never Died in the First Place" theory (proponents of which pointed to the moment when Picard said "au revoir" to Yar, rather than "good-bye," in the episode "Skin of Evil," and to the fact that fans never saw Yar's body disposed of); and the various "Alternate *Enterprise*" theories. Fans had to wait through the long summer to learn the answer to Yar's mysterious reappearance in the guise of a Romulan.

It was an idea that had originally been proposed by Crosby herself: Sela, Yar's half-Romulan daughter, was born after Yar had been captured by the Romulans prior to the destruction of the *Enterprise-C* following the events portrayed in "Yesterday's Enterprise." Young Sela was portrayed as the epitome of evil: her own mother, Tasha Yar, was killed in an escape attempt after the four-year-old had turned her in. This confusing plot thread, in which Tasha Yar was alive, died, was alive again, returned to the past, was alive simultaneously in two different places, had a half-Romulan daughter, and ultimately died (again) in both places, is so convoluted and twisted that fans continue to actively debate it to this day.

Crosby's Commander Sela would appear three more times over the course of *The Next Generation*: in the episode "The Mind's Eye" and opposite Leonard Nimoy's Spock in the two-part episode "Unification." "I had the best roles after my character *died*," Crosby joked. Denise Crosby would appear one final time on *Star Trek: The Next Generation*, in the series finale, "All Good Things . . ." As Lieutenant Yar, she was instrumental in the scenes featuring the "past" *Enterprise*. Her appearance on the bridge lent credibility to the difficult "time displacement" scenes, in which Picard is whisked by Q seven years into the past.

Denise Crosby's career has maintained a steady bearing. She was cast in the short-lived comedy-drama *Key West* (1993) as the homosexual, pro-growth, alcoholic, Republican mayor Chauncy Caldwell, one of the show's more mainstream characters. She appeared in well-regarded roles on both *Sisters* and *Lois & Clark*, and in two steamy episodes of Showtime's soft-core *Red Shoe Diaries*. On stage, Crosby portrayed a self-assured lesbian in *Last Summer at Bluefish Cove*, as well as appearing in an all-female production of *Richard III* with the Los Angeles Women's Shakespeare Company. She also was cast in the independent film *Dream Man* alongside Andrew McCarthy, and the direct-to-video B-movie *Mutant Species*.

Divorced from husband Geoff Edwards in 1990 after seven years of marriage, Crosby lived simply in a rented West Hollywood home with her English bull terrier, Julius. Her new life was quiet and content; she was most happy about forgoing the L.A. driving requirements. "I've not been in a car here except when being picked up to go on location. I bought a bicycle, put a basket on it, and ride it everywhere. That's my BMW." Romantically linked for a time with actor George Clooney (before his popularity exploded with roles on *ER* and as *Batman*), she finally settled down once again, this time with writer Ken Sylk. Married in 1995 to Sylk, her first child was born in 1996.

Crosby has spoken to the producers of *Deep Space Nine* about appearing as Sela. Although "they love the idea, I haven't seen any scripts yet," she remarked in 1996. She is also producing a documentary about *Star Trek* fandom, tentatively titled *Trekkies* (fan publications have already expressed their extreme displeasure at her choice of title). She has been filming footage at *Star Trek* conventions around the world, and intends to portray the avid fans of the program in a sincere, loving, and respectable light.

Crosby may be a footnote in the history of *Trek*, having only appeared on 27 of the show's 176 episodes, but she is unforgettable. Some fans never forgave her for leaving the show and brand her a prima donna. Others relish every appearance she made, respecting her decision to take chances with her career. As for Crosby, she is happy living simply in West Hollywood with her husband and new child, and is content about the decisions she has made regarding her career. "I live in boxers and T-shirts," she claims. "I've even taken the laces out of my Keds."

D E N I S E   C R O S B Y

Lieutenant Tasha Yar and Romulan Commander Sela

STAGE:
Stops Along the Way ('81)
Tamara ('84)
Last Summer at Bluefish Cove ('94)
Richard III ('96)

TELEVISION:
Days of Our Lives ('82)
Cocaine: One Man's Seduction ('83)
Gable and Lombard ('84)
The Family Martinez ('84)
Brisco County Jr. ('85)
Hunter ('85)
Malice in Wonderland ('85)
My Wicked, Wicked Ways . . . The Legend of Errol Flynn ('85)
Stark ('85)
Dallas ('86)
L.A. Law ('86)
Ohara ('87)
Star Trek: The Next Generation ('87–'88, '90, '91, '94)
Reading Rainbow ('88)
Mancuse, FBI ('89)
WIOU ('90)
The Flash ('91)
Jack's Place ('92)
Dark Justice ('93)
Desperate Crimes ('93)

Johnny Bago ('93)
Key West ('93)
The Red Shoe Diaries ('93, '95)
Diagnosis: Murder ('94)
Lois & Clark: The New Adventures of Superman ('94)
Sisters ('94)

FILM:
10 ('79)
48 Hours ('82)
Trail of the Pink Panther ('82)
Curse of the Pink Panther ('83)
The Man Who Loved Women ('83)
Desert Hearts ('85)
The Eliminators ('86)
Arizona Heat ('88)
Crime Zone ('88)
High Strung ('89)
Miracle Mile ('89)
Pet Sematary ('89)
Skin Deep ('89)
Tennesseee Nights ('89)
Dolly Dearest ('92)
Desperate Crimes ('93)
Black Water ('94)
Max ('94)
Relative Fear ('94)
Mutant Species (direct-to-video) ('95)
Dream Man ('96)

WHOOPI GOLDBERG

"Guinan is a combination of myself, Yoda, and Andrei Sakharov."
—WHOOPI GOLDBERG, QUOTED IN STAR TREK: THE OFFICIAL FAN CLUB
MAGAZINE, APRIL/MAY 1991

Of the stars on *Star Trek: The Next Generation*, perhaps the one *least* associated with the program is Whoopi Goldberg. While puzzling to some that an Oscar, Golden Globe, Grammy, and Emmy Award–winning actress who has headlined Broadway stages and feature films would join the cast of the weekly, syndicated science fiction drama, her presence validated the program for many viewers and critics. Named for famous female bartender Tex Guinan, her character was mysterious and helpful, calm but earnest. Troi may have been the ship's counselor, but Guinan had the captain's ear.

Born Caryn E. Johnson on November 13, 1949, in New York City, Goldberg began performing at the age of eight near the Chelsea neighborhood of the city. She first appeared on stage at New York's Hudson Guild Theatre as part of a children's program and was also involved in the Helena Rubenstein Children's Theatre. "My first coherent thought was probably, 'I want to be an actor,'" she recounted in a 1991 interview. "I believe that. That's just what I was born to do. I liked the idea that you could pretend to be somebody else and nobody would cart you off to the hospital."

High school in the Big Apple in the 1960s found Goldberg lost, drug addicted, and without vision. "I took drugs because they were available to everyone in those times. As everyone evolved into LSD, so did I. It was the time of Woodstock, of be-ins and love-ins." A self-professed "junkie," she dropped out of high school and never completed any further formal education. When she hit rock bottom she sought help and, with the assistance of a drug counselor, cleaned herself up. In 1972, Goldberg and her drug counselor were married. Two years later she gave birth to her daughter, Alexandrea, divorced her husband, and moved to San Diego to pursue her dreams of the stage.

Though she did not imagine the success she would ultimately realize, she dreamed big. "I always felt that if I kept going and pushing myself that something would happen. But nobody encouraged me in this business. I encouraged myself. I was very shy as a child and rather dull. I was the last person you would expect to be a successful actor. I knew what talents I had when I was doing theater and comedy, but I kind of shocked myself when I found out that I could be funny all by myself on stage."

While in San Diego, she helped found the San Diego Repertory Theatre. She starred in the company's productions of Bertolt Brecht's *Mother Courage* and Marsha Norman's *Getting Out*. She also performed with an improvisational comedy troupe, *Spontaneous Combustion*.

She was not yet known as "Whoopi Goldberg," though. She used her given name or often performed under the name "Whoopi Cushion." (She employed the French pronunciation, "Kush*on*.") Her mother, Emma Johnson, a nurse and teacher, told her daughter how completely ridiculous the name sounded, so Goldberg adopted a name from her family's history.

Despite regular stage work, her income from performing was not sufficient to appropriately care for her daughter. Goldberg took a variety of jobs while in San Diego, including bricklayer, bank teller, and a mortuary cosmetologist. She also spent a few years on public assistance.

Moving to San Francisco in the late 1970s, Goldberg became a member of a comic avant-garde troupe Berkeley's Blake Street Hawkeyes. The characters she developed there led her to create *The Spook Show*. Goldberg toured the country and Europe with the one-woman show. After performing it for an enthralled Mike Nichols, she accepted his offer to produce it on Broadway (which came to pass in September 1984). Rob Nagel, in his biography of Goldberg published in *Contemporary Black Biography*, discussed four of the "rueful—and sometimes sublime—characters" she portrayed: she played Fontaine, a profanity-spewing drug dealer with a Ph.D. in literature who travels to Europe looking for hashish, only to openly weep when he comes across Anne Frank's secret hiding place. She also took on the guise of a shallow thirteen-year-old surfing Valley Girl who is left barren after a self-inflicted abortion with a coat hanger. She effectively portrayed a severely handicapped young woman who tells her prospective suitor, who wants to go dancing, "This is not a disco body." Finally, Nagel praised her performance as a nine-year-old black girl who bathes in Clorox and covers her head with a white skirt, hoping to become white with long blond hair so she can appear on *The Love Boat*.

After the tour of *The Spook Show* ended (but prior to her Broadway debut), Goldberg returned to San Francisco to star as Moms Mabley in *Moms*, another one-person play she also cowrote. *The Spook Show* opened at Broadway's Lyceum Theatre in 1984. It was televised on HBO the following year and the recording garnered Goldberg a Grammy for the best comedy album of 1985.

In a story that is now Hollywood legend, in 1984 Goldberg had heard about the impending Steven Spielberg feature film of Alice Walker's *The Color Purple*. Never having appeared in a movie, Goldberg called Walker directly and asked to be involved in some way, however small, with the film. "I told her that whenever there was an audition I'd come. I'd eat the dirt, I'd play the dirt, I'd *be* the dirt, because the part is perfect." However, Walker was already a fan of Goldberg's and had already recommended her to filmmaker Spielberg. He requested that she perform her act at his famed and intimidating private screening room in Los Angeles for a group of onlookers that included Spielberg himself, Quincy Jones, and Michael Jackson.

Hoping only for a small part or perhaps the supporting role of Sophia, Goldberg found herself accepting the lead of Celie. "This is powerhouse acting," wrote *Newsweek*'s David Anson of the finished product. "All the more so because the rage and the exhilaration are held in reserve." Yet many critics took aim at the movie, criticizing both the screenplay and the selection of white male Spielberg to helm a movie focusing on the southern black experience from a female point of view. Goldberg defended Spielberg, which prompted filmmaker Spike Lee to retort in *Harper's*, "I hope people realize, that the media realize, that she's not a spokesperson for Black people." Goldberg defines herself as a humanist, and responded to Lee in a conversation published in *Interview* magazine, "What I am is a humanist before anything—before I'm a Jew, before I'm black, before I'm a woman. And my beliefs are for the human race—they don't exclude anyone."

In the years that followed *The Color Purple*, Goldberg was in demand for a host of television and film roles. Some were very successful, such as her Emmy-nominated appearance on *Moonlighting* in 1986 and her hosting stints (alongside Billy Crystal and Robin Williams) on *Comic Relief*. Some were less so, including feature films *Jumpin' Jack Flash* (1986), *Burglar* (1987), *Fatal Beauty* (1987), *Clara's Heart* (1988), and *The Telephone* (1988).

In 1986 she married for the second time to cinematographer David Edward Claessen, a marriage that ended in divorce two years later. She returned to the stage in 1988, with an all-new original one-woman show, introducing a different cast of her unique characters.

Goldberg also spent much time campaigning on behalf of such social causes as AIDS, drug abuse awareness, and abortion rights. She won the 1989 Starlight Foundation Award as Humanitarian of the Year for her involvement in these issues as well as *Comic Relief*, which benefited the homeless.

Though her work was charitable, the critics were not. Since *The Color Purple*, her career in film had been stagnant. Laura B. Randolph wrote in *Ebony* in March 1991, "In less than five years she went from Hollywood's golden girl to a rumored lesbian/Uncle Tom with a bad attitude and a career on the skids. In Hollywood, that combination is almost always terminal, and insiders whispered that she should pack it in and be happy to do guest spots on the *Hollywood Squares*." Nonetheless, Goldberg remained stoic. "I've stopped listening to them. I've taken crazy movies that appeal to me. I don't care what other people think about it. If it was pretty decent when I did it, I did my job."

In 1987, when friend LeVar Burton told Goldberg that he was preparing to appear on the new *Star Trek*, Whoopi told him, "Great, let them know I'm interested in doing it." She heard nothing from the producers the first year the show was on the air. "When I heard Denise Crosby was leaving, I thought that maybe I could fill a gap, not take her place, but fill a gap and I hoped that they would let me do it. When they finally realized I was serious, then, of course, everything was expedited—but that's basically how it came to be." However, it took quite a bit of cajoling to convince the Paramount executives that she seriously wanted to join the crew and not just make a one-time guest appearance. Ultimately, she called *The Next Generation* offices and just blurted, "Hey, I know I'm no blond, but . . ."

"Since I was a little girl on the streets, *Star Trek* was always my guide to morality and my philosophy," Whoopi Goldberg told Gene Roddenberry when explaining to him why she wanted to appear on *The Next Generation*. "Then, later, Nichelle Nichols showed me what a Black girl could do. I just want to be made a part of that and make it better if I can."

Goldberg was pleased with the character Roddenberry created for her. He built her a set (Ten-Forward, named for its location on the *Enterprise*, deck ten, forward) and a bar, a sort of recreation lounge where viewers could see how the *Enterprise*'s crew behaved off duty. Goldberg was excited. "I go in and I'm really sage and I get to wear great hats. I also get to hang out with some extraordinary people."

According to Roddenberry, Guinan was "patterned after Whoopi and patterned after what the whole group of us thought the character should be. We felt that Whoopi would have some mysterious, but not clearly stated, relationship with the captain. We needed a philosophical context for her. It just worked as we began to write it and play with it and as she began to make suggestions, it sort of all came together."

Her recent career setbacks on the big screen also made her decision to join *Star Trek* easy. "I did it because, frankly, I couldn't get any work then. I liked the show, so I asked if I could be on it. I did it as a tribute for my love of the show."

Much of Goldberg's role on *The Next Generation* consisted of giving advice, prompting one reviewer to write that "she was as much the ship's counselor as Troi." Guinan premiered on the opening episode of the second season, "The Child," and helped Wesley decide whether or not to join his mother at Starfleet Medical. She appeared in a total of five episodes during the second season, twenty-seven over the course of a six-year recurring role.

Yet she remained a mystery. Fans endlessly debated what was meant by Guinan's cryptic comment in the season-four premiere, "Best of Both Worlds Part II," when she claimed her relationship with Captain Picard was "more than family, more than a friend." Goldberg responds, "I can't tell you! I wish I could. But it did leave you wondering and I think that was the idea. It is those things that keep you guessing. But there is something there." This episode provided her one of her most significant moments on the series, as she offered advice to Riker that gave him the impetus to defeat the insidious Borg.

Nonetheless, Goldberg did not want to see Guinan develop beyond the bounds that had been drawn for her. "I actually don't want her to do too much. I just want her to be able to help them do what they need to do in the gentlest possible way. I don't think Guinan can do much more than that or be more than that on the show because then it would take away from the other characters. So, I think that just what she's doing is right."

A number of other episodes featured Goldberg in a significant role. In the fifth season's "I, Borg," viewers learned the fate Guinan's race had befallen at the hands of the Borg. As a result, she is adamant regarding what fate should befall the captured Borg Hugh. In the fifth-season cliff-hanger, "Time's Arrow," Data finds himself in nineteenth-century San Francisco and is surprised to see Guinan in a local newspaper. However, when he meets up with her she has no recollection of him. The conclusion to the story, the sixth-season premiere, "Time's Arrow, Part II," would be one of Goldberg's final appearances, due to her burgeoning schedule.

It was not until the 1994 feature *Star Trek: Generations* that fans learned significantly more about Guinan's elusive past. A refugee rescued by the *Enterprise-B* after the Borg destroyed most of her race and dispersed the surviving few, Guinan plays a vital role in getting Picard and Kirk together in the Nexus by explaining to Picard (and to moviegoers) the nature of the Nexus time-ribbon. Goldberg appeared in *Generations* without screen credit, and reportedly, gratis.

Goldberg's career was anything but stagnant during her run on *Star Trek*. Actually, it can be argued that her role on the *Enterprise* jump-started a stalled career. Her portrayal of the flamboyant yet heroic psychic Oda Mae in *Ghost*, the highest-grossing movie of 1990, garnered Goldberg an Oscar statuette. (She is only the second black female in the history of the Academy Awards to win such an honor.) She was pragmatic about the certifiable blockbuster hit that revitalized her screen career. "You can never know

whether a movie is going to do really well so you're always glad
when it does, and you hope that the next one will and if it doesn't,
maybe the one after that."

Goldberg followed *Ghost* with a serious dramatic film
about the 1955 Montgomery, Alabama, bus boycott, *The Long Walk
Home* (1990). She portrayed Odessa Carter, a housekeeper who is
forced to walk almost ten miles to work because of the boycott,
despite blistering and bleeding feet. Director Richard Pearce
claimed: "What her portrayal of Odessa revealed about Whoopi was
a complex inner life and intelligence. Her mouth is her usual
weapon of choice—to disarm her of that easy weapon meant that
she had to rely on other things. It's a real actress who can bring off
a performance like that. And she did."

In a 1990 performance that may not have made headlines,
but is of note to fans of *Star Trek*, Goldberg appeared with Patrick
Stewart and actor/singer Charles Keating on stage in *So Many
People Have Heads*, two evenings of skits, songs, poetry, and prose,
held as benefit performances. The program included one skit in
which Goldberg was hailed for "making real the painful experience
of drugs and its concomitant grief and loss." Though the benefit
lasted two evenings, Goldberg only appeared one night, being
replaced the second evening by Gates McFadden.

Subsequent years have brought a mixed bag of successes
and near-misses. Goldberg starred as the proprietor of a small
restaurant in a weekly situation comedy based on an offbeat 1988
German film, *Bagdad Café*. She abruptly walked off the program,
which costarred Jean Stapleton, after nine episodes, and it sputtered
to a halt. *The Whoopi Goldberg Show* (also known as *Whoopi*), a
1992 late-night program featuring Goldberg interviewing a single
guest for a half hour each weekday evening without the benefit of
studio audience, was canceled after one season. Successes included
a turn as a homicide detective in Robert Altman's *The Player* (1992);
and in a significant box-office draw, she donned a habit for the whim-
sical *Sister Act* (1992). Other films that have met with recent success
include *Sarafina!* (shot on location in Soweto, South Africa), *The
Lion King*, *Corrina, Corrina* (which featured a cameo by Brent
Spiner), *The Pagemaster* (costarring Patrick Stewart), and many others. "None of my films cure cancer," she explained, "but they have

allowed me to not just play one kind of person, which is important to me. Nobody knows how long this stuff is gonna last, and you want to have it and enjoy as much of it and be as diverse as you can."

These days Goldberg is prominent both in the gossip pages (linked romantically at various times with costars Ted Danson and Frank Langella) and in the financial sections (once again one of Hollywood's highest-paid actresses, buoyed by the success of *Sister Act*). She was married yet again, in 1995, this time to Lyle Trachtenberg. In 1996 she appeared in *Boys on the Side*, bringing her "own experience of being in love, even if it was with a man." However, her third marriage ended in divorce one year after the nuptials had been proclaimed.

Whoopi Goldberg's calendar remains more than full. She recently costarred with Alec Baldwin and James Woods in the Rob Reiner–directed film, *Ghosts of Mississippi*, about the murder of civil rights activist Medgar Evers. She is filming *High Strung* (formerly *Women on the Verge of a Nervous Breakdown*), and is signed to play the fairy godmother in *Cinderella* opposite Natalie Portman in the title role. She will also star in a faux-documentary, *An Alan Smithee Film*, performing in a role originally written for Arnold Schwarzenegger. (The part has been substantially rewritten.) Goldberg has also found the time to return to Broadway, having replaced Nathan Lane in the starring role in *A Funny Thing Happened on the Way to the Forum*. She has also signed a two-year deal with Caravan Pictures and plans to produce and costar in *Lily White* for them. She even has a book deal with an imprint of William Morrow & Sons for a freewheeling collection of her observations on many issues, comedic and serious, scheduled for publication in the fall of 1997. (However, this is not her first time taking pen to paper: she previously authored the children's book *Alice*.)

When given the honor of leaving her handprints and autograph in the cement outside Mann's Chinese Theater in Hollywood, Goldberg snipped off three of her trademark dreadlocks and added their imprint. She is content with herself and her success. "I think I'm as successful as I would like to be. I do long for more work and *good* work. But some stuff will be terrible and some will be great. I've done some good stuff and some bad stuff but I guess that's what careers are all about."

Her rapid climb from poor single mother to Hollywood royalty has not, Goldberg insists, significantly changed her outlook on the world. "I think it was rather bizarre for me because it happened so fast. It was peculiar. But most people who know me can see that nothing much is going to change about me. I'm still going to wear my hair the same way. You know I like working. I haven't had the perfect past; I grew up in a different world than a lot of people in this business so I haven't learned to guard my tongue yet or do things the way they're 'supposed' to be done. I just have a good time working and I'm grateful for the success I have."

What are the goals of a woman whose heroes include Lady Bird Johnson and Andrei Sakharov? "I want to win a Nobel Prize. It's a goal that I want to achieve in my lifetime. I plan to make the world a safer, better place. Basically, I want to save the world!" she jokes. "I just hope I can keep working and have some fun too."

W H O O P I   G O L D B E R G

Guinan

STAGE:

Hair ('71)
Jesus Christ Superstar ('72)
Pippin ('74)
Spontaneous Combustion ('74–'76)
Mother Courage ('76)
Getting Out ('77)
The Spook Show ('81–'84)
Moms ('83)
Whoopi Goldberg ('84)
Living on the Edge of Chaos ('88)
So Many People Have Heads ('90)
A Funny Thing Happened on the Way to the Forum ('97)

TELEVISION:

Comedy Tonight ('85)
Funny, You Don't Look 200 ('85)
Night of 100 Stars ('85)
The Spook Show ('85)
Whoopi Goldberg: Direct from Broadway ('85)
Comic Relief ('86)
Free to Be . . . A Family ('86)
Miami Vice ('86)
Moonlighting ('86)
Scared Straight: 10 Years Later ('86)
Carol, Carl, Whoopi, and Robin ('87)
Comic Relief II ('87)

First Annual American Comedy
  Awards ('87)
Happy Birthday Hollywood ('87)
The Best of D.C. Follies:
  Superstar Comedy ('87)
A Different World ('88)
Captain EO—Backstage ('88)
Comic Relief III ('88)
Dolly ('88)
Star Trek: The Next Generation
  ('88–'93)
The Tonight Show Starring
  Johnny Carson ('88)
Whoopi Goldberg's Fontaine . . .
  Why Am I Straight? ('88)
All-Star Tribute to Kareem
  Abdul Jabbar ('89)
Kiss Shot ('89)
My Past Is My Own ('89)
The Debbie Allen Special ('89)
Bagdad Café ('90)
Comic Relief IV ('90)
Reading Rainbow ('90)
Sesame Street ('90)
Tales from the Crypt ('90)
Whoopi Goldberg Live ('90)
Alan King: Inside the Comedy
  Mind ('91)
Silent Screen: Hollywood and
  the AIDS Crisis ('91)
The New Adventures of Captain
  Planet ('91)
Comic Relief V ('92)
Rock the Vote ('92)
Tales from the Whoop ('92)
The Whoopi Goldberg Show
  ('92–'93)
Mo' Funny: Black Comedy in
  America ('93)
Comic Relief VI ('94)

Science Fiction: A Journey into
  the Unknown ('94)
50 Years of Funny Females ('95)
Afterschool Special ('95)
Coach ('95)
Comic Relief VII ('95)
Grace Under Fire ('95)
Lois & Clark: The New
  Adventures of Superman ('95)
Murder One ('95)
68th Annual Academy Awards
  ('96)
Comic Relief's American
  Comedy Festival ('96)
Mad TV ('96)
Muppets Tonight! ('96)

FILM:

The Color Purple ('85)
Doctor Duck's Super Secret
  All-Purpose Sauce ('86)
Jumpin' Jack Flash ('86)
La Ladrona ('86)
Burglar ('87)
Fatal Beauty ('87)
Clara's Heart ('88)
The Telephone ('88)
Beverly Hills Brats ('89)
Ghost ('90)
Homer and Eddie ('90)
The Long Walk Home ('90)
House Party 2 ('91)
Soap Dish ('91)
Wisecracks ('91)
Sarafina! ('92)
Sister Act ('92)
The Magical World of Chuck
  Jones ('92)
The Player ('92)
Made in America ('93)

National Lampoon's Loaded Weapon I ('93)	Boys on the Side ('95)
	Moonlight and Valentino ('95)
Sister Act 2: Back in the Habit ('93)	The Celluloid Closet ('95)
	Bogus ('96)
Corrina, Corrina ('94)	Eddie ('96)
Liberation ('94)	T. Rex (direct-to-video) ('96)
Naked in New York ('94)	The Associate ('96)
Star Trek: Generations ('94)	An Alan Smithee Film ('97)
The Lion King ('94)	Cinderella ('97)
The Little Rascals ('94)	Ghosts of Mississippi ('97)
The Pagemaster ('94)	Lily White ('98)

COLM MEANEY

"I was in the transporter room for fifteen shows and they just kept referring to me as 'Transporter Chief.' Then I get a script and I see 'Transporter Chief O'Brien.' I freaked. I said, 'Hey! I'm the transporter chief! What's going on here?' And then Jonathan Frakes goes, 'Relax, Colm. They just gave you a name.'"
—COLM MEANEY, QUOTED IN *TV GUIDE*, DECEMBER 11, 1993

Background actors sitting in a restaurant, shopping in a store, walking down the street, or operating a control panel at an unnamed console on the bridge of the *Enterprise*: if you're not a scriptwriter, you call them "extras." In *Star Trek* scripts, they are referred to as "superluminaries," or "nondescript crew members." Famous actors have begun their careers in these roles, working as extras on television and in film until getting their "big break" somewhere else. However, rarely does one rise from the ranks to obtain as much as a speaking role on the program upon which they toiled as an extra, never mind a regular slate of appearances or the opportunity to headline a sequel series. Yet Colm Meaney has accomplished this—while consistently working in feature films as well—making him perhaps the most descript "nondescript crew member" ever to appear on any incarnation of *Star Trek*.

And no, he is not patterned after Scotty: the accent is real.

Born May 30, 1953, in Dublin, Ireland, Colm (pronounced "Kolum") Meaney started acting at age fourteen. A few years later, he was accepted to the Abbey Theatre School of Acting (the drama school of the Irish National Theatre), prompting him to happily leave his job aboard a fishing boat. After completing his education at the age of twenty, Meaney spent eight years on the London stage with the company of the Irish National Theatre. During this time he was also cast in a recurring role on the BBC police drama Z Cars.

In 1978 Meaney, along with his new bride, Bairbre Dowling, made the first of several trips to New York; and they spent the next four years shuttling back and forth between the Big Apple and the Emerald Isle. Looking to break onto the New York stage, Meaney felt his strong accent cost him some acting jobs because it thrust him into a narrow role in the minds of producers and directors. "Initially, I was considered a heavy," he explained in 1990. "But I've started to get away from that a bit, I think, and perhaps the O'Brien character has helped with that. I don't feel I've been badly typecast in film and television."

Meaney quit his transoceanic commuting and moved to New York in 1982, ultimately relocating to Los Angeles in late 1984. The impending birth of his daughter, and the requisite need for steady employment, prompted the move. It was here that his acting fortunes began to blossom. "In terms of work it certainly changed. I started to do some film and television," he said in 1990. "It's a very different world because I now have a five-year-old daughter; and working in regional theater and going out and doing three months here and six months there, I think it's a young man's game.

"There's a couple of different kinds of life here. It's like life in Los Angeles is very different than life in New York, both in terms of the lifestyles and in terms of the industry. I lived in New York from '82 to almost '85 and I tended to work mostly in regional theater and some off-Broadway as well. In Los Angeles, theater is not as big as it is out there and you tend to work in film and television.

"As far as the differences workwise between the U.S. and either Ireland or England . . . it's easier to have a career in everything over there: theater, film, television, and radio. You can have that in England because it's smaller. In London, you can be doing theater at night and doing a movie during the day or a TV or radio show, and also there's one union that represents actors in all the different mediums. So that's the real difference, you tend to do more of a variety of work. In this country, when you're deciding you want to pursue film and television, that kind of takes over and it's very hard to keep working in the theater. You have to set a period of time aside and say, 'Okay, for the next six months I want to do some theater work.'"

Meaney is sensitive to the obvious distinctions between his homeland and his adopted country, although those differences are narrowing. "You can walk into a bar in Ireland and the customers are watching *Monday Night Football* or they're watching the highlights of the previous day's games in the NFL. But there's still differences in terms of socializing. I think the people in Ireland tend to socialize more than they do here. People here tend to retreat into their own little land, boxes, or whatever. People see each other at work and stuff like that, but there isn't the same kind of general socializing that you find in Ireland."

Upon arriving in Los Angeles, Meaney raised his profile with guest roles on popular television dramas such as *Moonlighting* and *Remington Steele*. When the casting call for *Star Trek: The Next Generation* came, he auditioned for a couple of regular roles but failed to be cast. Nonetheless, the producers liked what they saw. They cast him in the unnamed role of "Conn Ensign" for the pilot episode "Encounter at Farpoint," in which he made a notable appearance helming the *Enterprise*'s Battle Bridge. He was seen once again during the first season, in "Lonely Among Us," an episode in which he was billed as the "First Security Guard." Again, he was nameless, and wore the insignia of an officer, an "error" that would be resolved only years later.

After the first half of *The Next Generation*'s premiere season, Meaney left California to appear once again on the New York stage. He was cast opposite Derek Jacobi on Broadway in the acclaimed drama *Breaking the Code*, a role that would last nine months—"the longest I had ever appeared in anything!" He was intent upon returning to Los Angeles after the play's run. However, because of the strike that halted the beginning of the 1988 Hollywood season,

Meaney stayed in New York City and landed a recurring role as an English thief on the soap opera *One Life to Live*. Yet Meaney was in touch with *The Next Generation* producers while the strike was on, and he was told that they might cast him as the transporter chief. He returned to Los Angeles in time to film the first episode of the second season, "The Child."

Meaney actually appeared, albeit briefly, in most of the episodes of *Star Trek: The Next Generation*'s second season. But it was not until "A Matter of Honor," the eighth episode of the season, that he was given a last name. It would take two more years for viewers to learn his full name, Miles Edward O'Brien.

By the end of the second season, although not a significant player in the plots—and with only a minute or two of screen time per episode—Meaney enjoyed the relationship that he and the viewers were gradually developing with O'Brien. "In terms of an acting job, I'd describe him as an irregular regular. He's obviously on the ship and part of the crew, but it's pretty much on the periphery. Then, in terms of the type of character, there were things in [the second] season that developed that I liked, like a sense of humor that, perhaps, isn't in some of the other characters—being the Starfleet graduates that they are. They all tend to have nerves of steel and are superprofessionals. I think the O'Brien character showed moments of vulnerability that were interesting, which gave him an edge of humor as well. I like that."

Even with such a minor role, Meaney had developed favorite episodes up to that point. "I really enjoyed the Sherlock Holmes episode ["Elementary, Dear Data"]. It's the marriage of two periods, the future and the past, and also Brent's acting was wonderful. What's wonderful about the show is the holodeck, which gives the actors the chance to play roles that they wouldn't normally get in a series like that. It gives them the chance to develop and expand. I also liked the one I had quite a bit to do in. I can't remember the name—the one where Dr. Pulaski is aging rapidly ["Unnatural Selection"]. I liked that one because, again, it touched on things outside of the normal routine."

Although Meaney appeared in about one-half of the third-season *Next Generation* episodes, little was done to advance his character beyond that of a peripheral player with only a few lines each week. At a *Star Trek* convention during the summer hiatus, he proclaimed his hope that his character might grow and even develop a love interest. Little did he know that in a few short months he would make *Star Trek* history in the romance department.

The fourth season aired back-to-back episodes that featured O'Brien as none had previously. In "Data's Day," the first *Star Trek* marriage took place, between Miles O'Brien and *Enterprise* botanist Keiko Ishikawa, played by Rosalind Chao. "The one thing that science fiction shows tend to lack is simple, real family business, like making tea or having dinner," Meaney explained. "There's usually no time for that. Interpersonal relationships and the like don't get much air time on science fiction shows, either. Having Keiko and Molly [the daughter who would be born to the couple the following season] there gives me more aspects of my character to explore. That's a tremendous plus. It's funny, Rosalind and I had an immediate rapport when we started on *Next Generation*. When we were getting married on *Next Generation*, her real-life husband, Simon Templeman, was actually working on a play in Costa Mesa with my wife, Bairbre. It was very strange. My wife would go to work with Simon and I would come here to work with Roz. We had a lot in common: Rosalind is married, I'm married; Rosalind recently had a baby. I have a child. Plus, she's great to work with. There really wasn't much time to develop a relationship, to sit at a table and rehearse. We just seemed to click from the beginning."

On "Data's Day," the episode that was *Star Trek*'s first real day-in-the-life-of program, O'Brien commented, "It was funny, so much was happening all over the ship that O'Brien melted into the background. It was really Keiko changing her mind, deciding yes, no, yes, no, and Data taking it all in. It was a fun episode because it shows that even in the twenty-fourth century, getting married is still a big step."

Immediately following "Data's Day" was the episode "The Wounded," in which O'Brien talks his emotionally frazzled former commander, Ben Maxwell, out of provoking the Cardassians. This episode not only introduced the Cardassians (who would of course figure very prominently in the plots of space station sequel *Deep Space Nine*), but also opened up O'Brien's life to *Star Trek* viewers for the first time. He was a peaceful, nature-loving boy who had never killed until a Cardassian patrol forced it upon him; and he had served as tactics officer aboard the USS *Rutledge* under Maxwell. Viewers of this episode also heard him croon an Irish drinking song with his former commander, which ultimately served to defuse a difficult situation and return Maxwell to some semblance of sanity. "It was one of the rare occasions on *The Next Generation* where we could explore a bit of O'Brien's past. It gave me a great dramatic dilemma to play. I had great loyalty to the man, but he had lost his mind and I had to deal with the fact that he had cracked."

His status as a recurring character, which did not require his presence on the *Star Trek* set every day or even every week, left Meaney open to appear in other projects. It was outside the confines of the *Enterprise's* transporter room that he first began to gain real fame. Starring in Roddy Doyle's *The Commitments* (1991), *The Snapper* (1993), and the recently released *The Van* (1997)—the three films combine to form the "Barrytown trilogy"—Meaney won his first wide-scale critical recognition. He earned a Golden Globe nomination as best actor in a comedy for his role in *The Snapper*, and critics lauded him with praise along the lines of "Colm Meaney may never again have to venture into outer space to earn his living after his incredible performance in *The Snapper*."

Meaney understood the trials and tribulations of his *Snapper* character, Dessie, a normal working-class Dubliner. "He cares very much about his family, and there's a strong sense of community; Dubliners feel very much part of a city that has a very strong identity of its own. They feel quite proud of that. They're not alienated from their environment. There's also a great sense of humor there; there's a great ability to converse and to *hold opinions*. Dublin people can be very opinionated. The problems of the world are dealt with seriously yet in a very humorous way as well."

Meaney became a household name in Ireland after his appearances in the Doyle films and became popular in the States after smaller roles in big-budget movies, including *Die Harder* (1990), *Last of the Mohicans* (1992), *Under Seige* (1992), and *The Road to Wellville* (1994). In 1992 he also had a significant role as an aviator in the pilot episode of *Dr. Quinn, Medicine Woman*. Shortly thereafter he appeared on stage alongside Patrick Stewart, Jonathan Frakes, Brent Spiner, and Gates McFadden in the Stewart-directed *Every Good Boy Deserves Favour*. Reviewing the play, *Variety*'s Jim Farber singled Meaney out as "impressive."

Meaney's appearances on *The Next Generation* were curtailed significantly during the fifth season (1991–92) due to his film commitments. In his last significant appearance before the series finale, the fifth season's "Power Play," Troi, Data, and O'Brien are possessed by ghostly alien entities who proceed to take hostages aboard the *Enterprise*, among them Molly and Keiko. "Again, it gave me a good dramatic dilemma. I've just married this woman and here I am threatening her with a phaser. And the baby was there, too. It was a bit shocking. Playing bad guys is often more fun than playing good guys. Brent, Marina, and I had a lot of fun." Off camera, Sirtis, Spiner, and Meaney invented nicknames for their "possessed" alter egos: Slugger, Buzz, and Slash.

Meaney would appear only briefly on *The Next Generation* after this episode, for his character received a transfer and a promotion. His final appearance on *The Next Generation* would come in the "flashback" scenes in the series finale, "All Good Things . . ."

It took Colm Meaney six months to finally agree to appear weekly as a central character on *Star Trek: Deep Space Nine*. On the spin-off, he would be central to the stories, central to the operation of the station, and central in viewers' eyes, as he was the most significant, most obvious link between the neophyte series and the much-beloved *Next Generation*. "Colm, just try saying it—try saying yes, yes, yes," his agent pleaded, noting Meaney's reluctance to commit to the weekly grind, potentially limiting his opportunities on the big screen.

It was more than his professional career that initially kept him from saying "yes," Meaney explained. "As a freelance actor, there is always a terrible insecurity in you. When I was debating with myself whether or not to do *Deep Space Nine*, I remember thinking that freelance actors become addicted to their insecurity and enjoy the insecurity. One of the fears I had in doing the series was losing my insecurity, which is so ridiculous. I would really like to just keep going as I'm going. I feel very good about the mixture I have. I'm fortunate to be able to get home to Ireland every so often

and to work there as often as I do. I get to do a lot of interesting projects on film and TV here in America and in England, too. And I
have steady, interesting work on *Deep Space Nine*. It's really a nice
mix, and I'm quite lucky to have it."

The producers of *Deep Space Nine* were generous about
scheduling so that Meaney could continue to pursue his opportuni-
ties in films. Most significantly, he missed a number of *Deep Space
Nine* episodes to film *The Englishman Who Went Up a Hill but Came
Down a Mountain* opposite Hugh Grant. "It's a nice mixture. For
Englishman we shot in London, I came back, did some episodes, and
then six weeks in Wales. Hugh complained about sitting around
waiting for me to get back from space." *Englishman* director
Christopher Monger dubbed Meaney "The Celtic Gerard
Depardieu," for his womanizing role as the "goat" whom Meaney
described as "the male equivalent of the hooker with the heart of gold."

Meaney has been the central focus of many of *Deep
Space Nine*'s best episodes. The first season's "Captive Pursuit"
found O'Brien attempting to save a hunted warrior, Tosk, in an
episode that questioned the Prime Directive. "The Storyteller"
placed O'Brien as the reluctant leader of a Bajoran village. "In
the Hands of the Prophets" was, according to Meaney, "probably
my favorite episode. The great thing about *Star Trek* is that it
takes on serious issues and deals with them. That episode dealt
with religious fundamentalism. . . . People [in the real world] are
getting into very rigid ideas about how other people should
behave. *Star Trek* is at its best when it's dealing with something
that has a contemporary echo and I'm very glad to see that we're
carrying on that tradition."

Meaney's performances have continued to impress fans. His
turn in "Hard Time" as a convict who lives an entire lifetime in his
head in the span of a few weeks for a crime he did not commit was
one of the most memorable *Deep Space Nine* episodes, and had
lasting repercussions on the character.

In all, Colm Meaney appeared in 52 of the 176 *Next
Generation* episodes, most of them in relatively small cameos in the
confines of the ship's transporter room. However, had Michael
Dorn not joined the cast of *Deep Space Nine* in 1995, Meaney,
once he completed his six-year commitment on *Deep Space Nine*,

would have held the record for the "actor to have appeared in the single greatest number of *Star Trek* episodes."

His perspective on *Next Generation* versus *Deep Space Nine* is unique: "On *Next Generation* they were dealing with more philosophical ponderings, where we on *DS9* tend to deal with more hands-on immediate crises that I think of as more resonant with the problems we have in the world today. The two-part episode last year with the homeless ["Past Tense"] I thought was superb. And the response to that from all the people involved in homeless social action was extraordinary! To find a show on popular TV where you can do work like that is extraordinary! I think that's probably the single main difference. We connect more with contemporary issues, issues relevant to the 1990s, than did *Next Generation*.

"When you attempt to do what some fans might see as moving away from the original vision of an idyllic futuristic thing—when you start doing that—you're taking a big risk. You're dealing with more confrontation and immediately relevant issues. Perhaps we should have foreseen it, but you will antagonize a lot of people perhaps who have the original vision and want to continue with that. But what you will also achieve, which is what we've managed to do, is generate a new audience because of the changes that we've made. Hopefully you can win back the people who originally resisted because of a previous incarnation of the show. I think for it to stand still and to do carbon copies of what's gone before would be stupid. It would be stultifying!"

One thing is for certain. Colm Meaney is no "carbon copy," and his future, within and without the confines of the *Star Trek* universe, promises to be anything but "stultifying."

COLM MEANEY

Chief Miles Edward O'Brien
Also on Star Trek: Deep Space Nine

STAGE:	TELEVISION:
Breaking the Code ('87–'88)	Z Cars ('77–'80)
Every Good Boy Deserves	Remington Steele ('85)
Favour ('92, '93)	Moonlighting ('86)

Tales from the Darkside ('86)
Star Trek: The Next Generation
   ('87–'92, '94)
The Gambler III: The Legend
   Continues ('87)
MacGyver ('88)
One Life to Live ('88)
Perfect Witness ('89)
The Father Dowling Mysteries
   ('90)
The New Adam-12 ('91)
Dr. Quinn, Medicine Woman
   ('92)
Jack's Place ('93)
Star Trek: Deep Space Nine
   ('93–present)
Scarlett ('94)
Gargoyles ('96)

FILM:
The Dead ('87)

The Omega Syndrome ('87)
Dick Tracy ('90)
Die Hard 2: Die Harder ('90)
The Field ('90)
Come See the Paradise ('91)
The Commitments ('91)
Far and Away ('92)
Last of the Mohicans ('92)
Under Siege ('92)
Into the West ('93)
The Snapper ('93)
The Road to Wellville ('94)
War of the Buttons ('94)
The Englishman Who Went Up
   a Hill but Came Down a
   Mountain ('95)
Sydney ('96)
ConAir ('97)
The Last of the High Kings ('97)
The Van ('97)

DIANA MULDAUR

"I'm kind of a pain in the neck."

—DIANA MULDAUR, COMMENTING ON THE INTRODUCTION OF HER
CHARACTER, DR. KATE PULASKI, QUOTED IN THE *LOS ANGELES TIMES*,
NOVEMBER 26, 1988

As Dr. Ann Mulhall in the *Star Trek* episode "Return to Tomorrow," Diana Muldaur's character was inhabited by the disembodied alien entity Thalassa. As Dr. Miranda Jones in the *Star Trek* episode "Is There in Truth No Beauty?" her character was blind but possessed telepathic powers and ultimately saved the *Enterprise*'s first officer. However, these two doctor roles were not found in the scripts of the 1988–89 *Star Trek: The Next Generation* episodes: they were guest-starring parts, portrayed by Muldaur, in 1968—on the original *Star Trek*.

From Captain Kirk's love interest and Mr. Spock's savior to a one-season role in twenty-one episodes as the chief medical officer on *The Next Generation's Enterprise-D* eighty fictional years and two real decades later, Diana Muldaur holds a unique place in the pantheon of *Star Trek*.

Born August 19, 1938, Muldaur, by the age of fifteen, was performing in summer stock theater during her vacations on Cape Cod and Martha's Vineyard. The acting bug seemed to stop biting when she reached Sweet Briar College and she enrolled in the art history program.

However, the lure of the stage proved to be overwhelming and she switched majors, graduating with a degree in drama. "What happened to me was I fell in love with the theater. I just couldn't believe the magic of it. I painted sets, worked in the office, and acted. I covered all of it because that's what fascinated me. Then I found out I happened to be good at acting and that it was easy for me. Acting was magic to me and I loved performing." Since graduation from Sweet Briar, she has been honored by her alma mater as one of the first to receive the school's Distinguished Alumni Award.

Throughout most of the 1960s, Diana Muldaur called New York City home. Her professional theater association was with APA, a group that was based in New York and New Jersey and re-created the classics. While with APA, she earned $25 a week and premiered off-Broadway in *The Balcony* at the Circle in the Square Theatre. In subsequent years she made her way to the Broadway stage, appearing in *Seidman & Son* with Sam Levine, *Poor Bitos* with Donald Pleasence, and *A Very Rich Woman*. She also performed on some New York–based daytime soap operas, including the venerable *The Secret Storm*. While finding regular employment in New York, Muldaur became fascinated with the world of film and television, and began commuting to the West Coast while still performing in plays back East.

Her commuting lifestyle paid off with guest-starring roles in many high-profile television series. She appeared in episodes of *Dr. Kildare* (1966), *Gunsmoke* (1967), and *The Invaders* (1968). She befriended Gene Roddenberry, who cast her in two episodes of *Star Trek* in 1968.

"It's funny, but the thing I remember most about the original show was that we broke every day at 6:12! Paramount in those days stopped all their shooting at 6:12 in the evening. I also remember having wonderful lunches at Nickodells with all the cast. Another thing I remember was how fascinating the wardrobe department was and throwing all these things together and creating all these costumes in a flurry. It was all very vivid to me in those days because I was new out here [Hollywood] and all my impressions were new and exciting. Both roles I played on the original series were wonderful. They were both good, meaty parts that you could put your hooks into and have a lot of fun with. The joy of this show is the imagination and creativity involved with it. And you're restricted with everything else made for television. You are totally restricted as to how far your part can go—but there are no restrictions on this show. You can go anywhere, any galaxy, create people and things and bring them to life—it's very exciting. You can't do that on your everyday cop show."

Relocating to Hollywood full time in 1968, Muldaur was regularly employed on both television and the big screen. Her first role as a regular member of a program's cast was on the ill-fated *The Survivors*. In the expensive hour-long show created by novelist Harold Robbins and starring Ralph Bellamy, George Hamilton, and Lana Turner, Muldaur portrayed Belle, Bellamy's secretary. The series only ran from September 29, 1969, to January 12, 1970, before being canceled, and was described in Alex McNeil's *Total Television* as "one of the biggest flops of the decade."

Nonetheless, Muldaur's career continued unfettered. Immediately following the demise of *The Survivors*, she was cast opposite Dennis "McCloud" Weaver as his friend Chris Coughlin, and appeared regularly throughout *McCloud* for the show's seven-year run. She also traveled to Africa to portray game warden Joy Adamson in the 1974 conservation-minded adventure series *Born Free*, and was a regular cast member on *The Tony Randall Show* (1976–78) as Judge Eleanor Hooper, Randall's romantic interest.

Diana Muldaur's television career was augmented throughout the 1970s with roles on the big screen and guest appearances on dozens of television programs. Her first feature film was *The Swimmer* (1968) with Burt Lancaster. She followed that up with roles in *The Lawyer* (1969) with Barry Newman, *Number One* (1969) with Charlton Heston, *One More Train to Rob* (1971) with

George Peppard, and *McQ* (1974) opposite John Wayne. She also guest starred on dozens of successful television programs in all genres throughout the late 1960s and the 1970s, ranging from *The Courtship of Eddie's Father* (1969) to *The Love Boat* (1979).

She was also cast in *Planet Earth*, Gene Roddenberry's failed 1974 pilot in which an American astronaut (John Saxon) is displaced to the year 2133 through suspended animation and ends up in a female-dominated society. *Planet Earth* costarred *Star Trek* denizen and Roddenberry's spouse, Majel Barrett Roddenberry.

Having gained recognition nationwide as a popular face on television, Diana Muldaur off camera was gaining respect in the Hollywood community for her intelligence and leadership abilities. In 1983, she was elected president of the Academy of Television Arts and Sciences, the only woman to ever serve in that post. Through her two-year tenure (she chose not to seek reelection), she is credited with being instrumental in bringing together two warring factions of the television academy, the New York– and the Los Angeles–based branches. During that time, she also inaugurated the TV Hall of Fame, which in 1984 under the aegis of the academy inducted its first "seven outstanding contributors to the medium," including Milton Berle, Lucille Ball, and Edward R. Murrow.

After stepping down from her position at the academy, Muldaur moved with her husband, writer/producer Robert "Harry O" Dozier, to Bear Valley, California, in the High Sierras, north of Yosemite and accessible only "by skis or snowshoe." Muldaur curtailed her professional appearances to settle into her new life and to pursue a number of hobbies, including sailing, skiing, fishing, and raising Airedale terriers.

In 1987, Diana Muldaur was cast as Dr. Alice Foley in the critically acclaimed *A Year in the Life*, which *TV Guide* called "remarkable television entertainment." She achieved recognition from the American Women in Radio and Television, and claims that on the series she found ". . . a very important part of my life. And a very important product for America." Although she was able to work on *A Year in the Life* while living in her mountain hideaway, she would be forced to move back to Hollywood ("a very tough decision, my husband was the happiest man on earth up in the mountains") when she agreed to accept her next role, offered her by good friend Gene Roddenberry.

Star Trek fans were up in arms when it was revealed that the producers of *The Next Generation* had decided to go in a different direction for the show's second season in terms of the *Enterprise's* chief medical officer. The producers, wanting a character more in the mold of DeForest Kelley's crusty "Bones" McCoy, devised Dr. Kate Pulaski as a replacement for Dr. Beverly Crusher. (Fans were appeased somewhat at the casting of Muldaur, remembering her two well-regarded turns on the original series. However, also very close to landing the role was Christina Pickles, a regular at the time on *St. Elsewhere*.)

Joining the cast at the same time was Whoopi Goldberg, who with Muldaur opted to accept "special guest appearance" billing rather than be listed with the regular cast in the show's opening title sequence. Muldaur's reason was simply that she was cautious. "I just won't do a series normally unless I totally believe in it, because I never want to be tied down like that." But when the opportunity to appear on *The Next Generation* arose, she knew she had to accept it. "I feel the old show was very much like this one; the chances for acting were great. I've done sitcoms and all that, but I thought this had greater opportunities. It was like doing theater again."

She admitted that joining a close-knit cast in their second season was not easy. "I think it was a very difficult thing to adapt to, but everyone was warm and wonderful. Nobody knew who I was and they were all staring at me strangely and wondering what I would do next. I think it took a couple of shows to begin feeling close to being at home. It took a lot of adjustment. Not being able to really explore the character and just beginning with the first show was hard."

On camera, however, Dr. Pulaski had no growing pains, coming in "full bore" and taking "right over." In a newspaper interview published at the start of the second season, Muldaur explained, "They're using me to aggravate Captain Picard from time to time and to upset our dear Data a great deal. I don't deal with him as a human but as a machine, and that upsets the rest of the crew. I'm kind of a pain in the neck."

Muldaur outlined her strategy for approaching the character of Pulaski, and emphasized the warm reception she received from the rest of the cast. "I try to put as much of me in her as I can and that's happening in a positive way. But the adjustment has been lovely, the people couldn't be nicer, and the crew is probably the most professional I've ever worked with. It's been a very exciting group to be a part of."

One thread running through Muldaur's acting career seems to be her penchant for being cast in roles as doctors. "Well, I think it's because I have a strength that comes out and they assume that I can realistically portray a doctor. Maybe it's because I honestly have a real interest in medicine as well. . . . I always have. I remember as a kid I would pick up *Time* magazine and read the medical news first. It's always fascinated me—how they can give their time, which is total. In my day, doctors still came to the house and sometimes in their pajamas with an overcoat in the middle of winter at three in the morning if you needed them. And they weren't making a fortune either. But even today, I don't know how they do what they do."

The Next Generation's second season, Muldaur's lone year on the program, featured a number of episodes in which her character figured prominently. Two early second-season episodes began to flesh out Pulaski: "Elementary, Dear Data," in which Dr. Pulaski challenges Data to solve a computer-generated case in the style of Sherlock Holmes, and "Unnatural Selection," in which the *Enterprise* discovers a ship on which the entire crew has seemingly died of "hyperaging" (a virus that ultimately affects the doctor). "I think we showed a little bit of her personality in 'Elementary, Dear Data.' There is a little hint of where she's going and who she is. 'Unnatural Selection' had a lot of her in it. There's not a lot of humor but a lot of everything else. Each show, we have put a little here or grabbed a little snippet there and put it in. Of course, we had the writers' strike and that delayed our script sessions and they had to push Kate Pulaski back a little bit until we got a lot of other things worked out. I think we have more time now to think about it and as the writers see who I am becoming they can do some more interesting things with her. And that will happen progressively."

Fans began noticing the obvious similarities between Dr. Pulaski and the beloved Dr. McCoy, though Muldaur was not as certain. "It's difficult for me to compare. In other words, I can't study his character to do my character. I have to do mine as only I could do it and somebody else would do it as only they could do it. So it's hard to draw the comparisons. I've seen DeForest Kelley twice already since he's shooting *Star Trek V* here at the studio and we've had some good talks. He's very pleased I'm doing it and I'm very pleased that he's very pleased. He told me, 'Who would've guessed years ago when you did the show that you would be back here again!?' And he's right, I never would have guessed it!"

Two additional episodes during the second season of *The Next Generation* gave Muldaur opportunities to shine. In "The Icarus Factor," Riker is reunited with his estranged father, who also happens to be an old flame of Pulaski's. In this episode, which did more than any other to bring Pulaski closer to the rest of the crew, viewers learned more of her backstory, including the fact that she had been married three times (and remained close friends with each ex-husband). Muldaur was featured one final time in "Shades of Grey," which Larry Nemecek called "probably the weakest *Trek* script ever written for either generation." She is forced to save Riker from an alien organism invading his body, despite potentially life-threatening consequences whichever course of action she decides to pursue.

The final appearance of Dr. Pulaski in the second season may have been the result of a yearlong letter-writing campaign by fans of both Gates McFadden and the chemistry of the first-season cast. Although Paramount never acknowledged the campaign, Muldaur was dropped during the off-season hiatus. "Technically, she's just not returning," was the way it was put by a key member of Gene Roddenberry's staff. "Diana Muldaur is a most talented actress, and the decision to let her go was made solely because the hopes for chemistry between her and the rest of the cast did not develop." He would add, "It was always our intention to leave the door open for [McFadden] to return to the show." Contractually, the process was simple: McFadden agreed to come back, and Muldaur's option for another year was not renewed.

Patrick Stewart is tactful in discussing Muldaur's fate. Although always vocal regarding his friend Gates McFadden ("I was always puzzled by the initial move to detach Gates from the show. . . . I think she's being offered up somewhat sacrificially"), he liked and respected Muldaur. He blamed poor writing and character development for her failure to catch on. "Dr. Pulaski kept flying off in so many different directions because the character never became firmly rooted. It was a mess—they got it wrong." Muldaur herself acknowledged in 1990 that her year on *The Next Generation* had not been a happy one. "The imagination and joy wasn't there."

Her career in space aborted, Muldaur landed a role in the 1989 television movie *The Return of Sam McCloud*. During the filming, she received a call to play a part that would win her national acclaim and would keep much of the country talking around the office water cooler. Cast as Rosalind Shays, a new partner on the megahit *L.A. Law*, she was called by reviewers "the first great barracuda of the '90s."

"Not my kind of lady at all," Muldaur claimed. "I often read a script and am just horrified. I can't believe they'd be having me do these things. I find very little to like about Rosalind, but I'm shocked by the reaction of people. They say, 'Yea! Rosalind!' I don't think anybody had a clue that the character would be such a big hit. I have to say I was surprised by the reaction—I had no idea people loved to hate so much."

She reflected upon the roles she had played throughout her career—a devoted game warden on *Born Free*, the nice girlfriend on *McCloud*, supercapable doctors in space—and commented, "Normally I'm Miss Goody. I was everybody's mistress for twenty years. But even then I was a good mistress. I never broke up anybody's marriage."

The dynamic of her character on *L.A. Law* intrigued a nation coming to grips with powerful women in the workplace, and intrigued Muldaur herself. "Interestingly, I find men far more ready to accept a woman of power than women [are themselves]. There are a lot of ladies who send me letters or that I run into on the street who are just horrified at the image of powerful women. I don't know why that is. Possibly it's jealousy, or perhaps Rosalind challenges them—that maybe they should be out doing something, somewhere. And Rosalind is rude, and women don't like to see that in other women." She acknowledged, however, "If it were a man doing the same things, no one would blink. In fact, it wouldn't even be good copy."

Muldaur appeared regularly on *L.A. Law* for two years before the plot called for her to plunge to her demise down an empty elevator shaft. She was nominated both years for an Emmy. Reviewer Tom Dorsey wrote of her second nomination, "One of the most-deserving, unsung actresses is Diana Muldaur . . . for her superb performance as the villainous Rosalind Shays." She admitted that the role had really grown on her. "I miss her terribly. I'll miss her all my life. She was terrific."

Muldaur has slowed her pace in order to return to the mountains, raise her dogs, and enjoy the outdoors. She has picked and chosen her projects sparingly since leaving *L.A. Law* (although she played yet another doctor, or voiced one at least: Dr. Tompkins on *Batman: The Animated Series*).

Nonetheless, despite her less-than-ideal experience on *Star Trek: The Next Generation*, Diana Muldaur remains optimistic regarding what *Star Trek* stands for, and why it continues to survive. "I think the show depicts faith in the future and hope for mankind. I think we all spend all of our days and all of our lives watching horrible things happen, things we're very frustrated about—like drugs—and it all becomes very consuming. Then you see *Star Trek* and see that indeed we made it and we made it in a positive way and we're out there doing some good. I think that's why *Star Trek* will continue for years to come."

D I A N A   M U L D A U R

Dr. Katherine Pulaski
Also appeared on the original Star Trek *as Dr. Ann Mulhall*
and Dr. Miranda Jones

STAGE:
Poor Bitos ('64)
The Balcony
Seidman & Son
A Very Rich Woman

TELEVISION:
The Americans ('61)

The Doctors and the Nurses ('65)
The Secret Storm ('65)
Dr. Kildare ('66)
Gunsmoke ('67)
I, Spy ('68)
Star Trek ('68)
The FBI ('68, '72)

The Felony Squad ('68)
The Invaders ('68)
Insight ('69)
The Courtship of Eddie's Father
 ('69)
The Survivors ('69–'70)
Dan August ('70)
McCloud ('70–'77)
McCloud: Who Killed Miss
 USA? ('70)
Mod Squad ('70)
Ironsides ('71)
Alias Smith and Jones ('72)
Banyon ('72)
Hawaii Five-O ('72)
Marcus Welby, M.D. ('72)
Medical Center ('72)
Owen Marshall, Counselor at
 Law ('72, '73)
Tender Comrade ('72)
The Bold Ones ('72)
A Special Act of Love ('73)
Call to Danger ('73)
Hec Ramsey ('73)
Kung Fu ('73)
Ordeal ('73)
Born Free ('74)
Cannon ('74)
Planet Earth ('74)
The Rockford Files ('74)
The Wonderful World of Disney
 ('74)
Charlie's Angels ('76)
The Streets of San Francisco
 ('76)
The Tony Randall Show
 ('76–'78)
Pine Canyon is Burning ('77)
Police Woman ('77)
The Deadly Triangle ('77)
Black Beauty ('78)
Lucan ('78)
Maneaters Are Loose! ('78)

The Word ('78)
To Kill a Cop ('78)
$weepstake$ ('79)
Hizoner ('79)
The Incredible Hulk ('79)
The Love Boat ('79)
The Miracle Worker ('79)
B. J. and the Bear ('80)
Fantasy Island ('80)
The Return of Frank Cannon
 ('80)
Fitz and Bones ('81)
Hart to Hart ('81)
Quincy, M.E. ('81)
Terror at Alcatraz ('82)
Too Good to Be True ('83)
Murder, She Wrote ('85)
Murder in Three Acts ('86)
A Year in the Life ('87–'88)
Matlock ('88)
Star Trek: The Next Generation
 ('88–'89)
L.A. Law ('89–'91)
The Return of Sam McCloud
 ('89)
Perry Mason: The Case of the
 Fatal Fashion ('91)
Batman: The Animated Series
 ('92, '93)
Empty Nest ('92)
Locked Up: A Mother's Rage
 ('92)
Prince Valiant ('94)

FILM:
The Swimmer ('68)
Number One ('69)
The Lawyer ('69)
One More Train to Rob ('71)
The Other ('72)
Chosen Survivors ('74)
McQ ('74)
Beyond Reason ('77)

CHAPTER 10

FACES YOU KNOW

MAJEL BARRETT RODDENBERRY

orn Majel Lee Hudec in Columbus, Ohio, on February 23, 1939, Majel Barrett has seen a successful career span over thirty years. She has played officers, aliens, and a computer voice in four incarnations of one television series, as well as in five movies and a cartoon series—*Star Trek*.

The acting bug bit her at the age of ten when her mother enrolled her in a workshop at the Cleveland Playhouse. Barrett continued acting at Shaker Heights High School and Flora Stone Mather College for Women of Western Reserve University, where she graduated with a degree in theater arts. She toyed with a year of law school before finally moving to New York and fully committing herself to acting.

In the 1950s, Barrett performed summer stock in Bermuda, and nearly landed a role on Broadway in the play *Models by Season*. She toured the country in *The Solid Gold Cadillac* and appeared in a series of productions at the Pasadena Playhouse. But it was not until she began studying with Anthony Quinn that her motion picture career took off. Impressed with Barrett, Quinn introduced her to moguls at Paramount Studios, for whom she ended up appearing in a number of motion pictures.

When her Paramount contract expired, she concentrated on television. Under the tutelage of Sanford Meisner, Barrett was introduced to Lucille Ball. Miss Ball taught her comedy and invited her onto several episodes of *The Lucy Show*. In 1964, Barrett landed a role in the MGM series *The Lieutenant*, produced by the man who would become her husband, Gene Roddenberry.

Roddenberry and Barrett were married in Japan, where Roddenberry had been sent to scout locations for MGM. Because one could not hire an American minister in Japan at the time, the couple chose to exchange their vows in a traditional Japanese Shinto ceremony. (Barrett had to bear a dagger in the event Roddenberry dishonored her, wear a hat that was said to hide the woman's horns of jealousy, and carry a purse of coins so she could get home in case her groom changed his mind.)

Barrett was thrilled to be cast in the powerful role of "Number One," Captain Pike's (Jeffrey Hunter's) first officer, in the original *Star Trek* series. However, NBC, which had commissioned the pilot, could not accept a woman in the second-in-command role in 1966. The network commissioned a new pilot with most of the cast changed. Although Roddenberry recast her as Nurse Christine Chapel midway through the first season, the role was a letdown compared to her original part. Nonetheless, she had no idea (nor did anyone at the time) what a phenomenon she had associated herself with.

As Nurse Chapel, Barrett appeared periodically on screen as a member of Dr. McCoy's staff. Throughout the original series' three seasons, a recurring plot thread revolved around her love for Mr. Spock. Sometimes played as a joke, but often vital to the plot, Chapel participated in away missions, assisted in surgery, and developed a unique voice of her own on the classic series. She was firm and serious, and obviously very smart, but portrayed rather stereotypically as a weak-kneed woman-in-love whenever Spock was around or, worse, in trouble.

Throughout the 1970s, Barrett not only voiced Nurse Chapel on the Filmation animated *Star Trek* series, but also had roles in Gene Roddenberry's television pilots *Genesis II* (1972), *Planet Earth* (1974), *The Questor Tapes* (1974), and *Spectre* (1977).

In 1970, Barrett and Roddenberry formed Lincoln Enterprises to satisfy the demand for *Star Trek* memorabilia. Barrett is still in charge of the company—the only one licensed to sell, among other items, copies of actual *Star Trek* television screenplays.

In 1974, Eugene Wesley "Rod" Roddenberry III was born. When he was six years old, according to *People* magazine, his classmates in the first grade inquired about his last name, wondering if he was any relation to the creator of television's cult space program. He did not know; so one evening when his mother was preparing dinner and he was just sitting quietly, he blurted, "Mr. Spock!" When he received no response from either of his parents, he yelled, "Captain Kirk!" Again, no response. He returned to school the next day and reported to his classmates that, in fact, he was not related to "that" Roddenberry. *Star Trek* simply wasn't a factor in the Roddenberry's Beverly Hills home: no memorabilia and no "shop talk."

According to *The Official Fan Club* magazine, when Roddenberry created the role of Lwaxana Troi for *The Next Generation*, he informed his wife, "Majel, I've got a great part for you; you don't have to act." As Lwaxana Troi, Barrett appeared six times on *The Next Generation*, once each season (except the sixth), and has made recurring appearances on *Star Trek: Deep Space Nine*. (She has also appeared as Lady Morella, the third wife of the late Centauri Emperor Turhan, on *Deep Space Nine* competitor *Babylon 5*. Again, the role was written specifically for her.)

Barrett's annual appearances as Lwaxana Troi on *The Next Generation* were events fans anticipated. In the first season's "Haven," she barges on board the *Enterprise* insisting upon having her daughter, Deanna, consummate an arranged marriage. This episode also introduced a plot thread that ran through all of Lwaxana's appearances, that of her aggressive flirtatious behavior toward Captain Picard (reminiscent of the actress's behavior toward Mr. Spock over two decades earlier). In the second season's "Manhunt," Lwaxana appears during her midlife Betazoid "phase," in which her sex drive has quadrupled. Again, she has set her romantic sights on Picard. The flirtation continued in her next appearance, the third-season Ferengi episode "Ménage à Troi."

In the fourth season's "Half a Life," Lwaxana visits again and this time finds herself romantically drawn to the doomed scientist Dr. Timicin, played movingly by David Ogden Stiers (of M*A*S*H fame). In the fifth season's "Cost of Living," Lwaxana has gone so far as to get herself engaged, and arrives for the wedding ceremony in traditional Betazoid garb—completely nude (a body double was used in filming the scene). In Barrett's final appearance as Lwaxana on *The Next Generation*, the seventh season's "Dark Page," Lwaxana appears ill, moody, and despondent. It remains up to her daughter to find the cause and save the impending diplomatic negotiations that hinge upon her mother's health.

Barrett can also be heard on the three most recent *Star Trek* series and all of the movies as the voice of the computer. When asked at a 1996 Los Angeles *Star Trek* convention if the voice of the computer took a lot of time, she laughed. "I go in for about fifteen minutes one day every two or three weeks. We sit around and tell some dirty jokes, I say my lines [which are taped and edited into the show later], and I go home! It takes no time at all!" An interesting trivia bit arose from *The Next Generation* episode "Cost of Living," where Barrett as Lwaxana Troi has a conversation with Barrett as the *Enterprise* computer.

An accomplished actress, and appreciated for her own achievements by fans of *Star Trek*, she will also always be fondly remembered as the spouse of *Star Trek*'s creator, Gene Roddenberry. Interviewed by Michael Logan, Barrett was very defensive regarding her deceased husband and some of the unflattering material that has been written about his life. She insisted, "Gene instilled a hope and a brightness in people. He gave us reason to look forward to the future and he did it with a great deal of love and energy." She also reacted to *The Next Generation*'s cancellation. "Paramount has come up with a whole bunch of excuses and reasons—but so far none of them holds water. One exec will point in one direction, one will point in the other. I have a feeling it has to do with what goes on behind that little door marked 'Accounting.' Maybe I'm wrong, but I don't think we've heard the truth yet."

Barrett was quoted in Larry Nemecek's *Star Trek: The Next Generation Companion* as stating, "I said facetiously once that *Star Trek* was bigger than Paramount, and since then I've started to think back on that, because it's true: we've had three new groups of owners/managers come in, but they've changed and we're still here—we've been the ones to keep a roof over everyone's head!"

More recently, Barrett has been working on producing and appearing in a series based upon *Battleground Earth*, a concept developed by her late husband. When not working on *Battleground Earth*, running Lincoln Enterprises, or making appearances and voice-overs on the *Star Trek* series, Barrett keeps busy with many hobbies, including golfing, gourmet cooking, gold-working, and gem-cutting. She has also coestablished a scholarship in Gene Roddenberry's name at California State University, Long Beach, College of Engineering. Despite a lengthy recent feud with Gene Roddenberry's first wife and a daughter from that marriage, Barrett has kept a positive attitude and is dedicated to keeping Gene Roddenberry's spirit alive.

Majel Barrett is a unique talent. Perhaps more than any other single actor, she has been affected by, influenced by, and wrapped up in the *Star Trek* universe that is her late husband's legacy.

MAJEL BARRETT RODDENBERRY

Lwaxana Troi and Computer Voice
On Star Trek—*Nurse Christine Chapel and Number One*
On Star Trek: Deep Space Nine—*Lwaxana Troi and Computer Voice*
On Star Trek: Voyager—*Computer Voice and Narrator*
On Star Trek: The Animated Series—*Nurse Christine Chapel*

STAGE:
All for Mary
Models by Season
The Solid Gold Cadillac

TELEVISION:
Westinghouse Desilu Playhouse ('59)
The Untouchables ('60)
Leave It to Beaver ('61)
Pete and Gladys ('61)
Window on Main Street ('61)
Bonanza ('62)
The Lucy Show ('62)
77 Sunset Strip ('63)
Dr. Kildare ('63)
The Lieutenant ('64)
Many Happy Returns ('64)
Love on a Rooftop ('66)
Please Don't Eat the Daisies ('66)
Star Trek ('66–'69)
The Wackiest Ship in the Army ('66)
Here Comes the Bride ('68)
The Second Hundred Years ('68)

Genesis II ('73)
The Questor Tapes ('73)
Star Trek: The Animated Series ('73–'75)
The FBI ('74)
Planet Earth ('74)
Spectre ('77)
The Man in the Santa Claus Suit ('78)
The Next Step Beyond ('78)
The Suicide's Wife ('79)
General Hospital ('83)
Star Trek: The Next Generation ('87–'94)
Star Trek: Deep Space Nine ('93–present)
Babylon 5 ('95)
Star Trek: Voyager ('95–present)
Battleground Earth ('97)

FILM:
As Young as We Are ('58)
The Buccaneer ('58)
Black Orchids ('59)
Love in a Goldfish Bowl ('61)

The Quick and the Dead ('63)	Star Trek IV: The Voyage Home ('86)
Sylvia ('65)	Star Trek V: The Final Frontier ('89)
Country Boy ('66)	
A Guide for the Married Man ('67)	Star Trek: Generations ('94)
Track of Thunder ('68)	Teresa's Tattoo ('94)
Westworld ('73)	Mommy (direct-to-video) ('96)
The Domino Principle ('77)	
Star Trek: The Motion Picture ('79)	Star Trek: First Contact ('96)

BRIAN BONSALL

Brian Bonsall didn't much care for his role as Worf's son, Alexander, in *Star Trek: The Next Generation*—as he relayed to Yardena Arar of the *Los Angeles Daily News*—due to "the Klingon makeup hassles, two hours to put it on and half an hour to take it off." He was cast to replace the child actor who originated the role of Alexander, Jon Steurer. Bonsall was a proven commodity with a television series track record, a necessity for what was to be a recurring role.

Recognized as the headlining star of Disney's *Blank Check*, Bonsall has often been compared to Macauley Culkin. He is best known from his role as the youngest Keaton, Andrew, in the last three seasons of *Family Ties* (1986–89). Bonsall was only ten years old when he first appeared as Alexander in *The Next Generation*'s fifth season, in the 1992 episode "New Ground." He only appeared twice during the sixth season. This was due both to Bonsall's busy career and to the *Star Trek* producers' concern that too much focus on Worf's young son would turn the Klingon into a character similar to any suburban father. They feared turning a unique role into one that could appear on any contemporary television program.

Even with the reduced *Star Trek* load, Bonsall had memorable episodes, such as the sixth-season episodes "Rascals" and "A Fistful of Datas." In the season-seven "Firstborn," the mysterious K'mtar is revealed to be Alexander, back from the future, seeking to affect his upbringing. Director Jonathan West was concerned during the filming of "Firstborn," according to Nemecek's book, due to the lateness of the day and the number of hours Bonsall had been working. Although Bonsall's time limit for a minor working in Hollywood had run out, his parents consented to an extension, and Bonsall filmed the last three angles of the Klingon battle ritual in one take without a mishap.

Bonsall played Alexander Keaton on *Family Ties* from the time he was four until he was seven, but "doesn't remember much about making the show," he told interviewer Arar. He has appeared with Art Carney in television advertisements for Coca-Cola, and has been the television son of Linda Hamilton, Pam Dawber, Richard Thomas, Jane Seymour, and Donna Mills. In 1993, he appeared as Patrick Swayze's son in the feature film *Father Hood*.

As Preston Waters in *Blank Check*, he had $1 million at his disposal. If he were actually in that situation, Bonsall mused, "I'd just buy all the toys [featured in *Blank Check*]. I wanted them all. I didn't get 'em — they were all rented." He was critical of Disney, a common practice among his older cohorts in Hollywood. "It was hard to film it all in forty days. The acting itself wasn't difficult, but it was very hot outside [they filmed in Texas in the height of summer] and we had to wear wool suits and stuff."

Considering the hours all actors who portray Klingons must endure in the makeup chair, it is a testament to Bonsall's professionalism and drive to perform that he was able to handle the pressure, the discomfort, and the inconvenience at all at such a young age. His role, as the first young son dealing with parental pressures and growing up on the *Enterprise*, was a model for future performances on all three new *Star Trek* incarnations. (Wesley Crusher, on the other hand, was practically a member of the crew. Viewers never experienced his childhood.) Bonsall was a favorite among young *Star Trek* viewers, and his few episodes remain popular among all *Next Generation* fans to this day.

B R I A N   B O N S A L L

Alexander Rozhenko (Worf's son)

TELEVISION:

Family Ties ('86–'89)
Go to the Light ('88)
Do You Know the Muffin Man?
  ('89)
Angel of Death ('90)
Booker ('90)
Mother Goose Rock 'n Rhyme
  ('90)
False Arrest ('91)

Shades of L.A. ('91)
Star Trek: The Next Generation
  ('92, '94)
Father and Scout ('94)
Lily in Winter ('94)

FILM:

Mikey ('92)
Distant Cousins ('93)
Father Hood ('93)
Blank Check ('94)

ROSALIND CHAO

Rosalind Chao, born Chao Jya-len, is the daughter of aristocratic, wealthy Chinese parents who fled their country shortly before the Communist takeover. Born in 1958, Chao attended Catholic High School, Pomona College, and the University of Southern California, graduating with a degree in broadcast journalism.

Much to her chagrin, because she did not want to be different from other Americans, she was the only Asian in her high school and neighborhood. She told a UPI interviewer in 1983, "I wanted to be blond and blue eyed. I dated Caucasian boys and still do. My parents were liberal about that in view of the fact that their parents were married by prearrangement in China."

One day the producers of a local stage production of *South Pacific* came into Chao's parents' Chinese restaurant and asked permission to use their daughter in the play. At the time, Chao was four years old. Since her father and mother had both appeared in Peking Opera productions and knew the rigors of an actor's lifestyle, they were initially unenthusiastic about the idea of her appearing in a stage production at such a young age. As it turned out, she was too scared to perform in *South Pacific*, but her talent finally led her onto the stage in *Teahouse*. From that point on, she was hooked. "I loved being on stage. I still do. It's a drug. An addiction." An agent spotted her in *Teahouse* and started casting her in commercials, including ones for Crest toothpaste and Barbie dolls. Chao admits that while being on stage is her first addiction, food is her second. "I always feel most at home in a restaurant."

As Chao grew older, she embraced her ethnicity and desired to be as Chinese as possible, studying Chinese dance and Asian culture at Pomona. "At USC I tried to emphasize my Chineseness. Now I've reached a happy medium." Although Chao remains a Catholic, she still visits a Buddhist temple to worship her ancestors on the wedding anniversary of her grandparents.

Because of the paucity of roles in Hollywood for Asians, her family and friends tried to talk her out of acting. Chao persevered, appearing in kung fu movies with Jackie Chan and Chuck Norris.

Connie Chung was admittedly an inspiration leading to her decision to attend journalism school at USC. After graduating, she turned down a "good job" as a television news anchorwoman—even though she insists television needs minority faces—because she wanted to act.

After appearing as Corporal Klinger's Korean girlfriend during the final (1982–83) season of *M*A*S*H*, in 1983 *After M*A*S*H* premiered, featuring Chao in a costarring role. This was the first time a Chinese woman had starred in a major prime time series. Over the next seven years, Chao landed guest roles on television, appeared on stage, and had small parts in movies.

In 1991 Chao was cast as Polly Bemis in *1,000 Pieces of Gold*, a story of a strong-willed Chinese woman who refused to become a prostitute in a gold-mining camp in Idaho. So impressed was she with the story that she threw herself into the history of the Chinese pioneers in the West. "I fell in love with the character [known as China Polly]. I felt it was a very important story to tell particularly because of the huge wave of immigration from Asia."

But her most famous role, perhaps, was in the movie version of Amy Tan's novel *The Joy Luck Club*. Receiving rave reviews for her work in this movie with an ensemble cast, Chao read Tan's book and was able to relate to the story, and the identity crises described. "After reading the book and talking about it with others, I realized that I was not alone, but a lot of my Jewish American and Italian American friends went through it, too. What I thought of as Chinese American issues are universal."

She has been cast as Chinese, Vietnamese, Korean, and, on *Star Trek: The Next Generation* and *Star Trek: Deep Space Nine*, presumably Japanese. The role of Keiko was conceived when it was decided to finally feature a wedding on *Star Trek*. Chao was a close friend of Elizabeth "Commander Shelby" Dennehy, and had been an earlier candidate for a recurring role on the show. Keiko Ishikawa and Miles O'Brien were married in Chao's first episode, the fourth season's "Data's Day." She appeared a total of eight times, with roles in "The Wounded," "Night Terrors," "In Theory," "Disaster" (in which Worf is forced to assist in the delivery of her child; the birth was a first for *Star Trek*), "Violations," and "Power Play." Chao's last *Next Generation* episode was the sixth season's "Rascals." In an interesting coincidence, Chao's husband, Simon Templeman, was performing in a play with Colm Meaney's wife during the time Chao and Meaney were shooting their first episode together, "Data's Day."

The summer before the sixth season, Chao, along with her "husband" Colm Meaney, agreed to the move and the weekly commitment of appearing on *Star Trek: Deep Space Nine*. Although Chao has spent months at a time off the *Deep Space Nine* station (her character was said to be living and working on the planet Bajor), she has been featured in many notable episodes. She is unique on the show and in the *Star Trek* universe. She is a mother, in an alien environment, who is unaffiliated with Starfleet and is raising two young children (the second was born during *Deep Space Nine*'s fifth season). She has been seen struggling with the danger and long hours her husband is constantly exposed to—as well as her own quest for a fulfilling and successful career. Although Keiko O'Brien's quest may remain unresolved for many years, Rosalind Chao is a proven success and an accomplished actress.

ROSALIND CHAO

Keiko Ishikawa O'Brien
Also appeared on Star Trek: Deep Space Nine

STAGE:
Teahouse
Green Card ('87)

TELEVISION:
Anna and the King ('72)
PJ and the President's Son ('76)
The Amazing Spider-Man ('78)
The Chinese Web ('78)
The Hardy Boys Mysteries ('78)
How the West Was Won ('78)
A Man Called Sloane ('79)
Mysterious Island of Beautiful
   Women ('79)
The Ultimate Imposter ('79)
One Day at a Time ('80)
Almost American ('81)
The Harlem Globetrotters on
   Gilligan's Island ('81)
Lobo ('81)
Twirl ('81)
Diff'rent Strokes ('82–'83)
Moonlighting ('82)
After M*A*S*H ('83–'84)
Bring 'Em Back Alive ('83)
M*A*S*H ('83)
The Terry Fox Story ('83)
American Playhouse ('84)
Falcon Crest ('84)
Riptide ('84)
The A-Team ('85)
An American Portrait ('85)
Paper Angels ('85)
Jack and Mike ('86)
St. Elsewhere ('86)

Max Headroom ('87)
Private Eye ('87)
Spies ('87)
Stingray ('87)
Beauty and the Beast ('88)
Miami Vice ('88)
Shooter ('88)
Island Son ('89)
Jake and the Fatman ('89)
Tour of Duty ('89)
Against the Law ('90, '91)
Drug Wars: The Camarena
   Story ('90)
Last Flight Out ('90)
1,000 Pieces of Gold ('90)
Star Trek: The Next Generation
   ('91, '92)
Intruders ('92)
Star Trek: Deep Space Nine
   ('93–present)
Chicago Hope ('95)
Under Suspicion ('95)
Live Report: Mission to Mars ('96)

FILM:
The Big Brawl ('80)
An Eye for an Eye ('81)
Slamdance ('87)
White Ghost ('88)
Denial ('91)
Memoirs of an Invisible Man ('92)
The Joy Luck Club ('93)
Web of Deception ('93)
Love Affair ('94)
North ('94)

JOHN DE LANCIE

B orn March 20, 1948, in Philadelphia, John de Lancie first discovered acting at the age of fourteen when he performed in a high school production of *Henry V*. By his own admission, he was a terrible student, though much of his difficulty was caused by his dyslexia. He credits his ultimate triumph over the learning disability to a teacher, David Biddle, who threw Shakespeare's *Henry V* into de Lancie's chest and told him that he had two months to learn the part of Prince Hal. "And to everyone's surprise," de Lancie claims, "I was good at it." By the time he left high school, de Lancie had performed in six of Shakespeare's plays.

Although he loved acting, he resisted the urge to take it seriously and went on to college instead. But once graduated, he started to perform in local theater and eventually enrolled at Juilliard. After graduating from Juilliard, he realized, "I found myself, in my thirties, with no experience other than acting." Upon making a full-time commitment to act, he worked initially at Stratford, then Seattle Repertory. He was at Universal when he was offered a contract doing episodic television for them.

Although many people felt that the studio contract system was anachronistic even then, it often meant steady work for actors lucky enough to have a contract. In 1977, de Lancie was a twenty-eight-year-old "hot prospect," working out of the stable of Monique James—the head of Universal's New Talent Development Program. De Lancie had arrived in Hollywood from New York in October 1976. By January 1977, he had already appeared in *The Six Million Dollar Man*, *McMillan*, *Captains and Kings*, and had landed the lead role in the ABC television movie *Flight of the Maiden*, which aired in February 1977. As it was clear at this point that he would no longer spend the majority of his time on the classical stage, de Lancie told the *Washington Post* in a 1977 interview, "I was once prepared for years of banging my head against the wall, but I don't worry anymore about becoming a star. I've got Monique and that's what she's all about. That's her job."

Years of work on stage and in television, combined with his struggles dealing with dyslexia, have left de Lancie serious and sober regarding his career and his life. He does not watch much television or see many movies because they are a "a bit of a busman's holiday. I know too much of what is going on outside the frame to relax. So for me the idea of being able to relax with a book or listen to classical music truly means relaxation." The son of the principal oboist in the Philadelphia Philharmonic—John de Lancie Sr. (who held that chair at the age of nineteen)—and the brother of Christina de Lancie—now a successful playwright and also a Juilliard-trained actress—John de Lancie has always had difficulty turning off his "critical mind." Nonetheless, he does know how to relax: his favorite place is on a sailboat holding a glass of Wild Turkey bourbon ("at the end of the day, of course").

Despite being surrounded by classical music and training at one of the country's great schools of the arts, de Lancie points to his three and a half years on *Days of Our Lives* as being his real training ground. It was on this soap opera, playing Eugene Bradford (the campy psychopathic comedic inventor who eventually left the show in a time machine), that he achieved his initial fame. "I probably learned more on the soap than I did while studying at Juilliard," he stated. During these television years, de Lancie was also the recipient of many awards, including an Emmy for a featured performance in *The Common Pursuit* and a Soap Opera Award for best supporting actor for his role as Eugene on *Days of Our Lives*.

De Lancie was cast in 1987 as the omnipotent and bothersome Q for the pilot episode of *Star Trek: The Next Generation*, "Encounter at Farpoint." Many fans drew a connection between his character and the powerful, childlike Trelane from the original series (in the episode "Squire of Gothos"). A couple of years later, de Lancie simply explained in *Star Trek: The Official Fan Club* magazine that Trelane is Q's son. As for the name of his character, de Lancie always assumed Q stood for "Question," or "Questioner," because "that seemed to be what I was doing," he told a *Star Trek* convention audience in Sacramento in 1990. However, on a trip to Scotland a couple of years later, a woman showed him a letter from Gene Roddenberry, which said in part that he would be naming a character after her. The woman's full name, de Lancie revealed, was Janet Quarton.

Although he only appeared in eight *Next Generation* episodes, de Lancie's—and therefore Q's—popularity among fans is a bit overwhelming. However, de Lancie explained in *Star Trek Communicator*, "Those eight episodes . . . are held aloft sometimes a little more than they should be because there are only eight. It's kind of like the Marx Brothers. They did six movies and only two of them are really, really good. But we hold them with such love that we say, 'God, everything they did was just so wonderful.' Well, that's not quite true. Not all the episodes I did were wonderful."

The most difficult scene for de Lancie on *The Next Generation* was the final scene from "Deja Q," in which he appeared with a mariachi band, among other things. Filming started the morning of Thanksgiving Eve at 7 A.M. It was not until sixteen hours later that the final takes were shot. The first scenes shot that day were Q's nude scenes, but the crew was unable to figure out how to shoot around his jockstrap. De Lancie just told anyone who might be offended to leave the set, then proceeded to drop the strap. The scene was filmed in one take.

De Lancie is married to actress Marnie Mosiman, who played one-third of Riva's chorus in the episode "Loud as a Whisper." The couple have a son, who tells his friends that if they're not good, "My dad will freeze you." Jokingly, at a convention, de Lancie referred to his child as "R."

De Lancie does not much enjoy appearing at *Star Trek* conventions or being asked such questions as "what's Q doing now?" He told *Entertainment Weekly* in 1995, "I don't answer questions like 'If Q met Godzilla, who'd win?' It's kind of like 'If my aunt had balls, would she be my uncle?' I don't answer 'if' questions."

De Lancie now devotes much of his time to "Alien Voices." A multimedia production company he formed in partnership with Leonard Nimoy, it is dedicated to bringing adaptations of classic science fiction to audio and CD-ROM. The first title from Alien Voices, H. G. Wells' *The Time Machine*, features Nimoy, de Lancie, Roxann Biggs-Dawson (B'elanna Torres on *Star Trek: Voyager*), and Armin Shimerman (Quark on *Star Trek: Deep Space Nine*). This marks the first time actors from all four *Star Trek* series have performed together in a single production.

De Lancie has made appearances as Q on *Star Trek: Deep Space Nine* and *Star Trek: Voyager*. He has also signed with Baen

Books to write a novel for its Starline series for young adults. In addition, he starred in the critically acclaimed *Legend*, an adventure drama produced and shown during the United Paramount Network's first season of broadcasting. *Legend* was unfortunately a ratings disappointment.

The future of Q and the Q Continuum on the various incarnations of *Star Trek* is uncertain, but as de Lancie once told an online audience, "There's a little Q in all of us."

JOHN DE LANCIE

Q

Also appeared on Star Trek: Deep Space Nine *and* Star Trek: Voyager

STAGE:
As You Like It
Aunt Dan and Lemon
The Cherry Orchard
Child Byron
Dracula, A Musical Nightmare
Golden Girls
Le Bourgeois Gentilhomme
Lion and the Portuguese
Man and Superman
A Month in the Country
The Mound Builders
Taming of the Shrew
Terra Nova
Saint Joan
Scapino

TELEVISION:
Emergency ('75)
The Six Million Dollar Man ('75)
Barnaby Jones ('76)
Captains and the Kings ('76)
Police Story ('76)
Another World ('77)

Flight of the Maiden ('77)
The Man with the Power ('77)
McMillan and Wife ('77)
Testimony of Two Men ('77)
The Bastard ('78)
Black Beauty ('78)
Little Women ('78)
As the World Turns ('79)
Battlestar Galactica ('79)
Common Pursuit ('80)
Scruples ('80)
The Miracle of Kathy Miller ('81)
Days of Our Lives ('82–'86, '89)
Missing Pieces ('83)
The Thornbirds ('83)
Murder, She Wrote ('85)
Houston: The Legend of Texas ('86)
It's a Living ('86)
Miami Vice ('86)
On Fire ('87)
Star Trek: The Next Generation ('87, '89, '90, '91, '92, '93, '94)
Trial and Error ('88)

The Twilight Zone ('88)
Christine Cromwell: Things
   That Go Bump in the Night
   ('89)
Get Smart, Again! ('89)
MacGyver ('89)
Matlock ('89)
Mission: Impossible ('89)
The Nutt House ('89)
L.A. Law ('90)
Searching for ETs: National
   Geographic Special ('90)
The Young Riders ('91)
Nightside ('92)
Arcade ('93)
Time Trax ('93)
Batman: The Animated Series
   ('94)
Prince Valiant ('94)
Star Trek: Deep Space Nine
   ('94)
Without Warning ('94)
Duckman ('95)

Legend ('95)
Star Trek: Voyager ('95, '96)
Murder One ('96)

FILM:
Legacy ('75)
SST: Deathflight ('77)
The Onion Field ('79)
A Change of Seasons ('80)
Loving Couples ('80)
Roxanne ('87)
Blood Red ('89)
Weekend at Bernie's ('89)
Angel of Death ('90)
Bad Influence ('90)
Taking Care of Business
   (a.k.a. Filofax) ('90)
The Fisher King ('92)
The Hand That Rocks the
   Cradle ('92)
Fearless ('93)
Deep Red ('94)
Evolver ('95)
Multiplicity ('96)

MICHELLE FORBES

Michelle Forbes appeared only nine times on *The Next Generation*. She first played Dara in the episode "Half a Life." Because the producers were so impressed with her, she was cast as Ensign Ro in eight later episodes. Not bad for a young actress (born February 17, 1965, in Houston) who left home at sixteen to pursue an acting career.

Forbes and her sister started out as dancers, but only her sister had an affinity for it. Forbes' mother was working in the theater. When her daughter saw her perform, "My eyes just opened up," she told *Star Trek: The Official Fan Club* magazine. This prompted her to attend the Performing Arts High School in Houston. A rebel, she dropped out of school at sixteen and made her way to New York in a bid for independence.

Forbes' first audition, for a role in *The Black Stallion Returns*, was unsuccessful. Nonetheless, she soon signed with the venerable William Morris Agency. However, she had trouble landing other than minor off-Broadway parts, and this she attributes to the fact that she looked older than she was. Directors had difficulty figuring out just what kind of roles she was suited for. Rejection was difficult for Forbes. When she could no longer face it, she packed her bags and moved to Los Angeles with her fiancé.

It was two years later and after the relationship had fizzled that she returned to acting. This time she landed a role she was most eager for, Solita on *The Guiding Light*. Her first major acting part evolved into a three-year stint on the soap opera. She played the dual role of good and evil twins Sonni and Solita Lewis, a portrayal that earned her critical raves. Forbes did not view the scheming Solita as evil. Instead, she perceived her as a woman trying to find her place in the world. "I played a schizophrenic psychologist from Venezuela, thank you very much," Forbes told columnist Ian Spelling. "I had a three-year contract, and two and one-half years into it, I said, 'I can't do this anymore.' They were very nice and let me out of my contract." In 1989, Forbes garnered an Emmy nomination for her role on *The Guiding Light*.

The following year, Forbes was cast as Dara for her first *Star Trek: The Next Generation* episode, "Half a Life." Forbes' performance in her only scene of this episode had such an impact on the producers that they chose her for the part of Ensign Ro in the fifth-season episode of the same name. As the rebellious Bajoran Ensign Ro, who disliked taking orders and being out of control, she stated that she "would not at all hesitate to sign a long-term contract and become a regular cast member of this series." However, she also hedged her statement. "Part of the joy of a recurring [as opposed to regular] role is that you can do other things, yet have the comfort of being a part of a regular series."

Since then, Forbes has turned down regular roles as Ro on *Star Trek: Deep Space Nine* and *Star Trek: Voyager*. In 1994, she told Spelling, "There was a lot of talk of my going onto *Voyager* [as a Maquis officer], but I'm not ready to commit to that any more than

I was ready to commit to *DS9* [in the role of the Bajoran first officer, which eventually evolved into the character of Major Kira Nerys] or any other series. If they ask me to make guest appearances as Ro, and my schedule allows, that I'd do. I like Ro very much and always enjoyed playing her."

According to Larry Nemecek's *Star Trek: The Next Generation Companion*, Forbes' appearance on the last regular episode of *The Next Generation*—the Patrick Stewart–directed "Preemptive Strike"—almost did not happen. Forbes' agent had told the producers of the show to leave them alone, but one *Star Trek* producer, Jeri Taylor, tried anyway. The agent told Taylor to call Forbes directly and explain the story line behind the episode. Taylor did and hooked Forbes on the story of "a woman torn, choosing between loyalties."

Since her last appearance on *The Next Generation*, Forbes' career has been in overdrive. She starred with David "X-Files" Duchovny in *Kalifornia*; appeared in *John Carpenter's Escape from LA*; performed in *The Prosecutor*, a two-hour NBC drama with Stockard Channing; and has joined the cast of *Homicide: Life on the Street* as chief medical examiner.

Although she may be a "hot" actress, Forbes is happiest when she is hiking with her dogs. Still single, she can be found "skimming bad scripts or reading good books . . . that'll probably be turned into bad movies." By her own admission, "I lead a pretty quiet life."

MICHELLE FORBES

*Ensign Ro Laren**

STAGE:	The Father Dowling Mysteries
Call It Clover ('94)	('90)
	Shannon's Deal ('91)
TELEVISION:	Star Trek: The Next Generation
The Guiding Light ('87–'90)	('91, '92, '94)

Seinfeld ('92)
Homocide: Life on the Street
  ('96–present)
Murder One ('96)
Outer Limits ('96)
The Prosecutor ('96)

FILM:
Reel Film ('92)
The Playboys ('92)
Kalifornia ('93)

Love Bites ('93)
Roadflower ('93)
The Road Killers ('94)
Black Day/Blue Night ('95)
Swimming with Sharks ('95)
John Carpenter's Escape from
  LA ('96)

*also Dara in the episode
"Half a Life"; promoted to
lieutenant in the episode
"Preemptive Strike"*

DWIGHT SHULTZ

A graduate of Towson State University in Maryland and founder of the touring company Baltimore Theater Ensemble, Dwight Shultz boasted an early career on Broadway that any stage actor would envy: David Mamet's *The Water Engine, Crucifer of Blood* with Glenn Close, and *Night and Day* with Maggie Smith. He was critically acclaimed in roles ranging from Ibsen to Ionesco. Yet even with this success, in 1982 at age thirty-five, Shultz was struggling—sleeping on couches, barely eking out a living as an actor. He almost gave up on show business.

It was when he picked up a copy of Heinz Pagels' *The Cosmic Code*, an attempt to explain quantum physics to the layman, that a new perspective was added to his life. Pagels' book taught Shultz to look at the world in more relative terms and not to take himself or his profession so seriously. Shultz explained to *The New Republic* in 1989 that "in the micro world of particles, when scientists view photons, if they want to view photons as a wave, it's a wave. If they want to look at it as a particle, they behave as particles. There was a lot of philosophical discussion about this: is it what I want it to be at the moment?" Applying these musings to his own life and his situation at the time, Shultz realized that "when someone props you up and another tears you down, it's not a question of wrong or right. And for you to try to beat yourself on the breast and say you're a terrible person—or say that you're a wonderful person because everyone loves you—is probably going a little too far."

In 1983, with renewed spirit, he took a trip to Los Angeles to visit his girlfriend, the actress Wendy Fulton (who eventually became his wife). While there, he auditioned for "an implausible TV pilot." The show was *The A-Team*, hailed as one that helped turn NBC's fortunes around. Shultz's portrayal of "Howling Mad" Murdoch brought "distinction to an otherwise shallow, if profitable, four-year enterprise," wrote the *National Review*.

Shultz said of his famous role on *The A-Team*, "It's the way you want to see it. If you want to see it as the epitome of art, it will be. If you want to see it as the height of exploitation and degradation, it will be. Neither of them is true. The truth is you're simply scratching out a living: I'm a song and dance man. That's the truth and there's a relaxation that comes with that." Clearly, Pagels' book had influenced Shultz. His classically trained friends in the theater tried to talk him out of doing *The A-Team*, warning him that he would be typecast for life. "Yes, it *[The A-Team]* is farcical and cartoonish . . . but at least the show does it well. There is something to be said . . . for quality of execution," Shultz told the *Los Angeles Times* in 1985.

After completing *The A-Team* in 1987, Shultz was approached to star in a controversial feature film about J. Robert Oppenheimer, *Fat Man and Little Boy*. The producers took a chance in casting Shultz in this, his first feature film, since he was still so closely identified with *The A-Team*. But Shultz's performance as Oppenheimer, which emphasized both the human dilemma behind the making of the bomb and the political forces at work, was convincing. He portrayed Oppenheimer as a victim of the period, a brilliant man torn over his role in building the bomb. Nonetheless, headline writers could not resist the chance to give the reviews such titles as "From A-Team to A-Bomb."

Interestingly, Shultz was cast for the role because director Roland Joffe had asked his casting director to "round up all the actors on American stages who were currently portraying Valmont in *Les*

Liaisons Dangereuses." The character was a manipulative man notorious for objectifying human beings. At the time Shultz was playing the role at the Williamstown (Massachusetts) theater festival.

The following year, Shultz had finished making the film *The Long Walk Home* with Whoopi Goldberg. They had discussed their joint appreciation for *Star Trek*, and she suggested that he do the show. Shortly thereafter, Dwight Shultz was cast as neurotic, hypochondriac Lieutenant (j.g.) Reginald "Reg" Endicott Barclay III.

His first appearance was in the third-season episode "Hollow Pursuits." He played an engineer who retreats to the holodeck because he cannot handle the pressures of real life. This led to a recurring role over the four remaining years of the program. Perhaps most notably, he costarred in the complex episode "Genesis," which marked Gates McFadden's *Star Trek* directorial debut, and in which Shultz as Barclay devolved into a spider-creature. Other memorable *Next Generation* scenes had him creating an ancient western holodeck program for young Alexander and caring for Data's cat, Spot, during her delivery of kittens.

In a guest appearance on the *Star Trek: Voyager* episode "Projections," directed by Jonathan Frakes, Shultz was praised for his performance opposite Robert Picardo. Frakes commented, "The chemistry between them turned out great. So, I just turned on the camera and watched them work. Bob [Picardo] and Dwight are two very funny men."

Director Frakes asked Shultz to make an appearance in the feature *Star Trek: First Contact*. He has a significant and poignant, if nervous, scene with Zefram "James Cromwell" Cochrane and LeVar Burton. The awkward Barclay is even more tongue-tied than usual when meeting his childhood hero.

Shultz continues to act regularly in television, in movies, and on the stage. In 1993, he starred in a television pilot that was not picked up as a series—*Boomtown*, about a dreamer in search of a pot of gold. More recently, he guest starred in a 1996 *Hart to Hart* television movie. In his spare time, Shultz still counts physics as something of a hobby.

DWIGHT SHULTZ

Lieutenant Reginald Barclay
Also appeared on Star Trek: Voyager

STAGE:

Crucifer of Blood
Night and Day
The Water Engine
Sherlock Holmes: The Case of
   Alice Faulkner ('81)
Les Liaisons Dangereuses ('88)

TELEVISION:

Bitter Harvest ('81)
Dial M for Murder ('81)
Hill Street Blues ('81)
Nurse ('81)
Thin Ice ('81)
CHiPs ('82)
The A-Team ('83–'87)
When Your Lover Leaves ('83)
Alfred Hitchcock Presents ('87)
Perry Mason: The Case of the
   Sinister Spirit ('87)
Perry Mason: The Case of the
   Musical Murder ('89)
Jake and the Fatman ('90)
A Killer Among Us ('90)

Star Trek: The Next
   Generation ('90, '91, '92,
   '93, '94)
Last Wish ('91)
Past Imperfect ('91)
Child of Rage ('92)
Woman with a Past ('92)
Victim of Love: The Sharon
   Mohr Story ('93)
Menendez: A Killing in Beverly
   Hills ('94)
Babylon 5 ('95)
Diagnosis: Murder ('95)
Nowhere Man ('95)
Outer Limits ('95)
Touched by an Angel ('95)
Hart to Hart: Till Death Do Us
   Hart ('96)

FILM:

The Fan ('81)
Alone in the Dark ('82)
Fat Man and Little Boy ('89)
The Long Walk Home ('90)
The Temp ('93)
Star Trek: First Contact ('96)

PATTI YASUTAKE

Patricia "Patti" Yasutake's career has spanned television situation comedy, theater (as both an actor and a director), and movies. As *Star Trek: The Next Generation*'s Nurse Alyssa Ogawa, she debuted during the fourth season in "Future Imperfect." She continued on the show in a recurring role through the final season, and in both

Star Trek: Generations and *Star Trek: First Contact*. Yasutake's career is notable to *Star Trek* fans because it has led her to cross paths with quite a few stars of the other *Star Trek* incarnations.

Yasutake's acting career began on the stage. In a role she originated in 1986, and then revived in 1987, she starred in *I Don't Have to Show You No Stinking Badges*, about a Mexican American couple putting their son through Harvard Law School. All is going well until he shows up on their doorstep with his new Japanese American girlfriend and announces that he's quitting school to become an actor. Yasutake, as the girlfriend, Anita, was hailed by the *Los Angeles Times* as "graceful, attractive, and funny," and the *San Diego Union-Tribune* said she "danced well in her part. . . . An invigorating performance." The role of Sonny Villa, the son, was played by *Star Trek: Voyager's* Robert "Chakotay" Beltran. In 1987 Yasutake also appeared in *Tea*, a one-act play about Japanese war brides.

Yasutake's first major television role was in the short-lived, poorly conceived ABC sitcom *Gung Ho*. Based on the film, it starring Gedde Watanabe as a Japanese auto-plant manager living temporarily in the United States. Yasutake played Watanabe's wife, Umeki.

In 1988, the year after *Gung Ho* was canceled, Yasutake played daughter Marsha in Michael Toshiyuki Uno's first feature film, *The Wash*. The wire service review by Joseph Mazo praised Yasutake's performance as "one of the few subtle points of the film, and one of the most interesting." Interestingly, *The Wash* was eventually reworked into an off-Broadway stage play featuring George "Mr. Sulu" Takei.

Although Yasutake's and Takei's lives did not cross paths with *The Wash*, they appeared together in 1995 at a fund-raiser to benefit the California State University at Sacramento library's Mary Tsukamoto Japanese American Collection.

After *The Wash*, Yasutake sat in the director's chair for two plays: Velina Hasu Houston's *Father I Must Have Rice* and Richard Polak's *The Singles' Guide*.

The year after Yasutake made her directorial debut was a disappointing one. The *Los Angeles Times* caught up with her in a Hollywood employment office. Frustrated by her difficulty in finding work, she told them, "I'm an actress, so it's tough because you're selling your face. You're selling your type." She lamented that the pattern of discrimination against women and minorities in the acting profession is difficult to track. Primarily, the dearth of good parts is due to the lack of women and minorities being represented in positions of writing and producing.

However, after being cast in 1990 as Nurse Ogawa on *The Next Generation*, parts became more plentiful for Yasutake. She starred as the wife of Gerald McRaney and the close friend of *Star Trek: Voyager's* Kate "Captain Janeway" Mulgrew in the 1991 NBC television film *Fatal Friendship*. Also, in the 1993 CBS movie *Donato and Daughter*, Yasutake appeared with *Next Generation's* and *Deep Space Nine's* Marc "Gul Dukat" Alaimo. Yasutake was also happy to appear in both *Star Trek: Generations* and *Star Trek: First Contact*. Her scene in *First Contact*, opposite *Star Trek: Voyager's* Robert "The Doctor" Picardo, was an audience favorite.

PATTI YASUTAKE

Nurse Alyssa Ogawa

STAGE:
I Don't Have to Show You No Stinking Badges ('87)
Tea ('87)
Father I Must Have Rice (director) ('88)
The Singles' Guide (director) ('89)

TELEVISION:
Gung Ho ('86–'87)
Tales from the Crypt ('89)
Star Trek: The Next Generation ('90, '91, '92, '93, '94)
Without Warning: The James Brady Story ('91)

Fatal Friendship ('92)
Picket Fences ('92)
Blind Spot ('93)
Donato and Daughter ('93)
Abandoned and Deceived ('95)
Dangerous Intentions ('95)
Murder One ('95)
Murphy Brown ('95)

FILM:
The Wash ('88)
Stop! Or My Mom Will Shoot ('92)
Star Trek: Generations ('94)
Star Trek: First Contact ('96)

POSTSCRIPT

A fan of *Star Trek* for as long as I can remember, I greeted the 1987 announcement of *The Next Generation* with mixed feelings: anticipation, trepidation, exuberance, caution. On the one hand, I was as excited as anyone that Paramount had committed to bringing *Star Trek* back. On the other, how dare they re-cast it? A bald captain. No Vulcan. A psychologist. A Klingon. No crusty doctor. A teenager. This was not the *Star Trek* I knew and loved.

The first season of the new show was uneven. I was not yet hooked. But over the course of the first three years, something amazing happened. Sure, the writing was better, but that can be attributed to maturity. The special effects were far superior, but again, placed in context, Hollywood had come a long way in two decades. I expected nothing less. It was something else.

There was a synergy among the cast. A magic. A chemistry. As I watched these professional actors recite impossible lines in impossible futuristic situations, it all became possible. I believed that Riker had once loved Troi, but now was torn as to his professional future. I felt Worf's torment as he struggled in a chasm between cultures. I understood Data's quest to understand and emulate humanity. I sympathized with Dr. Crusher's peace-loving, humanistic approach to even the Federation's most nefarious beings. Most amazingly, I actually preferred Picard's diplomatic, strategic style to that of an earlier era.

I was not alone.

When *Star Trek: The Next Generation* premiered, conversations around the globe—at the dinner table, on television news reports, and at *Star Trek* conventions—centered on one seemingly impossible question. Could this new cast ever equal that of the original show?

It took years for audiences to be convinced, but one thing was certain: *The Next Generation* cast *didn't* equal the original cast. They *surpassed* it. They proved, to themselves, to their audience, and to me, that they truly had become The Finest Crew in the Fleet.

BIBLIOGRAPHY

Adalian, Joseph. "Generations Treks." *The Washington Times*, November 20, 1994.

Aldridge, David. "Starship Captain." *Starburst*, 1994.

Alexander, David. *Star Trek Creator: The Authorized Biography of Gene Roddenberry*. New York: ROC/Penguin, 1994.

Altman, Mark A. "All Good Things . . ." *Star Trek: The Official Fan Club* 97, June/July 1994.

———. "All Good Things . . ." *Star Trek: The Official Fan Club* 98, August/September 1994.

———. "Brent Spiner on Data." *Cinefantastique* v. 24 No. 3/4, October 1993.

———. "Marina Sirtis, Betazoid Beauty." *Cinefantastique* v. 24 No. 3/4, October 1993.

———. "Star Trek's Next Spin-Off." *Cinefantastique* v. 24 No. 3/4, October 1993.

———. "Stephen Hawking's Star Trek Cameo." *Cinefantastique* v. 24 No. 3/4, October 1993.

———. "The Acting Ensemble." *Cinefantastique* v. 24 No. 3/4, October 1993.

———. "Will Riker, To Be or Not to Be?" *Cinefantastique* v. 24 No. 3/4, October 1993.

Antonucci, Mike. "'Star Trek' Doctor Likes Taking Command." *The Arizona Republic*, September 19, 1993.

Antonucci, Mike. "With 'Generation' Ending, Universe Gets Colder." *The Phoenix Gazette*, May 21, 1994.

Appleson, Gail. "'Trek' Captain Launches a Pair of New Enterprises." *Detroit Free Press*, March 30, 1991.

Arar, Yardena. "Brian Bonsall: The 12-Year-Old Star of 'Blank Check' Can't Remember a Time When He Wasn't an Actor." *Los Angeles Daily News*, March 3, 1994.

Arnold, William. "Stewart Adapts to Life as Captain Picard." *The Times-Picayune*, December 2, 1994.

Avins, Mimi. "The Joy Luck Club." *South China Morning Post*, December 5, 1993.

Bacall, Simon. "Troi: An Exclusive Interview with Marina Sirtis." *Star Trek Communicator* 102, May/June 1995.

Ball, Priscilla. "The Minneapolis Convention." *Stargazer* 13, 3rd Quarter, 1991.

———. "Dreamwerks Chicago." *Stargazer* 14, 4th Quarter, 1991.

———. "The Pasadena Grand Slam." *Stargazer* 23, 1st Quarter, 1994.

Beale, Lewis. "'Trek' Star: The Next Advocation." *Daily News* (N.Y.), November 25, 1996.

Beaufort, John. "'Gillian' Explores Family Tragedy with Care and Compassion." *The Christian Science Monitor*, March 29, 1984.

———. "Back Aboard The 'Enterprise.'" *Tribune Media Services*, August 28, 1989.

———. "Hollywood: Stewart's Enterprise Worth It." *The Press Democrat*, June 6, 1990.

———. "'Muldaur' Dropped From 'Star Trek' Crew." *The Bergen Record*, June 25, 1989.

———. "What's Fame Worth if He's Incognito?" *The Bergen Record*, December 1, 1991.

Bisbee, Dana. "TV Talk; Patrick Stewart Prepares for Another 'Trek' Adventure." *The Boston Herald*, May 28, 1995.

Blessed, Brian. *The Dynamite Kid*. London: Bloomsbury Books, 1992.

Bradley, Seamus. "A Close Encounter with the Captain." *View*, June 4–11, 1995.

Brantley, Ben. "Orton's Warped Wit, More Slapstick Than Verbal." *The New York Times*, March 6, 1996.

Bravin, Jess. "Down to Earth." *Los Angeles Times*, February 14, 1992.

———. "Trying to Break Out of 'Star Trek's' Orbit: Stage Roles Help Stars Fight Typecasting." *The Washington Post*, March 1, 1992.

Brotman, Barbara. "Trekkies Ponder the Fate of Tasha Yar." *Chicago Tribune*, September 23, 1991.

Buck, Jerry. "'Star Trek' Discovers Sex in the 24th Century." *Chicago Tribune*, March 3, 1990.

Bullard, Jim. "Crush is on for the 'Next Generation'." *St. Petersburg Times*, August 27, 1993.

Campbell, Bob. "Patrick Stewart Launches Inner 'Trek'." *The San Francisco Examiner*, July 29, 1995.

Canby, Vincent. "Film: 'Rent Control,' New York Cast." *The New York Times*, May 4, 1984.

Carr, Jay. "New Star Trek Makes Comfy Contact." *The Boston Globe*, November 22, 1996.

Carter, Gayle Jo, Mark Glubka, and Jonathan Walters. "Clips from the Stars' Prom Nights." *USA Weekend*, June 7, 1992.

Cerone, Daniel. "An Enterprise with Longevity." *The Bergen Record*, November 4, 1990.

Chambers, Colin. "Responsibility to the Future." *Plays and Players* (UK), July 1978.

Clements, Kathleen. "A Review of Merchant of Venice." *Stargazer* 15, 1st Quarter, 1992.
Cohen, Amy. "More Than Just a Country Doctor." *Star Trek: The Official Fan Club* 96, April/May 1994.
———. "LeVar Burton: The Vision of Geordi LaForge." *Star Trek: The Official Fan Club* 94, November/December 1993.
Corliss, Richard. "Aliens! Adventure! Acting!" *Time*, November 25, 1996.
Coutros, Evonne E. "Sirtis: From Shakespeare to 'Star Trek'." *The Bergen Record*, January 7, 1990.
Cunningham, Kamy. "A Galaxy of Stars." *Star Trek: The Official Fan Club* 86, July/August 1992.
Davis, John S. "Close-Ups: Colm Meaney." *Star Trek: The Official Fan Club* 76, October/November 1990.
———. "Close-Ups: John de Lancie." *Star Trek: The Official Fan Club* 66, February/March 1989.
DePaolis, Mark. "Doctor in Space, Role Model on Earth." *Star Tribune*, March 25, 1993.
Devlin, Ruthanne. "So Many People Have Heads!" *Stargazer* 9, Summer 1990.
Dier, Cary. "IAAPS Goes to New York City." *Stargazer* 6, September/October 1989.
Dorsey, Tom. "Emmy Monotony." *The Courier-Journal*, August 25, 1991.
Dougherty-Johnson, Lily, Ralph Mims and Amy Pacholk. "Talking with Wil Wheaton." *Newsday*, August 25, 1991.
Dumas, Alan. "Beyond the Final Frontier." *Rocky Mountain News*, February 25, 1994.
Easton, Nina J. "From 'A-Team' to A-Bomb." *Los Angeles Times*, November 1, 1989.
Ebert, Roger. "Resistance to 'Contact' Is Futile." *Chicago Sun-Times*, November 22, 1996.
Edmunds, Lynne. "Making Theatre Marriage Work." *Daily Times* (UK), September 9, 1982.
Edwards, Henry. "Patrick Stewart." *Details*, September 1995.
Esterly, Glenn. "Star Trek's Data Becomes More Human." *Chicago Tribune*, November 21, 1991.
Fanger, Iris. "'Loot' at Hartford Stage through March 16." *The Boston Herald*, March 7, 1996.
Farber, Jim. "Frakes Gets His Chance at Star Trek." *The State Journal-Register* (Springfield, Ill.), November 28, 1994.
———. "Legit Review: Every Good Boy Deserves Favour." *Daily Variety*, February 19, 1992.
———. "Stewart Plans 'Carol' Tour, with Final Stop on B'way." *Daily Variety*, July 11, 1991.
Fiaca, Nick. "Captain Picard's Log." *News of the World*, December 2, 1995.
Fiddick, Peter. "A Trek Around Dickens." *The Guardian*, January 4, 1994.
Fisher, Deborah. "Season Review/Preview." *Star Trek Communicator* 108, August/September 1996.
———. "Star Trek: First Contact." *Star Trek Communicator* 109, November/December 1996.
Flatow, Sheryl. "The Appeal Is Universal." *The Washington Times*, December 6, 1991.
Fleming, Michael. "Michael Dorn Will Return to Space." *Chicago Sun-Times*, July 6, 1995.
Florence, Bill. "Naren Shankar—Herald of 'The First Duty.'" *Star Trek: The Next Generation Magazine* 22, February 11, 1993.
Frankel, Martha. "Patrick Stewart: The Next Generation." *Movieline*, November 1994.
Freeman, Laurie. "Patrick Stewart: Actor, Director, and Writer." *Newsmakers* 1, 1996.
Frost, Bob. "Interview with Colm Meaney." *West*, February 1995.
Gabriel, Sandra, Natalie Smith, and Keith Warno. "Talking with Marina Sirtis." *Newsday*, October 28, 1990.
Geairns, Alex J. "By My Troth, Captain, These Are Very Bitter Words." *Satellite Times* (UK), 1993.
Geeslin, Ned. "Gene Roddenberry and Majel Barrett's Most Successful Enterprise Isn't a Starship; It's Their 17-Year Marriage." *People*, March 16, 1987.
Goldman, Gregory. "The Man in the Mask." *Axcess*, June/July 1996.
Goodman, Walter. "Theater 'Tea,' End of Trilogy." *The New York Times*, October 21, 1987.
Graham, Jefferson. "McFadden Trades Space for Paradise on Earth." *USA Today*, January 17, 1995.
Grant, James. "Q&A with Patrick Stewart." *Los Angeles Times*, August 3, 1995.
Green, Tom. "Playing Tactless Partner on 'L.A. Law' Presents a Challenge to Diana Muldaur." *The Courier-Journal*, May 6, 1990.
Greenstreet, Rosanna. "Questionnaire." *The Guardian*, January 21, 1995.
Greenwald, Jeff. "Masters of the Universe." *Details*, December 1996.
Gressel, Janine. "Album Offers New View of 'Star Trek' Star." *The Seattle Times*, September 8, 1991.
Grogan, David. "Star Trek's LeVar Burton Needs Space to Escape His Roots." *People*, March 7, 1988.
Gross, Edward. "Immortal Q." *Cinescape*, January 1996.
———. "John de Lancie: The Man Who Would Be Q." *Starlog*, March 1988.
Gussow, Mel. "Stage: 'Say Goodbye,' A Story of Family Life." *The New York Times*, December 2, 1986.
Guttman, Monica. "Frakes Continues Journey of 'Enterprise.'" *St. Petersburg Times*, November 5, 1987.

Hall, Steve. "Worf Beams Aboard 'DS9.'" *The Indianapolis Star*, October 1, 1995.
Hanauer, Joan. "Father Doesn't Always Know Best Anymore." *United Press International*, April 6, 1988.
Harmetz, Aljean. "The Boys of 'Stand by Me' Learn to Stand by Each Other." *Chicago Tribune*, September 25, 1986.
Hartl, John. "'Pieces': It Was a Golden Opportunity for Rosalind Chao." *The Seattle Times*, April 26, 1991.
Hartling, Judy. "'Star Trek' Actress Has Down-to-Earth Advice." *The Hartford Courant*, March 16, 1996.
Heinzen, Krystal. "To Boldly Go Where One Has Gone Before." *St. Petersburg Times*, May 13, 1988.
Helmbreck, Valerie. "Where No Man, No One, Has Gone: You've Come a Long Way, Betazoid." *Gannett News Service*, October 29, 1990.
Heyman, Karen, and Ileane Rudolph. "Surfing with Data." *Yahoo Internet Life* v. 2 No. 7, December 1996.
Hochman, David. "Lost in Space?" *Entertainment Weekly*, November 22, 1996.
Honeycutt, Kirk. "Teen Actor Wheaton Wants No Part of Trash." *Chicago Tribune*, August 21, 1986.
Hughes, Mike. "TV or Not TV." *Gannett News Service*, June 23, 1989.
———. "Worf Is on Board at 'Next Gen.'" *Gannett News Service*, October 5, 1995.
Hull, Pete. "Brent Spiner: A Pure Stream of Data." *Star Trek Communicator* 103, July/August 1995.
———. "Creation Salutes the Grand Slam Show." *Star Trek: The Official Fan Club* 92, July/August 1993.
———. "Michael Dorn, The Honorable Warrior." *Star Trek Communicator* 104, October/November 1995.
———. "The Big Goodbye." *Star Trek: The Official Fan Club* 97, June/July 1994.
———. "Trekbits." *Star Trek Communicator* 108, August/September 1996.
Hyman, Jackie. "Taking Chances: LeVar Burton Hopes to Create Literate Human Beings." *Chicago Tribune*, July 13, 1993.
Infusino, Divina. "Out of Character." *Star Trek TV Guide Collector's Edition*, Spring 1995.
Inman, David. *The TV Encyclopedia*, New York: Perigee, 1991.
Jackson, Kevin. "Theatre: The Final Frontier." *The Independent*, December 29, 1993.
Jacobs, A. J. "Patrick Stewart Makes It So." *Entertainment Weekly*, October 20, 1995.
Johnson, Allan. "Utility Klingon." *Chicago Tribune*, May 28, 1996.
Johnson, Lorie. "Kith & Kin: An Interview with Trevor Stewart." *Stargazer* 14, 4th Quarter, 1991.
———. "Kith & Kin: An Interview with Trevor Stewart, Part II." *Stargazer* 15, 1st Quarter, 1992.
———. "An Interview with Ruth Wynn Owen." *Stargazer* 12, Spring Quarter, 1991.
Johnson, Malcolm. "At Age 32, 'Loot' Still Fresh, Funny." *The Hartford Courant*, February 19, 1996.
Johnson, Peter. "Diana Muldaur Will Take a Challenge, But Not a Dive." *USA Today*, September 24, 1991.
———, and Brian Donlon. "Torturing Research for Stewart's 'Star Trek.'" *USA Today*, December 14, 1992.
Jones, Welton. "Patrick Stewart Finds Being Alien Is Part of the Job." *The San Diego Union-Tribune*, March 29, 1991.
Karlin, Susan. "LeVar Burton: Bridging the Gap." *Daily Variety*, April 20, 1993.
Kaufman, Joanne, and Michael Alexander. "For Star Trek's Marina Sirtis, Love Is on the Launching Pad." *People*, December 12, 1988.
Kavanagh, Linda. "Going Baldly." *RTE Guide* (UK), May 14, 1993.
Kenny, Glenn. "Brent Spiner." *Entertainment Weekly Special Star Trek Issue*, Fall 1994.
———. "Gates McFadden." *Entertainment Weekly Special Star Trek Issue*, Fall 1994.
———. "John de Lancie." *Entertainment Weekly Special Star Trek Issue*, Fall 1994.
———. "Michael Dorn." *Entertainment Weekly Special Star Trek Issue*, Fall 1994.
———. "Patrick Stewart." *Entertainment Weekly Special Star Trek Issue*, Fall 1994.
Kettman, Steve. "A Star Among Scientists." *The San Francisco Chronicle*, June 20, 1993.
Kiley, Fran. "The Two Captains Convention at the Penta in New York." *Stargazer* 12, Spring Quarter, 1991.
Kim, Albert. "Star Trip." *Entertainment Weekly*, January 20, 1995.
———. "Hot Seat." *Entertainment Weekly*, August 12, 1994.
King, Susan. "Jolly Good Shows: American Series Television Takes on a British Touch." *Los Angeles Times*, November 4, 1990.
Kishi, Russell. "Gates McFadden's Pragmatic View on Fame." *United Press International*, February 12, 1988.
Kitei, Mindy. "Prescription for the Future." *Star Trek TV Guide Collector's Edition*, Spring 1995.
Klein, Alvin. "Prairie Passion Fails." *The New York Times*, August 29, 1982.
———. "Theater: Barry Play Proves Durable." *The New York Times*, August 15, 1982.
Knutzen, Eirik. "'Star Trek's' Worf: Michael Dorn." *The Bergen Record*, July 3, 1988.
Koehler, Robert "Stage Beat." *Los Angeles Times*, March 6, 1987.

———. "Stage Beat." *Los Angeles Times*, January 1, 1988.
Koltnow, Barry. "Calling His Shots." *Orange County Register*, November 20, 1996.
Kotkin, Joel. "The Starmaker." *The Washington Post*, January 27, 1977.
Krol, Pamela V. "Patrick Stewart: His Career Is Zipping Along at Warp Speed." *A&E Monthly*, February 1996.
Kubasik, Ben. "Roz, Leland Lay Down the 'Law.'" *Newsday*, May 3, 1990.
Kurzman, Dan. "Worf Worked Into 'Trek VI.'" *Orlando Sentinal Tribune*, July 5, 1991.
LaFaso, Edward Jr. "Alien Role." *The Bergen Record*, July 7, 1988.
Lassiter, Jo Ann. "Boston Bound." *Stargazer* 15, 1st Quarter, 1992.
———. "Starcon '94—Denver." *Stargazer* 23, 1st Quarter, 1994.
———, and Priscilla Ball. "A Capital Convention." *Stargazer* 21, 3rd Quarter, 1993.
Lawler, Sylvia. "Jonathan Frakes Nears the End of His 'Trek.'" *The Morning Call* (Allentown, Penn.), February 27, 1994.
Lee, Luaine. "'Star Trek' Set No Place for Snobs." *Pittsburgh Post-Gazette*, November 22, 1994.
Lincoln, Christian. "An Interview with Jean-Luc." *Daily Nexus*, October 14, 1993.
Lind, Jane Nyback. "The Stewart in Sacramento." *Stargazer* 14, 4th Quarter, 1991.
Lipton, Michael A. "Can Data Find a Mate-A?" *People*, June 8, 1992.
Logan, Michael. "Frakes' Progress." *TV Guide*, November 23–29, 1996.
———. "Making 'Contact.'" *TV Guide*, November 23–29, 1996.
———. "Patrick Stewart." *TV Guide*, August 24–30, 1996.
———. "The Dawn of a New 'Deep Space' Age." *TV Guide*, October 7–13, 1995.
Louey, Sandy. "Ever Consider Acting?" *The Hartford Courant*, August 1, 1996.
Loynd, Ray. "One-Acts Paint the Coloring of a Culture." *Los Angeles Times*, January 27, 1988.
Madsen, Dan. "Gates McFadden: The Doctor Is In." *Star Trek: The Official Fan Club* 74, June/July 1990.
———. "Jonathan Frakes: Looking Out for 'Number One.'" *Star Trek Communicator* 105, December/January 1996.
———. "Michael Dorn: A Klingon Bound for Glory." *Star Trek: The Official Fan Club* 72, February/March, 1990.
———. "Patrick Stewart: Captain Picard on Shatner, Roddenberry and the Realm of Star Trek." *Star Trek Communicator* 100, December/January 1994/1995.
———. "Patrick Stewart: The Future of Captain Picard Part One." *Star Trek: The Official Fan Club* 87, September/October 1992.
———. "Patrick Stewart: The Future of Captain Picard Part Two." *Star Trek: The Official Fan Club* 88, November/December 1992.
———. "Star Trek Update with Jonathan Frakes." *Star Trek Communicator* 107, June/July 1996.
———. "Star Trek: First Contact Completes Shooting." *Star Trek Communicator* 108, August/September 1996.
———. "Welcome to Deep Space Nine (Part Three)." *Star Trek: The Official Fan Club* 91, May/June 1993.
———. "Whoopi Goldberg: Guinan's Guide to the Galaxy." *Star Trek: The Official Fan Club* 79, April/May 1991.
———. "Wil Wheaton—The Final Words of Wesley Crusher." *Star Trek: The Official Fan Club* 77, December/January 1990–91.
———, and John S. Davis. "Denise Crosby Protecting the Indomitable Spirit of Tasha Yar." *Star Trek: The Official Fan Club* 59, December/January 1987.
———. "Diana Muldaur: A New Member of the Family." *Star Trek: The Official Fan Club* 66, February/March 1989.
———. "Jonathan Frakes—Looking Out for 'Number One.'" *Star Trek: The Official Fan Club* 58, October/November 1987.
———. "Marina Sirtis: Understand Counselor Troi." *Star Trek: The Official Fan Club* 64, October/November 1988.
Magda, James. "Majel Barrett Nurses a Role." *Star Trek: The Official Fan Club* 95, February/March 1994.
Maloni, Kelly, Ben Greenman, Kristin Miller, and Jeff Hearn, *Net Trek*. New York: Random House Electronic Publishing, 1995.
Mano, D. Keith. "The Making of Fat Man and Little Boy." *National Review*, November 10, 1989.
Margulies, Lee. "Dwight Shultz: Typecast as Versatile." *Los Angeles Times*, July 20, 1985.

Marks, Peter. "Patrick Stewart: A Class(ical) Act." *The Houston Chronicle,* November 1, 1995.

Martin, Sue. "Faces: Continuing Mission." *Los Angeles Times,* November 26, 1988.

———. "Spiner Explores the Nuances of an Android Called Data." *Los Angeles Times,* June 24, 1989.

Martinez, Jose A. "An Intergalactic Rogues' Gallery." *TV Guide,* August 24–30, 1996.

Mavroudis, Christina. "Patrick Stewart: Live From Palo Alto, CA. 2/10/90." *Stargazer* 9, Summer 1990.

Maynard, Kate. "A Voice to Be Heard." *Stargazer* 21, 3rd Quarter, 1993.

McCarthy, John. "The Beauty of Idaho Nearly Took Chao's Speech Away." *Lewiston Morning Tribune,* April 26, 1991.

McDonnell, David. "Patrick Stewart Epic Hero." *Starlog Yearbook.*

McNeil, Alex. *Total Television.* New York:Penguin Books, 1996.

Metcalf, Steve. "Acting Career, as Measured in Light-Years." *The Hartford Courant,* February 7, 1996.

Meyers, Kate. "What Ever Happened To . . . Wil Wheaton." *Entertainment Weekly,* November 29, 1996.

Middlehurst, Lester. "The Unlikeliest Trekkie of All." *Daily Mail,* December 28, 1993.

———. "Ugly Duckling Who Fell in Love with Graeme Souness." *Daily Mail,* February 4, 1995.

Millar, John. "You'd Never Get Me up in One of Those Things." *Scottish Daily Record,* December 5, 1996.

Miller, Ron. "Emmy Drama." *Chicago Tribune,* June 28, 1990.

Minkowitz, Donna. "A New Enterprise." *The Advocate,* August 22, 1995.

Minor, Debra K. "That Macho Lt. Worf Is a Nice Guy—Really." *Sun-Sentinel* (Fort Lauderdale), April 4, 1993.

Modderno, Craig. "'Generations' Rap." *TV Guide,* October 8–14, 1994.

Mott, Sue. "Kinnear the Deadly Serious Joker." *Sunday Times* (London), August 15, 1993.

Naeye, Robert. "A Conversation with Patrick Stewart." *Astronomy,* December 1995.

Nagel, Rob. "Whoopi Goldberg," in *Contemporary Black Biography* v. 4. New York: Gale Research, 1994.

Nashawaty, Chris. "Most Illogical." *Entertainment Weekly,* December 6, 1996.

Nemecek, Larry. "Trekbits: London Convention." *Star Trek Communicator* 102, May/June 1995.

———. *The Star Trek: The Next Generation Companion.* New York: Pocket Books, 1995.

Nicholson, Debby. "Taking a Bite from the Big Apple." *Stargazer* 21, 3rd Quarter, 1993.

———. "The Brunch—At Last!" *Stargazer* 25, 3rd Quarter, 1994.

O'Hare, Kate. "Michael Dorn Reflects on Last Season of 'Next Generation' and Klingon Lt. Worf." *The Times Union,* January 9, 1994.

Ostroff, Bridgit, and Lindsay Feldman. "Talking with LeVar Burton." *Newsday,* November 16, 1994.

Parks, Louis B. "The Long Great Trek: Majel Barrett Goes Boldly Through TV's Final Frontier." *The Houston Chronicle,* September 1, 1992.

Pearlman, Cindy. "Patrick Stewart Finds Life After 'Trek.'" *Chicago Sun-Times,* August 27, 1995.

Peel, Lesley, and Claudia Wiegand. "Fanfare . . ." *Imzadi International* 2, Pipedream Publishers, September 1995.

Pickle, Betsy. "Time-Warp Brings Shatner, Stewart to Mutual Admiration." *Knoxville News-Sentinel,* November 18, 1994.

———. "While 'Star Trek's' Wesley Studies, So Will Actor Wil Wheaton." *Chicago Tribune,* October 27, 1990.

Preston, Andrew. "Out of This World." *Daily Express* (UK), June 4, 1993.

Provenzano, Tom. "Michael Dorn." *Drama-Logue,* August 25–31, 1994.

Reader, Stephanie. "Radio, TV, Music: 'DSN,' 'Next Gen' Fans Trek to Bellevue Convention." *News Tribune,* August 3, 1994.

Reichardt, Nancy M. "The Evil Twin at Work." *The Bergen Record,* July 17, 1988.

Reiner, Eric L. "'Trek' Actor Spiner Moves Boldly Ahead." *The Denver Post,* April 24, 1996.

Rensin, David. "Patrick Stewart—The Unpublished TV Guide Interview." *Stargazer* 23, 1st Quarter, 1994.

Rice-Oxley, Mark. "Star Trek Star Treks to Bosnia to Boost Troop Morale." *Agence France Presse,* March 4, 1996.

Rich, Frank. "Stage: BAM Company in Shakespeare 'Dream.'" *The New York Times,* January 12, 1981.

———. "Theater: A Musical 'Three Musketeers' Opens." *The New York Times,* November 12, 1984.

———. "Theater: 'To Gillian,' on the Death of a Wife." *The New York Times,* November 4, 1983.

Rich, Jason. "Michelle Forbes: The Return of Ensign Ro." *Star Trek: The Official Fan Club* 83, December/January 1991.

Roller, Pamela. "Much Ado About Q." *Star Trek Communicator* 101, February/March 1995.
———. "Patrick Stewart: The Legacy of Captain Picard." *Star Trek: The Official Fan Club* 99, October/November 1994.
Rondeau, Melody. "Patrick Stewart in Palo Alto." *Stargazer* 8, Spring 1990.
Rosenblum, Trudi. "Star Trekkers Present Alien Voices." *Publishers Weekly*, November 4, 1996.
Roush, Matt. "Dorn's 'Trek' to Acceptance." *USA Today*, June 18, 1991.
———. "On 'Star Trek,' Brent Spiner Is the Heart of Gold Data." *USA Today*, September 28, 1989.
Rousuck, J. Wynn. "'Capt. Picard' Prefers the Bard to Sci-Fi." *The Idaho Statesman*, October 1, 1990.
Rumerman, Joan. "Patrick Stewart Credit List." *IAAPS/PSRL*, 1995.
Ryan, James. "Rosalind Chao Strikes Gold in '1000 Pieces.'" *BPI Entertainment Newswire*, July 10, 1991.
Sanchez, Jose Luis Jr. "'Trek' Helps Boy Escape." *Sun-Sentinel* (Fort Lauderdale), November 27, 1994.
Sanello, Frank. "British Actor Relishes Role as Star Trek Captain." *The Sun* (Westerly, R.I.), March 7, 1990.
Sasitharan, T. "Patrick Stewart: Picard Is Modelled on My Father." *The Straits Times* (Singapore), April 8, 1995.
Schaefer, Stephen. "Stewart: Beyond the 'Trek' Horizon." *USA Today*, November 21, 1994.
Schenden, Laurie K. "Denise Crosby Treks to Stage Center." *Los Angeles Times*, May 17, 1994.
Scher, Valerie. "Soldier's Tilt with Satan Well-Told." *The San Diego Union-Tribune*, August 23, 1993.
Scheuer, Dorothy. "Young Wil Wheaton Stars in Young Harry Houdini." *Scholastic Update*, March 9, 1987.
Schwartzbaum, Lisa. "Space Jammin'." *Entertainment Weekly*, November 29, 1996.
Scott, Vernon. "Rosalind Chao: TV First for Chinese-American." *United Press International*, July 11, 1983.
———. "Scott's World: Hollywood Inaugurates TV Hall of Fame." *United Press International*, February 27, 1984.
Shales, Tom. "'North and South Book II': This Trial, Too, Shall Pass." *The San Diego Union-Tribune*, May 8, 1986.
Slotek, Jim. "Star Struck: Patrick Stewart's Trek to Become an American Hero and William Shatner's Pal." *The Toronto Sun*, November 22, 1994.
Smith, Liz. "Picard's Romance." *Newsday*, July 31, 1995.
Smith, Stacy Jenel. "Sirtis Boldly Warping into Unemployment." *Sun-Sentinel* (Fort Lauderdale), February 27, 1994.
Soriano, Cesar G. "Bad by a Hair: Frakes Dons His Evil Goatee." *The Washington Times*, November 25, 1994.
———. "The Bald Truth." *The Washington Times*, September 6, 1993.
Spelling, Ian. "Actor Spiner Stays Busy with Big-Screen Project." *The Houston Chronicle*, June 29, 1996.
———. "Colm Meaney—Chief O'Brien." *The Official Star Trek: Deep Space Nine Magazine* 5, 1994.
———. "Colm Meaney Never Bought into the 'Deep Space' Hype." *Chicago Tribune*, September 24, 1993.
———. "Denise Crosby Recalls Short, but Sweet 'Trek.'" *The Houston Chronicle*, March 25, 1995.
———. "DS9's Meaney Is Overworked—And Loves It." *Roanoke Times & World News*, May 23, 1995.
———. "Frakes Gains Responsibility as Well as a Few Pounds." *Chicago Tribune*, December 17, 1993.
———. "Frakes Has an Amazing Trek Record, Actor/Director Has 'Next Gen' on His Wish List." *The Denver Post*, January 19, 1996.
———. "Genesis of a Director." *The Toronto Sun*, March 6, 1994.
———. "Indeed an Actor." *Starlog*, December 1996.
———. "It's Mom: Gates McFadden When Junior Comes Crawlin'." *Chicago Tribune*, April 9, 1993.
———. "LeVar Burton Explores New Turf." *Chicago Tribune*, May 21, 1993.
———. "LeVar Burton's 'Yesterday,' Today, and Tomorrow." *Chicago Tribune*, July 28, 1995.
———. "Luck of the Irish." *Starlog* 227, June 1996.
———. "Majel Barrett Beams onto 'Babylon 5' as Lady Morella." *Chicago Tribune*, February 23, 1996.
———. "'Next Gen' Crew Takes the Next Step with Caution, Glee." *The Houston Chronicle*, May 14, 1994.
———. "'Next Gen' Star KOs Media on 'Strong' Women Roles." *Chicago Tribune*, August 13, 1993.
———. "Still a Way to Go on Worf, Busy Actor Says." *The Denver Post*, September 13, 1996.
———. "Testy 'NG' Fans Made an Enterpriser of Wil Wheaton." *Chicago Tribune*, February 25, 1994.
———. "Texas Native Dorn 'Clings On' to Worf." *The Houston Chronicle*, September 11, 1993.
———. "The 'Next Generation' of Michael Dorn's Busy Career." *Chicago Tribune*, June 2, 1995.
———. "This Bajoran Hesitant About Taking a Ride on 'Voyager.'" *Chicago Tribune*, August 5, 1994.
———. "Through the Generations." *Starlog*, December 1996.

———. "When She Was Down, 'The Next Gen' Beamed Her Up." *Chicago Tribune*, June 30, 1993.

Stever, Gayle S. "Mr. Goodwrench," *Star Trek Communicator* 105, December/January 1996.

Stewart, Bob. "Toward Equality; Exploring a World of Difference; Looking for Work." *Los Angeles Times*, February 13, 1989.

Stewart, Patrick. Letter to the editor. *Stargazer* 25, 3rd Quarter, 1994.

———. Letter to the editor. *Stargazer* 26, 4th Quarter, 1994.

———. "Me and My Tennis." *Perspective*, Winter 1990.

Stone, Judy. "Chao's Journey to '1000 Pieces.'" *The San Francisco Chronicle*, May 27, 1991.

Swanson, Debbi K. "Marina Sirtis." *Drama-Logue*, December 14–20, 1989.

Teitelbaum, Sheldon. "How Gene Roddenberry and His Brain Trust Have Boldly Taken 'Star Trek' Where No TV Series Has Gone Before." *Los Angeles Times Magazine*, May 5, 1991.

Terrace, Vincent. *Fifty Years of Television*. New York: Cornwall Books, 1991.

Terry, Clifford. "Flimsy Premise, Little Style Marks 'Wizard.'" *Chicago Tribune*, September 9, 1986.

Tesser, Neil. "Enterprising Sorts." *Chicago Tribune*, April 4, 1993.

Thompson, Anne. "The 'Englishman' CoStar Colm Meaney." *Entertainment Weekly Online*, May 19, 1995.

Todd, Anne Christine. "In His Own Words" (transcriptions of Patrick Stewart's interviews and informal remarks made at benefits for Amnesty International USA). October 1990, July and November 1991.

Toepfer, Susan. "Denise Crosby, Granddaughter of Bing, Beams Down from Star Trek for Some New Enterprise." *People*, May 2, 1998.

Trimble, Bjo. *Star Trek Concordance*. New York: Citadel Press, 1995.

Venant, Elizabeth. "Valdez—A Life in the River of Humanity." *Los Angeles Times*, February 2, 1986.

Vierria, Dan. "An Alien Adventure Propels Star Trek Star to Capitol Event." *Sacramento Bee*, November 3, 1995.

Vincent, Mal. "Captains Talk 'Trek.'" *Roanoke Times & World News*, November 22, 1994.

Walls, Rose. "Oedipus Tyrannus (a review)." *Stargazer* 6, September/October 1989.

Walstad, David. "Denise Crosby Well-Suited to the 'Key West' Lifestyle." *Los Angeles Times*, January 2, 1993.

Wankoff, Jordon. "LeVar Burton" in *Contemporary Black Biography* v. 8. New York: Gale Research, 1994.

Warren, Elaine. "'Star Trek' Is Born Again . . . Worrying How to Dress a Pig." *TV Guide*, October 24, 1987.

Weiskind, Ron. "In the Captain's Seat." *Pittsburgh Post-Gazette*, April 4, 1996.

———. "She Finds Life After 'Star Trek' in Hawaii." *Pittsburgh Post-Gazette*, March 26, 1995.

———. "Worf Clings to His Duty as Dorn Joins the 'DS9' Crew." *Pittsburgh Post-Gazette*, October 3, 1995.

Weiss, Hedy. "Audience Transported by 'Trek' Actors." *Chicago Sun-Times*, April 12, 1993.

Werts, Diane. "A 'First' for Him, Jonathan Frakes Takes Directing Controls of the Latest 'Star Trek' Film Enterprise." *Los Angeles Times*, November 29, 1996.

———. "Dorn Keeps His Goals Simple: Work, Work, Work." *Newsday*, May 25, 1996.

———. "The Bold and the Beautiful." *Star Trek TV Guide Collector's Edition*, Spring 1995.

Westbrook, Bruce. "Alien on the Set of TV's 'Star Trek.'" *The Houston Chronicle*, November 17, 1991.

———. "Beyond 'Star Trek'; 'Data' Ready for Unchartered Territory." *The Houston Chronicle*, February 6, 1994.

———. "Movies 'Star Trek' Voyage Takes Spiner from Television to Big Screen." *The Atlanta Journal and Constitution*, November 18, 1994.

———. "'Trek' Cliff-hanger Concludes." *The Houston Chronicle*, September 25, 1993.

Wilkerson, Marilyn. "Patrick Stewart: A Biography." *The Picardian*, 1993.

———. "Vulkon Atlanta 1992." *Stargazer* 15, 1st Quarter, 1992.

Williams, Mike. "Role That Changed My Life." *Stockton-on-Tees Evening Gazette*, May 20, 1993.

Williamson, Bruce. "The Wash—Movie Reviews." *Playboy*, September 1988.

Willistein, Paul. "Frakes Makes Contact." *The Morning Call* (Allentown, Penn.), November 22, 1996.

Wilson, Emily. "Ooh, You Are Bold." *Daily Mirror*, March 21, 1996.

Wulf, Steve. "To Die or Not to Die." *Entertainment Weekly Special Star Trek Issue*, Fall 1994.

ARTICLES PUBLISHED WITHOUT A BYLINE

Coventry Evening Telegraph. "All's Well That Ends Well for Double Act." May 25, 1971.

Data Entries 4. Special Theatrical Edition, Summer 1988.

Detroit Free Press. "Kira Goes Where No Woman Has Before." April 25, 1993.

Entertainment Today (UK). "Interview Patrick Stewart." December 16, 1988.
Entertainment Weekly. "Cybertalk." August 2, 1996.
———. "Fall Movie Preview: Star Trek: Generations." Fall Double Issue, 1994.
———. "News & Notes—Flashes, Riker's Peak." February 23–March 1, 1996.
———. "Great Performance, Patrick Stewart." December 29, 1995–January 5, 1996.
Imzadi International 1. "Horizon Generations Con." Pipedream Publishers, June 1995.
———. "Number One." Pipedream Publishers, June 1995.
———. "The Serene Betazoid." Pipedream Publishers, June 1995.
Imzadi International 2. "The Final Days . . ." Pipedream Publishers, September 1995.
Imzadi International 4. "Whispers . . ." Pipedream Publishers, July 1996.
Imzadi International 5. "Hyperspace Files . . ." Pipedream Publishers, December 1996.
———. "Whispers . . ." Pipedream Publishers, December 1996.
Irish Evening Herald (Dublin). "Starship to Success." May 14, 1993.
Kansas City Star. "Actress Goes Boldly to 'Trek' Fests." January 31, 1993.
Los Angeles Times. "Short Takes: Gender Key to 'L.A. Law' Villain." October 23, 1990.
News & Record (Greensboro, N.C.). "Frakes Makes Debut as 'Trek' Director." December 5, 1996.
People. "Diana Muldaur: Power Envy." April 8, 1991.
Playboy. "20 Questions: Patrick Stewart." November 1992.
PR Newswire. "Actor, Director LeVar Burton and Stephanie Cozart Burton Honored for Work Promoting Awareness About Infertility." September 16, 1996.
———. "LeVar Burton Accepts Mission to 'Bluestar' Space Station from Magnet Interactive Studios." July 14, 1995.
———. "The Klingons Are Back." July 5, 1995.
Red Alert 1. "Personal Log . . ." Pipedream Publishers, September 1994.
———. "Tidbits from 10-Forward." Pipedream Publishers, September 1994.
Red Alert 2. "A Dream for Genie & Jonathan." Pipedream Publishers, November/December 1994.
———. "Tidbits from 10-Forward." Pipedream Publishers, November/December 1994.
Star Trek: The Next Generation Poster Magazine 26. "LeVar Burton." July 1992.
Star Trek: The Next Generation Poster Magazine 27. "Cheryl Gates McFadden." August 1992.
Star Trek: The Next Generation Poster Magazine 48. "Majel Barrett Roddenberry." July 1993.
Stratford Nightly Programmes. "Profile Patrick Stewart." 1976.
Sun-Sentinel (Fort Lauderdale, Fl.). "Stewart's Kids Were 'Trek' Fans." June 20, 1993.
The Bergen Record. "Actress Gates McFadden Is Pushing to Have Women Go Where They Haven't Been Going on 'Star Trek: The Next Generation.'" December 21, 1990.
———. "LeVar Burton: Modern Day Rebel." December 11, 1988.
The Charleston Gazette. "Star Trek Pokes Fun at Writers." July 25, 1994.
The Commercial Appeal (Memphis). "Crusher Prescribes Romance." March 16, 1992.
———. "'Trek' Actor Frakes Likes Getting Labeled." November 28, 1992.
The London Express. "The Actor Who Boldly Went . . ." April 22, 1988.

WORLD WIDE WEB PAGES (all begin with http://)
copper.ucs.indian/~mmcdanie/delancie.html
members.aol.com/hheyer2003/colm/
members.aol.com/majelr/
members.aol.com/openface/ww.html
members.aol.com/soongme/
meritbbs.rulimburg.nl/Fun/Troi/
millennianet.com/lee/
ourworld.compuserve.com/Homepages/lskywa/
ourworld.compuserve.com/Homepages/psas/
spitfire.cid.com/~werdna/sttng/
us.imdb.com/cache/person-biography/
users.aol.com/oladler/bspiner.htm
vsonic.fi/~tommiph/info.html

world.std.com/~jhlee/bdft/bdft.html
www.asahi-net.or.jp/~ti3y-itu/
www.astro.umd.edu/~sgeier/obrien.html
www.bravotv.com/patrick.html
www.cdsnet.net/vidiot/
www.cris.com/~Carman/
www.europa.com/~mercutio/JDL.html
www.helsinki.fi/~mmtmakel/women_of_ST.html
www.ipacific.net.au/~gunther/gates/
www.pbs.port.ac.uk/~sis4381/beverly.html
www.pebbs.com/lonomyth/hl-ww.ntml
www.physik.uni-regensburg.de/~krt04517/Forbes
www.pricecostco.com/pcc/art/ar296e.html
www.Prtcl.com/html/Katherin/Kath2.html
www.scifi.com/frakes/
www.sfcm.edu/bios/de_lancie.html
www.TU-Berlin.DE/~gruhlke/
www.tut.fi/~pekka
www.ugcs.caltech.edu/st-tng/
www.umr.edu/~mrwilson/FAQ.html
www.vol.it/luca/startrek/

TELEVISION AND RADIO INTERVIEWS, AND TAPED CONVENTION APPEARANCES

A Tale of Two Captains. Vulcan Video (retail videotape, no date appended).
Castaway's Choice with Patrick Stewart. April 1981, KCRW radio, Los Angeles, transcription by Susan Wickham for Stargazer.
Charlie Rose. August 9, 1995, PBS, 11:00 P.M. EST.
CNN: Showbiz Today. January 9, 1996, 5:43 P.M. EST.
CNN: Showbiz Today. July 14, 1995, 11:12 A.M. EST.
CNN: Showbiz Today. November 28, 1994, 5:29 P.M. EST.
Interview Between Steve Wright and Patrick Stewart. April 29, 1993, BBC Radio 1 FM, 8:00 P.M. GMT.
Larry King Live. December 17, 1994, CNN, 9:00 P.M. EST.
Larry King Live. May 14, 1994, CNN, 9:00 P.M. EST.
Larry King Live. August 3, 1993, CNN, 9:00 P.M. EST.
Late Night with David Letterman. November 29, 1996, CBS, 11:35 P.M. EST (interview with Brent Spiner).
NPR: Weekend Edition. May 15, 1994, 10:00 A.M. EST.
Personality Video: Marina Sirtis. Vulcan Video (retail videotape, no date appended).
Personality Video: Patrick Stewart Vol. One. Vulcan Video (retail videotape, no date appended).
Personality Video: The Crew of the Next Generation Vol. One. Vulcan Video (retail videotape, no date appended).
Star Trek: The Next Generation Press Kits. Vulcan Video (retail videotape, no date appended).
Star Trek: The Next Generation Rarities Vol. One. Vulcan Video (retail videotape, no date appended).
The Tonight Show with Jay Leno. November 29, 1996, NBC, 11:35 P.M. EST (interview with Patrick Stewart).